IATEFL 2006
Harrogate Conference Selections

Edited by Briony Beaven

40th International Annual Conference
Harrogate
8–12 April 2006

Editorial Committee: Ingrid Gürtler, Amos Paran, Silvana Richardson

Published by IATEFL
Darwin College
University of Kent
Canterbury
Kent CT2 7NY

Copyright for whole volume © IATEFL 2007

Copyright for individual reports/papers remains
vested in the contributors, to whom applications for
rights to reproduce should be made.

First published 2007

British Library Cataloguing in Publication Data
Education
Beaven, Briony (Ed.)
  IATEFL 2006 Harrogate Conference Selections

ISBN 1 901095 09 6

For a complete list of IATEFL publications, please
write to the above address, or visit the IATEFL
website at www.iatefl.org

Copy-edited by Simon Murison-Bowie, Oxford.
Designed and typeset by Keith Rigley, Charlbury.
Printed in Britain by Information Press, Eynsham.

Contents

	Editor's introduction	8
1	**Conference reviews**	
1.1	The first and the fortieth (I)ATEFL conferences *Michael Swan*	10
1.2	IATEFL—The ultimate conference for creative teachers of English! *Maggie Bouqdib*	11
1.3	Finding out and being found out *John Hughes*	13
1.4	Relationships and ELT *Caroline Linse*	14
2	**Talk and texts**	
2.1	Plenary: 'It was so funny'—gender and humour in everyday talk *Jennifer Coates*	17
2.2	Classroom perspectives on the occurrence and benefits of negotiated interaction *Miroslaw Pawlak*	29
2.3	Task difficulties and learners' reactions to a monologic speaking task *Tomoko Horai*	31
2.4	Real lives, real listening: a new approach to listening training *Sheila Thorn*	34
2.5	A collaborative learning approach to listening *Anthony Green*	36
2.6	Writing—a neglected skill? *Audur Torfadottir*	38
2.7	Symposium on academic writing *Convenor: Edward de Chazal*	40
3	**Form, meaning and use**	
3.1	Plenary: Two out of three ain't enough—the essential ingredients of a language course *Michael Swan*	45
3.2	Easing your way into grammar *Joanne Collie and Hans Mol*	54
3.3	Language corpora and peer teaching in an English grammar course *Maria Estling Vannestål*	56
3.4	Discover your dictionary: book, CD-ROM, online *Birgit Winkler*	58
3.5	How we made an academic vocabulary syllabus *Adam J. Simpson*	60
3.6	What's in a name? Plotting lexical relationships in computer English *Andreja Kovacic*	62
3.7	Totally Wiki-ed: using Wikis in EAP—a swapshop *Tilly Harrison*	64

4 Classroom interactions

- 4.1 The nature and quality of classroom interaction in the primary classroom—three case studies *Zehang Chen* 68
- 4.2 Teacher-centred or learner-centred—does it have to be a dichotomy? *Qiang Wang* 70
- 4.3 Classroom questioning in Malaysia: mismatch of expectations and realities? *Habsah Hussin* 72
- 4.4 Aspects of teachers' feedback on students' contributions in class *Linda Taylor and Shan Fu* 74
- 4.5 Spanish cross-curricular issues and English teaching at some Andalusian schools *Diego Rascón* 76
- 4.6 Young learners developing foreign language literacy: voices from the classroom *Irma-Kaarina Ghosn* 78
- 4.7 Challenge not competition *Andrew Wright* 80

5 English for specific purposes

- 5.1 English competence and reading comprehension among first-year business students *Hans Platzer and Désirée Verdonk* 84
- 5.2 We don't teach, we coach: Team Academy in Finland—a new learning environment *Riitta Purokuru and Hannu Ryynänen* 87
- 5.3 A national ESP curriculum for universities: generating success *Oleksandr Shalenko and Nataliya Todorova* 89
- 5.4 Linking EAP courses and undergraduate assessment: a task-based approach *Katie Dunworth* 92
- 5.5 Implementing strategy training with low-level EAP learners *Alex Dawson* 93
- 5.6 Interactivity in EAP groups and students' views of effective learning *Clare Anderson* 96
- 5.7 An investigation into the effectiveness of time on the teaching of EAP *Robert Berman and Samira ElAtia* 98
- 5.8 Why students plagiarise: developing plagiarism prevention strategies among international students *Nadezhda Yakovchuk* 100
- 5.9 Teaching against plagiarism in the EAP classroom *Philip Nathan* 102
- 5.10 Literature and media in an ESP classroom *Aysha Viswamohan and Ursula Troche* 104
- 5.11 The fun side of business English *Marjorie Rosenberg* 106
- 5.12 City & Guilds Spoken English Test for Business. The BEST teaching ideas. *Vincent Smidowicz* 107

	5.13	Life and death situation—responding to the *real* needs of ESP learners *Marie McCullagh and Ros Wright*	109
	5.14	Meeting the linguistic and cultural needs of foreign nursing students *John Tremarco*	110
6	**According to teachers**		
	6.1	What price self-esteem? Image and self-image in TEFL *Jeremy Harmer, Rod Bolitho, Sagrario Salaberri and Luke Meddings*	113
	6.2	If you can't measure it, you can't manage it: implications of upward assessment *Esin Çağlayan*	115
	6.3	Examining the effectiveness of the four-week ELT training course *Valerie Hobbs*	117
	6.4	The impact of overseas in-service training on teachers' beliefs *Chizuyo Kojima*	119
	6.5	Teacher beliefs: an essential element of effective language teacher education *Simon Phipps*	121
	6.6	Constructing communities of learning and practice: a narrative approach *Christine Savvidou*	123
	6.7	Can primary school teachers be researchers? *Derin Atay*	125
	6.8	Two hats or the same one? Exploring the changing attitudes of TESOL teachers to classroom-based research *Tim Graham and Alice Oxholm*	127
	6.9	Pre-service training and the first year of teaching *Peter Watkins*	129
7	**Teacher development**		
	7.1	Plenary: The spirit of the dance—taking one step further *Bena Gül Peker*	132
	7.2	Understanding dynamics supportive of learning in the young learner classroom *Zeynep Onat-Stelma and Juup Stelma*	142
	7.3	Promoting knowledge of theory in teacher practice *Kristen di Gennaro and Bede McCormack*	144
	7.4	Killing twenty-five birds with two stones: strategies for implementing innovation *Andrew Sheehan*	146
	7.5	Peer observation in teacher development *Peter Beech*	148
	7.6	Giving your staff the best chance possible *Rachel Appleby*	150
	7.7	Task-based teacher training activities *Naďa Vojtková and Světlana Hanušová*	152
	7.8	Practical ideas for trainer training and teacher development *Briony Beaven*	155
	7.9	Issues in ELT in transitional countries: a presentation by Hornby scholars *Convenor: Rod Bolitho*	157

8 Focus on the learner

8.1	Nature and nurture, the best of both worlds *Dede Wilson*	163
8.2	Symposium on materials development: ways of developing materials to achieve affective engagement *Convenor: Brian Tomlinson*	166
8.3	The factors contributing to proficient English users' language classroom anxiety *Magdalena Keblowska*	168
8.4	Mission possible: English class as a learning organisation *Mojca Belak*	170
8.5	Towards autonomous learning *Sanja Wagner*	172
8.6	Learning in style! *Judy Garton-Sprenger and Philip Prowse*	174
8.7	An evaluation of English language teaching in Icelandic compulsory schools *Samuel Lefever*	175
8.8	Understanding the English language learner self-concept *Sarah Mercer*	177
8.9	'Learning difficulties' or teaching challenges? *Anne Margaret Smith*	180

9 Information and communication technology (ICT) in ELT

9.1	New technologies and instructional design models: a UAE experience *Aidan Thorne*	182
9.2	Enriching ELT with ICT *Jana Jilkova*	184
9.3	Making IT or faking IT? *Nicky Hockly*	186
9.4	The electronic language portfolio *Maggie Bouqdib and Beate Vogel*	188
9.5	Motivating Brazilian female ELT teenage learners using the rhetoric of digital genres *David Shepherd*	191
9.6	ChatBox: dynamically creating a resource for e-moderators *Valentina Dodge and Sheila Vine*	193
9.7	E-twinning: the Polish experience *Elżbieta Gajek*	195

10 Testing

10.1	Symposium on teaching for institutional exams *Convenor: Rubina Khan*	198
10.2	Who really uses tests? *Judith Mader*	200
10.3	Objective IELTS: meeting the challenges of IELTS *Michael Black*	202
10.4	Relating exams to the Common European Framework of Reference: the Trinity College London experience *Spiros Papageorgiou*	204

	10.5 Using the CEFR in the tertiary level context *Juliet Wilson and Senem Donancı Büyük*	206
	10.6 A brief history of a CEFR implementation: finding a common language *Maria K. Norton*	208
11	**Cross-cultural matters**	
	11.1 Plenary: Critical approaches to culture in English language teaching *Ryuko Kubota*	213
	11.2 Native-speakerism in ELT: *plus ça change …?* *Alan Waters*	223
	11.3 Symposium on the Chinese learner *Convenor: Melinda Whong-Barr*	225
	11.4 Understand Chinese culture through its keywords *Wei-Wei Shen*	228
	11.5 Dinner at the homesick restaurant *Irina Perianova*	230
	11.6 Interesting choices and untapped potential: what and who we teach *Elka Todeva*	231
	11.7 Questions around ELF: investigating teachers' attitudes *Nadia Benrabah-Djennane*	233
	11.8 Symposium on intercultural communication *Convenor: Alessia Cogo*	235
	Index of authors	239

Editor's introduction

The 40th International Annual IATEFL Conference took place in the Harrogate International Centre, Harrogate, UK, surely an ideal venue for such an international gathering. Outside the conference centre, Harrogate proved to be a popular choice with delegates who praised its friendliness and its food. The town was described as compact and accessible, while evening events helped delegates to become familiar with the area and with Yorkshire culture.

Our 1st conference, when we were just ATEFL, not IATEFL, was held at the end of December 1967 in London. One of the delegates was Michael Swan, the only delegate out of the 122 at that first conference who also made it to our fortieth, so it is fitting that he was one of our plenary speakers in Harrogate and that he has also written a special contribution for Chapter 1. Regular readers of *Conference Selections* will notice the new 40th anniversary cover and the expanded size, which we hope will make the selections more reader-friendly.

The four plenaries, one panel discussion summary, one debate summary, five symposium summaries, seventy-one reports of presentations and four conference reviews included in this volume represent a selection of all that happened at the conference. Reading the reports makes it clear that widely differing views on a number of common ELT topics are represented in IATEFL. This is in line with IATEFL's vision statement. All IATEFL activities and publications aim to conform to that vision. How does *Conference Selections* fit into the vision?

- It is *outward-looking and international*, including articles from authors world-wide. The Editor also actively seeks conference reviewers from different parts of world. Consequently *Conference Selections* provides a sample of international English, with its varied writing styles and approaches. As far as possible the mix of styles is deliberately retained although some features of the volume need to be uniform to provide maximum comprehensibility and clarity.
- Editorial policy is to include content with *different ELT perspectives and from different ELT contexts*. This makes us a major forum for debate, one of our strengths being the range of experiences we can consult from within our membership.
- *Conference Selections* solicits and includes contributions from both *experienced* and *inexperienced* members of our profession.
- It includes both *practical* and *theoretical* articles and welcomes contributions that seek to combine practice and theory.

Editor's introduction

This issue of *Conference Selections* is divided into eleven chapters with a chapter introduction at the beginning of each chapter. Each year the content of *Conference Selections* depends very much on the balance of submissions. This time EAP and the special needs of Chinese learners are strongly represented. The growing influence of the Common European Framework of Reference for Languages (CEFR) will also be apparent. Other frequent threads running through the chapters are teacher beliefs and skills, learner autonomy and classroom interactions. A new addition this year is an author index, which we hope will prove useful.

The job of editing could not be accomplished without the work of the Editorial Committee. The reviewers read all the reports 'blind', that is, they do not know who wrote the reports. Based on these 'blind' readings, members of the Editorial Committee make recommendations to the Editor as to which reports to include; they also sometimes make suggestions for the editing process. So my thanks go to Ingrid Gürtler, Amos Paran and Silvana Richardson. I would also like to thank our copy-editor, Simon Murison-Bowie, and Keith Rigley, for his work on layout and typesetting.

This year there were more submissions than ever to *Conference Selections* from presenters. The symposiums, debates and panel discussions are represented too, of course, but I would like to take this opportunity to invite more convenors of debates and symposiums to write for the next edition of *Conference Selections*, with the help of input from your speakers.

NOTE: References are given in full for plenary papers, with a maximum of three references in other reports. Readers wishing to follow up references can obtain details on application to the authors, or to the Editor in cases where no contact information is given.

Briony Beaven
Freelance, Munich, Germany, September 2006
Email: brionybeaven@t-online.de

1 Conference reviews

Chapter 1 of this volume traditionally opens with reviews from conference delegates and this year is no exception. However there is also a brief backward look at our first conference by **Michael Swan**. Michael Swan's comparison of our first and fortieth conferences is followed by reviews of the fortieth contributed by **Maggie Bouqdib**, **John Hughes** and **Caroline Linse**.

Reviewers write their reviews based on the sessions they attended and not knowing who will contribute articles to *Conference Selections*. They may therefore include descriptions or mentions of presentations which are not represented in this volume. In order to avoid readers vainly searching for absent articles, I include below a list of those presentations appearing in the reviews which are represented by a summary or article in one of the later chapters in *Conference Selections*.

2.1 Plenary: 'It was so funny'—gender and humour in everyday talk
Jennifer Coates
4.5 Spanish cross-curricular issues and English teaching at some Andalusian schools   *Diego Rascón*
6.1 What price self-esteem? Image and self-image in TEFL
Jeremy Harmer, Rod Bolitho, Sagrario Salaberri and Luke Meddings
7.1 Plenary: The spirit of the dance—taking one step further   *Bena Gül Peker*
7.3 Promoting knowledge of theory in teacher practice
Kristen di Gennaro and Bede McCormack

1.1 The first and the fortieth (I)ATEFL conferences

Michael Swan   *Freelance and Visiting Professor, St. Mary's College, University of Surrey, UK*

I was privileged to attend both the first and the 40th (I)ATEFL Conferences. As one might expect, the occasions were very different in character. Although in 1967 ATEFL was already an international association (in fact if not yet in name), the ninety-odd people who were able to attend its first conference were almost all British. The occasion was dominated by plenaries, and covered a pretty limited range of topics. We discussed methodology and the pros and cons of structure drilling and language labs; ways of improving testing; how to design teaching programmes for different contexts (especially immigrant education); and the training of EFL teachers. The 40th Conference, in contrast, had nearly 1,000 registered participants from all over the world; we were able to choose from parallel sessions dealing with a vast range of topics, some of which a 1967 audience might have found baffling. ('*Prefabs*—isn't that a kind of house? *ELF*—like in Lord of the Rings? *Critical Discourse Analysis*—?????')

Whatever the differences, however, the idealistic ethos which launched the 1967 conference remains the same. Participants and organisers alike are people who are prepared to devote time and resources to improving their command of their profession, and to helping others to do so. Speaking for myself, my first conference brought enormous benefits to a young language teacher who was desperately short of guidance; every conference I have attended since (and not least the 40th) has brought me something more. IATEFL's founders would have been proud of their legacy.

Email: michaelswan@grammar2.demon.co.uk

1.2 IATEFL—The ultimate conference for creative teachers of English!

Maggie Bouqdib *Bremer Volkshochschule, Bremen, Germany*

My impressions of the IATEFL Conference in Harrogate in 750 words? When Briony asked me to contribute to the Conference Selections 2006, I was both chuffed and honoured, but also somewhat stumped. My typical teacher's 'gift of the gab' rarely lets me down, but the daunting prospect of squashing a myriad of impressions and experiences, talks and discussions, presentations and workshops, exhibition stands and extra-curricular activities into such a brief report almost left me—albeit temporarily—at a loss for words!

What's an IATEFL Conference? Using an acrostic:

I ATEFL holds an
A nnual conference for
T eachers of
E nglish from
F ar flung
L ands.

If you've never experienced an IATEFL conference I can only say, 'Do your very best to attend at least once during your teaching life; you won't regret it!' Harrogate was only my third conference, after Brighton and Liverpool, but this year was particularly special in that I was a first-time presenter, which imparted a whole new flavour.

The IATEFL experience begins on arrival at the conference centre. The organisation is superb—programmes and badges here, free conference bags there—everywhere smiling, helpful young people ready and willing to give information and directions.

Chapter 1: Conference reviews

The tortuous decision regarding which sessions to attend plagues every delegate; we're simply spoiled for choice. The 'Great Names' of EFL can rarely complain of sparsely–filled conference rooms. They soak up their brief moments of fame, busily signing copies of their latest works, generously distributed free by the publishers (many thanks!), stoically embracing admiring delegates for the obligatory souvenir photos (keep smiling!) and chatting to yours truly about prospective INSET seminars in Bremen. The 'hitherto unknowns', however, also offer a wealth of experience and a colourful medley of interesting and thought-provoking ideas, research and methods in their sessions.

The extensive exhibition is always an absolute 'must', with freebies, competitions, cakes, sweets, wines and even the occasional delicious buffet. Our insatiable thirst for knowledge and voracious appetites for tips and tricks in teaching was just as adequately satisfied as were our physical needs. A wonderfully colourful display of Chinese dancing with ferocious, lettuce-eating dragons and numbingly-loud drumming was just one of the highlights of the extracurricular activities, though in this case definitely not for the faint-hearted.

One of the most positive and enjoyable aspects of the conference for me, though, is off the programme. I love meeting, listening and talking to the great variety of teachers, trainers, colleagues and authors, some familiar from previous conferences, of all ages, experience levels, colours and nationalities, all speaking my own beloved native tongue and all intrinsically bound by a common love of teaching and the English language, plus an incredibly dynamic, contagious enthusiasm, motivation and idealism. It's simply phenomenal. The atmosphere is open and friendly; delegates mix and compare notes during and after sessions, or over tea and coffee. These spontaneous exchanges are of great importance in sorting and cementing new knowledge, experiences and contacts; they reduce the danger of remembering mere snippets which, once home, merge into a general plethora of impressions.

Those enduring souls who hang in there until the final session are always well rewarded for their pains. This year's closing plenary (Bena Gül-Peker) was utterly uplifting, resulting in hundreds of happy delegates enthusiastically dancing between the rows and aisles of the lecture hall. It was an unforgettable experience.

Then, suddenly, thanks and applause, flowers and sad farewells and we were all left facing not only the unenviable task of fitting a huge collection of bulky teaching materials into cracks and crevices in our (already-full) suitcases, but also of casually pretending to airline staff that our (weighty) hand luggage was actually as light as a feather. Another fantastic, worthwhile conference was over; roll on Aberdeen 2007! Thank you IATEFL.

Learning
Fulfilling
Encouraging
Teaching
Amazing
I ATEFL!

E-mail: maggie.bouqdib@vhs-bremen.de

1.3   Finding out and being found out

John Hughes   *Freelance, Hucclecote, UK*

IATEFL 2006 began with my car engine over-heating on the M1 motorway up to Harrogate so the first day of the conference literally went up in a puff of smoke for me. When I did finally get there on Monday, the spa town of Harrogate was looking spring-like and offered attractive places to wander. The conference centre itself was a good choice in terms of facilities though it felt vast and intricate. To walk from the main auditorium to the other rooms needed keen navigation. On the days that followed, I don't think I ever did find the speakers' room called 'Restaurant'. I did find a restaurant, many of them in fact, but none with a workshop going on, so apologies to any of the speakers who found themselves being asked for steak and chips twice rather than, 'Do you have any good ideas for what to do with a computer in the classroom?'

Meanwhile, on the Monday, back in the main auditorium, Jeremy Harmer was running a debate on image and self-image in TEFL. Various panel members gave opinions on what it means to be a teacher, our self-esteem and professionalism in the industry. You got a sense of the UK native-speaker teacher somewhat in decline. For the non-native-speaker teacher Sagrario Salaberri, a Spanish teacher trainer, outlined the five years of study pursued by teachers in Spain, a stark contrast to the typical one-month initial certificate courses for many native speakers.

You couldn't avoid the themes of digital age, technology and the learner of the future at this year's conference (and I suspect for many more to come). First of all, the exhibition hall had stands demonstrating the latest in interactive whiteboards, online learning environments, and the latest in digital publishing. To try and make sense of all this, IATEFL conferences are increasingly becoming breeding grounds for futurologists—people who specialise in predicting the future and looking at the 'what-if' scenarios. (Nice work if you can get it!) Concerns were expressed at a number of formal events over the lack of training available and the gap between those with the knowledge and those without. But, as Caroline Moore (Director of IT Services, the British Council) said at the forum 'Meet the learner of the future', 'the problem with being a futurologist is that if you are wrong, after a few years you get found out.' So we'll all have to keep coming to IATEFL conferences for the next few years to find out if the Harrogate futurologists were right.

Finally, away from the glitz and PowerPoint, it's always reassuring at IATEFL to re-join the cut and thrust of chalk-face sessions going on elsewhere. Take, for example, the session 'Course books are killing teaching'. The speaker began with a wry look at some of the course book classics of the past. While commenting on an extract from *Strategies*, we were to discover that an author of the coursebook was in fact sitting in the audience. An uneasy but rather delicious tension settled in the room as the speaker delicately presented his views on the author's work. I also thought there were more practical sessions this year and it's pleasing to see how many presenters are still asking us to fiddle around with bits of cut-up paper, stand up, chat to someone else in the room and give us at least one good idea to use in class on Monday morning. Notable award in this category goes to Hanna Kryszewska whose workshop included lengths of wool to wrap round your finger, telling a complete stranger what concerns you in EFL and acting out chunks from a Queen song—ah yes, the true spirit of IATEFL was alive and well in Harrogate.

Email: jhnhghs@msn.com

1.4 Relationships and ELT

Caroline Linse *Sookmyung Women's University, Seoul, Korea*

Language is probably best used as a tool to build strong and satisfying relationships both in and outside of the classroom. In recent years the focus on communicative language teaching and task-based language instruction has led ELT theorists and practitioners to consider meaningful uses of language more actively. Initiating and sustaining relationships, in addition to the ones that exist between teachers and students, is not usually listed on a course syllabus. In addition, building professional relationships is not something that a school generally puts into their budget.

Different aspects of the Harrogate IATEFL conference made me consider the connections that I have with other professionals and the skills that ELT students need in order to develop satisfying relationships with individuals using English as the medium of communication. I like the fact that at the IATEFL conference, unlike TESOL, the opportunities to meet and initiate relationships are more prevalent. This year's conference was no exception even though the venue was a bit sprawling. For example, in Harrogate, morning and afternoon tea and coffee were served in proper crockery mugs. The subtle but nevertheless important message was that chatting and visiting amongst professionals are important parts of the conference.

The use of coffee-based meetings, albeit, on a slightly more formal basis was reported by Kristen di Gennaro and Bede McCormack of New York as a way to help teachers discuss theoretical premises and the latest developments in second language research. They see conversations about theory amongst faculty as benefiting learners. It was clear that although the aim was to build professional knowledge, another by-product was to help teachers build professional collegial relationships amongst one another. Such relationships may have an even stronger impact on learners than just the theoretical information discussed.

On another level relationships are important for teachers to consider. When we teach learners the language necessary to communicate we also need to be aware of how language can be used as part of both new and on-going relationships for learners of all ages. In her plenary address, Professor Jennifer Coates discussed the interplay between gender, humour and language. She reminded us that the way adult women interact with one another and use humour differs from that of adult men. Her remarks about how women use humour, in the form of stories, when they communicate in pre-existing friendships, were very illuminating. Professor Coates explained that the humorous anecdotes women tell amongst themselves serve to both 'create' and 'sustain' bonds between women. This type of information, how language is used to build relationships, is often absent from ELT course-books and curricula. Frequently there is no mention of the fact that women and men do communicate differently and that gender does impact on communication and the use of language.

On a slightly different note, Diego Rascón Moreno spoke about an innovative ELT curriculum in the Andalusian Primary Schools that includes discussions about relationships as part of the Peace Education component. Diego explained that students consider ways to solve problems within a relationship by dialoguing. He also mentioned that, as part of the Andalusian ELT curricula, children are taught to be aware of the importance of friendships and family relationships. In the primary school ELT classroom it is appropriate to discuss relationships that exist between family members and between friends and even between people and pets because that is when children are beginning to refine their interpersonal skills.

Conclusion

Relationships are important for us as members of the ELT community and their development deserves time and attention. As a result of the conference, I personally am lingering a bit more when I talk with my colleagues at the university about both professional and personal matters. Also as a result of the conference, I am beginning to think more about how the curriculum can better address the issues of relationships for learners of all ages and at all stages of English language development. In the era of purposeful and meaningful endeavours there is probably nothing more fulfilling than personal and professional relationships where all parties contribute and benefit.

Email: clinse@aol.com

2 Talk and texts

Jennifer Coates' plenary, which opens this chapter, considers the role of humour in everyday life. She analyses a number of humorous oral interactions to argue that humour can be used to emphasise power differences, for self-protection and to maintain or create solidarity. However, notions of what is funny vary along gender lines, with men generally preferring stories that focus on action, while women on the whole like humour that deals with people and relationships.

The theme of oral interaction is continued in the article by **Miroslaw Pawlak**. He conducted a study that looked at the interactive work done by interlocutors to overcome real or perceived communication breakdowns, finding that negotiation, in spite of its generally accepted role in raising the quality of learner oral output, was quite rare. He concludes that learner training in effectively negotiating form and meaning appears indispensable. **Tomoko Horai**, on the other hand, is interested in long monologues and what contributes to the degree of task difficulty within monologic tasks in speaking tests. He reports on the effects on candidate performance of manipulating the variables of permitted planning time, the amount of support provided, and the time allowed for responses.

Both **Sheila Thorn** and **Anthony Green** have devised listening materials that train listeners in decoding sounds, words and short utterances. Both presenters feel that traditional listening materials concentrate too much on listening for content and not enough on helping learners with their difficulties in recognising even words they know within the stream of connected authentic speech. Sheila Thorn surveys a variety of exercise types she has designed to support learners in listening while Anthony Green describes technology that assists them in transcribing what they hear and which encourages collaborative listening work.

Moving from listening to writing skills **Audur Torfadottir** reviews and discusses the results of a study on the writing skills of Icelandic learners of English. She proposes more training for the learners in the use of cohesive devices and states that this will have to be effected by means of greater teaching focus on texts as a unit, rather than individual sentences. **Edward de Chazal** convened the symposium on academic writing. In his own talk he recommended a three-stage cycle for expressing key meanings in training for academic writing. This would offer a toolkit of adverbials in three semantic areas which would help students to generate their own language based on prototypical patterns. **Amna Yousef** discusses the impact of peer collaborative revision on college students' essays, noting that the majority of students in her study incorporated revisions suggested by their peers into later drafts of their writing. **Alejandro Armellini** presents a practical approach to developing Chinese graduate students' writing. Amongst other useful features of the programme, regular, formative feedback appears to be the main factor in improving their writing. Finally **Lindy Woodrow** describes a project to address the academic writing needs of graduate students. She presents a course outline and explains that the most significant aspect of the course is the notion of ethnography of writing whereby students are trained to conduct research as insiders upon their own required writing tasks.

2.1 Plenary: 'It was so funny'—gender and humour in everyday talk

Jennifer Coates   *Roehampton University, London, UK*

In this paper, I want to look at language in a variety of contexts to explore the role of humour in everyday talk. I shall examine the variable of gender in relation to language and humour. One important goal of the paper is to show that the stereotypes about gender and humour are wrong: it is not true that women lack a sense of humour. But I hope to show that there are interesting ways in which women's humour differs from men's humour. This is hardly surprising given that gender has to be constructed as part of the ongoing performance of the self. When we engage in humorous talk, humour becomes a tool of gender construction.

It is important to distinguish between joke-telling (which involves set formulae) and conversational humour. Joke-telling is not common in friendly talk, for the simple reason that telling a joke interrupts the flow of conversation. In my entire corpus of friendly talk, there was only one example of joke-telling. (This was in a mixed group in a Belfast pub.) Conversational humour, by contrast, covers a wide spectrum of behaviour. It is helpful to invoke Bateson's (1953) idea of a play frame. Bateson argues that we frame all our actions as 'serious' or as 'play'. Conversational humour can be defined as 'a play frame created by the participants with a back-drop of in-group knowledge' (Boxer and Cortes-Conde 1997: 278).

In order for a play frame to be established in talk, conversational participants must collaborate with each other. In other words, it is not sufficient that a speaker says something humorous; it is also vital that the other conversational participants recognise this move into playful talk and continue with the play frame. To use the phrase coined by McCarthy and Carter (2004: 172), humorous talk requires conversational participants to adopt 'an interactive pact'.

Research into gender and humour is quite a new phenomenon. The evidence from both questionnaire data and spontaneous conversational data is that there are differences in the humour typical of women and men. In particular, men seem to prefer more formulaic joking while women share funny stories to create solidarity. (See, for example, Gibbs 2000, Hay 2000, Crawford and Gressley 1991, Holmes, Marra and Burns 2001.) Boxer and Cortes-Conde (1997: 290), working on conversational data from the USA and Argentina, argue that gender 'strongly conditions the type of verbal play that occurs in everyday talk'.

Humour is a highly significant part of everyday interaction and is a useful tool for the speaker because of its multi-functionality. Jennifer Hay (1995) identifies three main functions of humour:

- to emphasize power differences,
- to provide self-protection—used in self-defence or to cope with a problem, and
- to create or maintain solidarity within the group.

In what follows, I shall draw on Hay's three-part distinction to illustrate the different kinds of humour found in talk and to show how women and men have different preferences. I shall look briefly at examples of the first two functions listed here, before devoting the rest of the paper to an exploration of the solidarity function of humour and the contrast between men's and women's patterns of humorous talk. I shall draw on a wide range of sources as well as my own database of friendly conversation.

Humour's role in emphasising power differences

The first example comes from conversation involving four people on a train together. Three are women who know each other well and work in the same field—they are all reference librarians. The only man is the companion of one of the women. The women are talking about their work when the man interrupts with a joke:

Example 1
Woman 1
Woman 2   [talk about work]
Woman 3
Man   What's the difference between a feminist and a bin liner?
             A bin liner gets taken out once a week.
(Griffin 1989)

The joke produced no laughter—on the contrary, the women became silent. The man then started a new topic, a topic unrelated to the women's work talk, and took an active part in the ensuing conversation.

The second example comes from a very different context—a secondary school classroom. The pupils are participating in a problem-solving activity called 'The

Desert Survival Situation'. This brief extract comes from discussion involving the whole class. (Words following the symbol // were spoken at the same time.)

Example 2

Rebecca	But it's pointless trying to stay in one place. You have got to try and survive. You can't just stay in one place. [general hubbub as she speaks, some heckling from one boy]
Teacher	Hands up everyone. Hands up.
Rebecca	Until someone will, might come long, you've got to at least *try*. And without a compass, you don't know where //you are going.
Damion	//Yeah, but … Yeah, but …
Teacher	Damion
Damion	I think that, sorry, just a minute [pretends accidentally to fall off his chair. Everyone laughs.]

(Baxter 2002: 91)

Damion is one of the most popular boys in this class and here we see how he uses humour to maintain his dominant position. Damion appears to have something to add to the discussion but once he succeeds in gaining the teacher's and the class's attention, he pretends to fall off his chair. His clowning around interrupts Rebecca's contribution and makes him the centre of attention. Baxter argues that disruptive humour of this kind is a key strategy for dominant male speakers who want to stay in the limelight.

Both these examples show how male speakers can exploit humour to assert power. In both cases the male's disruptive humour means that he gains the floor while other speakers (female in both these examples) are silenced.

Humour used for self-protection

A second function of humour is to protect the self. I shall illustrate this function with two examples of talk produced in the context of a breast clinic involving women patients and radiology technicians in charge of the mammograph equipment. Having a mammogram (i.e. an X-ray designed to check for tumours indicating breast cancer) is not exactly a pleasant experience—the woman patient has to strip to the waist and have her breast clamped in a machine to be X-rayed.

Example 3

Radiology technician	need your arm outta your right sleeve
Patient	sorry, I'm just standing here waitin' for mother to tell me what to do! [both laugh]

(DuPre 1998: 93)

Example 4
[patient to technician as she arranges her breast ready for mammogram]
Patient   there's not very much to put on there
[compression begins]
Patient   you're going to squash what I have left! [laughter]
(DuPre 1998: 93)

In both these examples, the female patient says something humorous which results in laughter. Humorous exchanges like the ones reproduced here mitigate the discomfort and the anxiety. The humour, of course, also functions to create solidarity between the patient and the technician.

Humour and solidarity

The creation and maintenance of solidarity is the main function of humour in everyday conversation between equals. The main goal of most informal talk in the private sphere is the establishment and maintenance of good social relationships. So it is not surprising that humour emerges as an important component of conversational interaction between friends. I shall look first at examples of humorous talk from all-male talk, and will then turn to all-female talk.

All-male talk

'Having a laugh' is something which young males value very highly, to the extent that it is claimed that 'having a laugh' is central to being acceptable as masculine (Frosh, Phoenix and Pattman 2002: 205). In the classroom, one of the ways that boys 'do' masculinity is by fooling around. Boys try to be cool and to avoid the label of 'nerd' or 'boffin'. Damion, the boy who falls off his chair to make the class laugh in Example 2, is a good example of someone who is 'cool' and who knows how to have a laugh. One boy interviewed by Kehily and Nayak (1998) described the everyday classroom ethos as one where the 'normal' student is saying, 'What can we do for a laugh today?'. This boy claims he has had to change to fit in with this ethos: 'cos I was fairly quiet in the classroom and for a while everyone was callin' me gay' (Kehily and Nayak 1998: 83). Long term ethnographic research in London schools by Stephen Frosh and his colleagues (2002) revealed the pervasiveness of this ethos—'having a laugh' and being cool make it very difficult for boys to engage seriously with academic work.

Among older males, talk often takes the form of an exchange of rapid-fire turns. Example 5 was recorded by Jane Pilkington in a bakery in Wellington, New Zealand. Sam and Ray disagree over whether apples are kept in cases or crates:

Example 5
Ray   crate!
Sam   case!

Ray	what?
Sam	they come in cases Ray not crates
Ray	oh same thing if you must be picky over every one thing
Sam	just shut your fucking head Ray!
Ray	don't tell me to fuck off fuck (…)
Sam	I'll come over and shut yo-
Jim	yeah I'll have a crate of apples thanks [laughingly using a thick sounding voice]
Ray	no fuck off Jim
Jim	a dozen …
Dan	shitpicker! [amused]

(Pilkington 1998: 265)

There is a lot of disagreement in this extract, but, as Pilkington stresses, the participants here and in other similar exchanges seem to be enjoying themselves and their talk contains much laughter. It is friendly sparring, not a quarrel.

Another example of friendly but adversarial male talk comes from a conversation between two public-school boys, arguing about whether or not a fellow student speaks French:

Example 6

Julian	but the boy speaks French
Henry	he does not . do you want this knife embedded in your face?
Julian	do you want that tape-recorder inserted up your rectum?
Henry	[laughing] she'd get some pretty interesting sounds then

Male speakers build solidarity through this kind of competitive talk. However, if we turn to the private talk of friends in pairs or small groups (i.e. talk not recorded in the public domain), competition is not so evident. In Example 7, two men friends have met to have lunch together and in their talk they play with the idea of a parallel world in which Chris had become an academic rather than a solicitor:

Example 7

Chris	I would've been going down the shops for more . leather elbow patches for my cardigan.
Geoff	[laughs] yes and you would've been running a 386 machine and gasping at the graphics that that would produce.
Chris	a 386! I would've had a Style Writer or something.
Geoff	[laughs] 'what's wrong with the old pen and paper?' [old man's voice]

The two friends here collaborate in mocking the idea of the unworldly academic, rather in the style of the Monty Python 'sardine tin in the road' sketch. Each contribution takes a more extreme position and Geoff's laughter demonstrates their amusement at this sustained bit of joking. (Of course, by mocking the technological naivety of academics, they position themselves as technologically sophisticated.) Their ability to co-construct this joking fantasy is evidence of their shared understanding of each other. This builds solidarity between them.

The next extract, 'Jonesy and the lion', is a third person narrative. It comes from a conversation involving three male friends in their 20s and early 30s, Eddie, Geoff and Simon. They are talking in Simon's flat about a man who Eddie and Geoff used to know. Eddie is the narrator (Geoff's comments are in italics; Simon's are in italic capitals).

Example 8 'Jonesy and the lion' [MS02-1]
1   God that reminds me talking of lion cages d'you remember Jonesy?
2   *oh yeah Jonesy yeah*
3   well he lost his job at the um-
4   he worked at an army camp but lost his job there
5   [...]
6   but the one I was thinking of was when he was at er- he worked at the zoo
7   [...]
8   and somebody said that they needed some electrical sockets in the lion's cage
9   and they said that that would be his next task to put some electrical sockets in the- in the lion's cage
10 but- [laughs] but then [laughs] what he did
11 he just went and picked up the keys from the office one day
12 and he went IN to the lion's cage [laughs]
13 [G laughs]
14 and started drilling
15 and this lion . became sort of [laughs] quite aroused by the er- by this drilling
16 *OH NO* [laughing]
17 and he ended up being chased around the cage by the- by the lion
18 *OH NO*
19 and then the-
20 and well by this time there was quite a commotion in the zoo generally
21 *THERE WOULD BE* [laughing]
22 so the um head or- the head keeper discovered what was going on
23 so he was outside the cage you know
24 doing um whatever er lion um tamers do to keep the lion away from this guy

25 and eventually they managed to get him out of the cage
26 so um-
27 *HE WASN'T HURT?*
28 no he wasn't hurt
29 so there you go
30 he's just mad [laughs]
31 and it's just a miracle really
32 that he's still alive
33 but um he's always [laughs] been mad like that

The story focuses on an eccentric character, Jonesy, described by Eddie as 'just mad'.

The story gives an account of an episode when he acted in a very eccentric, not to say dangerous way. This portrait of someone as different, as 'other', serves to construct solidarity: the three friends are bonded by their shared amusement at the crazy behaviour of Jonesy. They position themselves as an in-group clearly distinct from people like Jonesy, and in so doing they reinforce their own group norms.

All-female talk

'Having a laugh' is not such an overt characteristic of female subculture, but having fun together is an aspect of friendship that women cherish. In fact, one of the things that struck me very forcibly when I transcribed the tapes I collected of all-female conversations was the amount of laughter involved.

In my interviews with women who participated in my research, several mentioned fun. Sitting over a cup of tea or a glass of wine in a private space was seen as a classic locus of good talk, and was explicitly contrasted with sitting round a table in a more public space such as a restaurant. The extract given in Example 9 comes from an interview with three women friends (words between the symbols / and \ were spoken simultaneously).

Example 9

Sue   we have [gone out for a meal] but I don't know that it's the same
Anna no
Liz   no it isn't as relaxing
Sue   I mean you can't shriek with laughter can you when you're out
Liz: no
Sue   you /have to be very controlled\
Liz   /well you CAN\ you CAN
Sue   yeah you can but you get chucked out
Jen   [laughs]

This extract suggests that the home is preferred because it's a place where women feel uninhibited about expressing themselves. I also asked participants in my research to tell me what talk with friends was like. This was Mary's answer:

Example 10
We probably laugh a lot and find things that are in common .... so that you would ... you would pick up on one thing and then the person reinforced that by saying well the same thing happened to them, or it happened in a different way, then you'd have a laugh because it's a shared thing.

Mary's words make an explicit link between laughter and solidarity: she claims that women establish common themes and take it in turns to tell stories arising from these themes, and that this results in a sense of shared understanding. Laughter, she argues, arises directly from the sense of a shared understanding.

To illustrate women's sense of humour, let's look at three examples. Example 11 is a 3rd-person narrative; it's a story told by a woman to two friends about her eccentric mother.

Example 11 'My mother and the jogger'
1 She took ... she's got these two dobermans who are really unruly but very sweet.
2 She took them for a walk on the beach one day,
3 and this was at the height of the Rottweiler scare,
4 and this jogger's running along the beach at Liverpool,
5 and Rosy, her dog that she can't control,
6 decided to run along after the jogger
7 and bit him on the bottom.
8 And this man was going absolutely mad,
9 and my mother started off by being nice to him
10 and saying, 'I'm terribly sorry, she's only a pup and she was just being playful'
and so on,
11 and he got worse,
12 so the more she tried to placate him,
13 the more he decided he was gonna go to the police station and create a scene about it.
14 So she said, 'Let me have a look',
15 and she strode over and pulled his ... [laughs] ... pulled his tracksuit bottoms down,
16 and said, 'Don't be so bloody stupid, man, there's nothing wrong with you,
17 you're perfectly all right'.

18 At which point he was so embarrassed he just jogged away.
19 [laughter]

This story constructs solidarity among the three friends by focusing on a non-present other, the narrator's mother. The mother is presented as an eccentric, a woman capable of doing the outrageous. The narrator implicitly contrasts the eccentric mother with the three (sensible) friends. The narrative positions the mother as 'other' while the three friends are bonded as the in-group who are not like this woman. At the same time, the story celebrates the mother as a woman who demonstrates agency, and a woman who inverts the normal order of things—at the end of the incident it is the man who is embarrassed and the woman who is triumphant. This overturning of normal expectations is another reason the story is so funny. So humour here both maintains notions of 'normal' femininity, while at the same time subverting those norms by celebrating a woman behaving badly.

More commonly, women narrators tell funny stories about themselves. Example 12 comes from a conversation involving four schoolgirls in their early teens. The story is told to Hannah by Becky with Claire's help—Claire's contributions are in italics—about an incident involving Becky, Claire and the school librarian which took place in school on a day when Hannah wasn't there—[xx] means that there were additional words which were not decipherable:

Example 12 'Knicker stains'
   It was so funny when you weren't there one day.
   Well we were in the library, right?
3 and we were in that corner where all the erm the picture books are.
   Claire's putting on some lipstick,
   I was putting on some lipstick,
6 and and and they said 'oh what are you doing in that corner?',
   and she said we were smoking [xx],
   no I said we were checking for people who were smoking,
9 and he said … and he said 'are you sure you weren't having a quick smoke yourself?',
   and I said, 'yes I must admit it',
   and I meant to say, 'Look at my nicotine stains',
12 and I held up my fingers like that,
   and I said, 'Look at my knicker stains'.
   [xx] we were rolling about the tables.
   It was so funny.

Notice how the evaluative clause 'it was so funny' frames this story, appearing both as a prelude to the story and as the final line. The telling of this story is followed by chaotic talk and laughter, with Jessica saying that she had told the story to her mother, and her mother too had been reduced to hysterics.

This story is about a funny (or embarrassing) slip of the tongue, and depends for its impact on Becky telling us what she *didn't* say, that is, 'Look at my nicotine stains'. The punch line, the words she actually said, 'Look at my knicker stains', only has such an impact because we know what she was trying to say. Overtly the friends treat this as yet another ridiculous story which they can laugh over—it fits a tradition of women's funny stories where a female protagonist finds herself in an impossible or humiliating or embarrassing position.

The final example, Example 13, shows how conversational participants can draw on what has been talked about in a serious frame earlier in the conversation. Sue tells her two friends that she has brought the school rabbit home for the weekend. They talk briefly about the rabbit before the conversation moves on through other topics to a discussion of marriage and relationships. Sue tells a story about a couple she knows where the wife has forbidden the husband to play his guitar, or even to have a guitar in the house. This raises issues about obedience and appropriate behaviour in relationships, and after some more serious talk about the husband's wild youth and near-alcoholism, Sue re-introduces the rabbit theme. The example below represents a very small part of the discussion of the obedient husband. (The final section is presented in stave notation. This means that all participants' contributions are to be read simultaneously, like instruments in a musical stave. Any word, or portion of a word, appearing vertically above or below any other word, is to be read as occurring at the same time as that word.)

Example 13 'Obedient husband'

Sue I told you I went round to a friends who had ((a)) guitar.
[...]
The wife right- his wife would not let him have a guitar.
She said no [A and L laugh]
and he's so obedient.
She's ... she said, 'You're not having a guitar',
so he didn't have one,
he just didn't play it ever.
And then for Christmas she allowed him to have a guitar
as long as he didn't play it in front of her ...

[final section]

1 ────────────────────────────────────

Anna
Liz   oh |bless him= |he   does |n't have much of a life=
Sue |he's-   =yeah |((he's just)) |

Gender and humour in everyday talk

```
2
Anna  =he doesn't       |by the sounds |of it/
Sue   =he doesn't real|ly/ [laughing] |he's like the rabbit/
3
Liz                         |he is really isn't he/  |she should
Sue   yeah [giggle]I think  |I should bring him-     |I think I should
4
Anna                                                 |introduce them/
Liz   get him- [giggling]  |I wonder why she doesn't |get him a RUN in
Sue   bring him home for   |weekends/[laughs]
5
Anna                  introduce them |((then you'll be able to-
Liz   the GARden [giggling]          |I'll be all ((6 sylls))
Sue                                               ((xxxx)) bring
6
Anna
Liz   ————————————>                              get him a few
Sue   him home at)) weekends and let him go out in a run/      yeah/
7
Anna                                      [laughs ————
Liz   lettuce leaves/ he'd be quite happy/'thank you Ginny' [name of wife]
Sue                                               [laughs———
8
Anna  ————————>]
Liz   <LAUGHS————>
Sue   ———>      oh don't/ poor thing [solemn tone]/
9
Liz   it's strange isn't it the life some people lead/
Sue
```

At the beginning of this extract, the three friends ponder on the obedient husband's life. Liz's utterance 'oh bless him he doesn't have much of a life' triggers Sue's laughter as she responds 'he doesn't really'. The switch to a play frame is achieved by the mocking, quasi-maternal tone which Liz adopts in relation to the obedient husband. Sue then introduces a new dimension with her simile: 'he's like the rabbit', and warms to her theme, continuing 'I think I should bring him home for weekends'. Liz joins in with the suggestion that the bossy wife should get the husband/rabbit a run in the garden, while Anna suggests the two 'rabbits' could meet. Liz fantasises that the husband/rabbit would be happy with a few lettuce leaves and adopts an ingratiating voice to mimic the husband thanking his wife for the lettuce. This is a very good example of Kotthoff's (2003) claim that the co-construction of humour relies on participants responding to what is said (playing with the theme of rabbits, of bringing pets home for the weekend, of making runs in the garden), rather than to what is meant (wives and husbands should have a more equal relationship and shouldn't order each other round). The repetition of the rabbit theme makes the talk of these friends textually cohesive. By reverting to the rabbit theme and using 'rabbit' as a metaphor for 'obedient husband', these friends are able to play with the parallels that this throws up and to say some pretty devastating things about the obedient husband.

In all these examples, we see how women achieve solidarity though the sharing of funny stories and the co-construction of humorous talk. The creation of solidarity is an inevitable consequence of this kind of talk since interactants who collaborate in humorous talk, 'necessarily display how finely tuned they are to each other' (Davies 2003: 1362).

Conclusions

In this paper, I've argued (following Hay 2000) that humour has three main functions: first, humour can emphasise power differences; secondly, humour can provide self-protection; and thirdly, it can be used to create or maintain solidarity within the group. I've shown how these three functions do not seem to be evenly distributed between male and female speakers: male speakers use humour as a way of exerting dominance, female speakers use humour as a form of self-protection, while both male and female speakers use humour to create solidarity. Moreover, banter and adversarial humour is relished in all-male groups but is uncommon in all-female talk, while in all-female groups speakers enjoy telling stories about their own disasters—times when things went wrong. So my data suggests that men and women in same-sex groups achieve solidarity in different ways.

As the examples we've looked at demonstrate, humour is used by women and men as a tool of gender construction. Men constitute themselves as masculine by engaging in verbal sparring and insulting each other. Competitive behavior of this kind counts as 'having a laugh' in male subculture. Men's humorous stories focus on non-present others who do idiotic things (like going into a lion's cage to fit a switch) or on their own laddish escapades where they managed to 'get away with' something. These stories focus on actions rather than feelings and function as boasts. Women, by contrast, constitute themselves as feminine through telling funny stories which focus on people and on relationships between people. Their playful talk explores the meaning of relationships and finds humour in embarrassing experiences and the betrayals of the female body.

So it appears that humour, language and gender are linked in multiple and complex ways. We all enjoy 'a good laugh', and medical research has shown that laughing is good for us. In this paper, I have argued that having a good laugh is important to all of us, both male and female speakers, in particular because of its capacity to construct solidarity. But what counts as 'a good laugh' varies along gender lines, to the extent that it can be claimed that conversational humour plays a key role in both the construction and of contemporary masculinities and femininities.

References

Bateson, G. 1953. 'The position of humour in human communication' in H. von Foerster (ed.). *Cybernetics*. Ninth conference. Josiah Macey Jr. Foundation, New York: 1–47.

Baxter, J. 2002. 'Jokers in the pack: why boys are more adept than girls at speaking in public settings'. *Language and Education* 16/2: 81–96.

Boxer, D. and F. Cortes-Conde. 1997. 'From bonding to biting: conversational joking and identity display'. *Journal of Pragmatics* 27: 275–94.

Crawford, M. 1995. *Talking Difference*. London: Sage.

Crawford, M. and D. Gressley. 1991. 'Creativity, caring and context: women's and men's accounts of humour preferences and practices'. *Psychology of Women Quarterly* 15: 217–31.

Davies, C. E. 2003. 'How English-learners joke with native speakers: an interactional sociolinguistic perspective on humor as collaborative discourse across cultures'. *Journal of Pragmatics* 35: 1361–85.

DuPre, A. 1998. *Humour and the Healing Arts*. Mahwah, N.J.: Lawrence Erlbaum Associates.

Frosh, S., A. Phoenix and R. Pattman. 2002. *Young Masculinities*. London: Palgrave.

Gibbs, R. W., Jr. 2000. 'Irony in talk among friends'. *Metaphor and Symbol* 15/1 and 2: 5–27.

Griffin, C. 1989. '"I'm not a woman's libber but…": feminism, consciousness and identity' in S. Skevingon and D. Baker (eds.). *The Social Identity of Women*. London: Sage: 173–93.

Hay, J. 1995. *Gender and Humour: Beyond a Joke*. Unpublished MA dissertation. Victoria University of Wellington, New Zealand.

Hay, J. 2000. 'Functions of humour in the conversations of men and women'. *Journal of Pragmatics* 32: 709–42.

Holmes, J., M. Marra, and L. Burns. 2001. 'Women's humour in the workplace: a quantitative analysis'. *Australian Journal of Communication* 28/1: 83–108.

Kehily, M. J. and A. Nayak. 1997. '"Lads and laughter": humour and the production of heterosexual hierarchies'. *Gender and Education*, 9/1: 69–87.

Kotthoff, H. 2003. 'Responding to irony in different contexts: on cognition in conversation'. *Journal of Pragmatics* 35/3: 1387–411.

McCarthy, M. and R. Carter. 2004. '"There's millions of them": hyperbole in everyday conversation'. *Journal of Pragmatics* 36: 149–84.

Pilkington, J. 1998. '"Don't try and make out that I'm nice": the different strategies women and men use when gossiping' in J. Coates, *Language and Gender: A Reader*. Oxford: Blackwell.

2.2 Classroom perspectives on the occurrence and benefits of negotiated interaction

Miroslaw Pawlak *Adam Mickiewicz University, Poznan, Poland*
  State Higher Professional School, Konin, Poland

According to many theorists and researchers, negotiated interaction, or the interactive work done by interlocutors to overcome real or perceived communication breakdowns, has the potential to facilitate L2 development and should therefore be encouraged in the language classroom. In particular, negotiation is believed to aid learners in understanding problematic language forms, to be a source of corrective feedback and to result in students producing more accurate, appropriate and coherent output. The presentation reported the findings of a study which sought to verify such claims by exploring the occurrence and value of negotiation of form and meaning in pair and group work activities.

The data comprised transcripts of 112 instances of pair and group work, 24 of which were instances of 'required information exchange tasks', where each participant holds some key data and interaction is thus indispensable, and 88 were 'optional information exchange tasks', in which all group members share the same information and their participation is far from guaranteed. The learners whose interactions were audio-taped were Polish secondary school learners representing pre-intermediate and intermediate proficiency levels.

The transcripts were analysed quantitatively and qualitatively. The numerical analysis involved counting the instances of negotiation, tabulating the cases where it led to modified output, and making comparisons in these respects between different task types (i.e. required vs. optional information exchange) and conversational strategies (i.e. clarification requests vs. confirmation checks). Qualitative analysis consisted in examining the nature of negotiated sequences, the quality of modified output and alternative means of solving communication breakdowns.

On the whole, negotiation was rather infrequent, with only 74 instances thereof being identified in the data, which means that there was on average 0.66 exchange of this kind per task. It turned out that its incidence was greater in required information exchange (26 cases or 1.08 per task) than in optional information exchange tasks (48 instances or 0.55 per task). As regards the types of conversational strategies employed to initiate negotiated sequences, 42 (56.76%) of those were confirmation checks whereas 32 (43.24%) clarification requests.

In 38 (51.35%) cases, negotiation led to reformulations of the original message, which indicates that there was on average 0.34 output modification per task. Somewhat in contrast to the results of previous research, the learners were equally likely to adjust their productions in response to clarification requests and confirmation checks, with 19 such instances in each category. However, the changes were minimal and did not lead to substantial elaboration or simplification of the utterance. Moreover, only on three occasions did a negotiated sequence lead to greater accuracy of learner output.

An important finding was that negotiated sequences were predominantly triggered by genuine problems with message comprehension rather than inaccuracies in interlocutors' output. This demonstrates that the students were reluctant to highlight errors in the speech of their peers and, as the analysis of the interactions showed, when they did so, they resorted to more explicit types of corrective feedback. It must also be noted that, on many occasions, confirmation checks appeared to act as time-gaining devices or acknowledgements of what a peer has said rather than signals of non-comprehension, which shows that we should be circumspect about interpreting the use of such strategies as a prelude to negotiation of form and meaning.

Moreover, many exchanges coded as instances of negotiation contained words and phrases in Polish, which would have doubtless rendered them ineffective had the interlocutors represented different L1 backgrounds. Of vital importance is also the fact that the transcripts contained numerous exchanges where only Polish was used to clear up misunderstandings or get complicated messages across, which proves that just getting students to interact in small groups does not guarantee the occurrence of negotiation or ensure its beneficial effects. Finally, it should be noted that there was a lot of variation between pairs and groups in all of the areas investigated.

In view of such findings, some kind of training in effectively negotiating form and meaning appears indispensable. This could involve raising students' awareness of the value of group work activities, demonstrating how negotiation can reduce L1 use, showing how conversational strategies can be used to respond to errors, providing examples of successful output modifications, teaching phrases that can be drawn upon to overcome communication breakdowns, setting up tasks necessitating negotiated interaction or regularly negotiating form and meaning in classroom discourse. It stands to reason that following such guidelines is likely to ensure greater reliance on the target language in resolving communication problems, more high quality output modifications and, ultimately, greater learning opportunities.

Email: pawlakmi@amu.edu.pl

2.3 Task difficulties and learners' reactions to a monologic speaking task

Tomoko Horai *Roehampton University, London, UK*

Introduction and methodology

'Individual long-turn (monologue)' is an established format in assessing speaking ability. Its practical advantages are that it can be delivered in a variety of formats, for example, live or recorded. Moreover, as a single speaker produces a long turn without interacting with other speakers, it does not suffer from the contaminating effect of the co-construction of discourse, seen by McNamara (1997) as potentially resulting in construct irrelevant variance. However, very little research exists on what contributes to the degree of task difficulty within monologic tasks in a speaking test and how it impacts on candidates' linguistic performance even though such tasks feature prominently in high stakes tests around the world.

The research that I reported on was designed to explore how candidates' performance on a monologic speaking task can be affected by 'deliberately manipulated' tasks (planning time, the amount of support, and response time) with the inclusion of quantitative and qualitative analysis of candidates' test scores and interlanguage measures (operationalised here as the three areas of accuracy, fluency, complexity).

Our study was based on the following research questions;

- Does *planning time (preparation time)* impact on task performance in terms of test scores, interlanguage measures of accuracy, fluency, complexity?
- Does *planning condition (support)* impact on task performance in terms of test scores, interlanguage measures of accuracy, fluency, complexity?
- Does *response time (length of talk)* impact on task performance in terms of test scores, interlanguage measures of accuracy, fluency, complexity?
- Do differences in respect of the above vary according to the participants' proficiency levels of English?

Four individual long-turn speaking tasks, which were demonstrated to be equivalent in difficulty from a quantitative and qualitative perspective by O'Sullivan, Weir and Horai (2005) were used for the investigation. 72 university level EFL participants (low, intermediate and advanced proficiency level) in Japan, Malaysia and a UK

Task B [UNCHANGED]	Task E [NO SCAFFOLDING]

You will have to talk about the topic for two minutes. Your have one minute to think about what you are going to say.
 	
B. Describe a part-time/holiday job that you have done.
You should say:
  How you got the job
  What the job involved
  How long the job lasted
And explain why you did the job well or badly.
	You will have to talk about the topic for two minutes. Your have one minute to think about what you are going to say.
	
	E. Describe a teacher who has influenced you in your education.
	And explain why this person influenced you so much.

Task D [NO PLANNING]	**Task F [REDUCED OUTPUT]**

You will have to talk about the topic for two minutes. Your should start speaking now, without taking time to think about what you are going to say.
 	
D. Describe an enjoyable event that you experienced when you were at school.
You should say:
  What the event was
  When it happened
  What was good about
And explain why you particularly remember this event.
	You will have to talk about the topic for one minute. Your have one minute to think about what you are going to say.
	
	F. Describe a film or a TV programme which made a strong impression on you.
	You should say:
	  What kind of film or TV programme it was
	  (e.g. comedy)
	  When you saw it
	  What it was about
	And explain why it made such an impression on you.

Figure 2.3.1: Manipulated tasks

institution were selected from a larger population (N = 146) based on 'fair average' scores from a Multi-Facet Rasch Analysis. They performed the four tasks in the present study (see Figure 2.3.1).

In data analysis, recorded performances were double-scored by two trained and experienced examiners and analysed quantitatively. All performances were then transcribed and analysed in terms of accuracy, fluency, complexity, based on Skehan and Foster (1995).

Results

Expressed as an ANOVA result, no significant differences among the four different tasks were found in the score comparisons. However, when proficiency level is taken into account (see Figure 2.3.2) we can see that there are different patterns of scoring across the three groups; post hoc analysis indicated that some of these differences were significant.

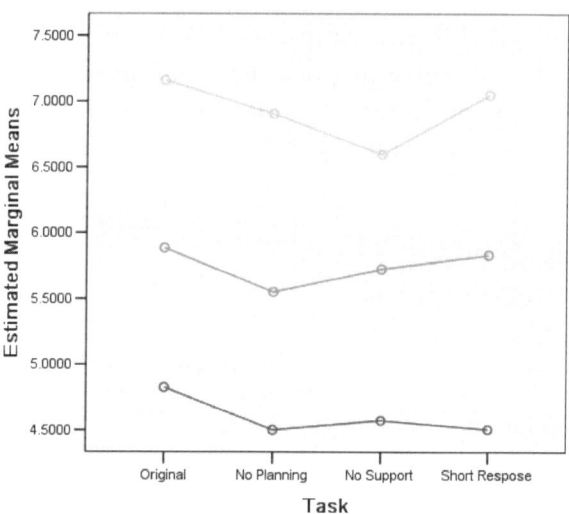

Figure 2.3.2: ANOVA result: comparison of means score

With respect to analysis of interlanguage measures, 15 Japanese (low, border and high level) were randomly selected from 146 participants for this paper. The results showed that no significant differences were found in *accuracy* and *complexity* among three levels and four different tasks. However, in terms of the measure for *fluency*, significant differences were found in *number of pauses*; first, between low and border levels (mean diff. = 3.70, p = .01); second, between *no planning* and *short response* task (mean diff. = 2.933, p < .05). Moreover, there were significant differences in *total silence*: first, between low and border levels (mean diff. = 17.718, p < .01]; second, between low and high levels (mean diff. = 14.798, p <. 05); and third, between *no planning* and *short response* tasks (mean diff. = 13.116, p < .05).

Discussion and conclusion

These results above are expected to have the following implications for teachers and test developers. Task difficulty in a test of oral performance or exercise for speaking in the classroom can be systematically adjusted by manipulating the parameters investigated here. However, the impact will depend on the level of students. Time allowed for 'monologue' type speaking test tasks could be critical, especially for lower level of learners. Therefore, they need more time to achieve a task. However, higher level students could complete the task in a shorter response time. For both teachers and test developers, it could be argued that there is little point in asking for longer responses for higher level students. As was seen in the interlanguage analysis, there is a possibility that scores do not reflect the actual overall linguistic performance, for example, grammatical accuracy in speech. However, some other aspects such as incompletion of the task within time or unintelligible pronunciation could significantly affect the scores particularly of low level students. Therefore, these features should also be investigated in further studies.

Email: t_horai@msn.com

References

McNamara, T. 1997. '"Interaction" in second language performance assessment: whose performance?'. *Applied Linguistics* 18/4: 446-66.

O'Sullivan, B., C. Weir and T. Horai. 2005. 'Exploring difficulty in speaking tasks: an intra-task perspective'. *IELTS Funded Research Project 2004 Final Report*. Cambridge: University of Cambridge ESOL Examinations.

Skehan, P. and P. Foster. 1995. 'Task type and task processing conditions as influences on foreign language performance' in *Thames Valley University Working Papers in English Language Teaching* 3. Thames Valley University.

2.4 Real lives, real listening: a new approach to listening training

Sheila Thorn *The Listening Business, London, UK*

We began the session by considering why the listening texts found in most coursebooks fail to prepare students for the English they will listen to outside the classroom.

This occurs because coursebook listening texts are mainly used to introduce students to new language, rather than specifically to improve their listening ability. These texts are generally scripted and read aloud by actors who tend to speak slowly and clearly articulate each word. Accents are mainly neutral and the recordings are usually made in a studio with no background noise. Even when authentic-sounding listening texts are included in coursebooks, the focus is almost exclusively on listening comprehension rather on training students to listen more effectively. The danger with focusing solely on comprehension is that students' answers are either right or wrong and the listening comprehension exercise then becomes a kind of test. This can lead to a sense of failure among those students who regularly score lower points, as well as a tendency for them to switch off during listening practice activities.

We next looked at the problems students have when exposed to authentic spoken English. Not only do they complain that everyone speaks too fast, but also that people don't speak clearly enough (unlike actors performing the scripted texts they are used to). They also have problems segmenting (i.e. separating words which have run together because of assimilation or linking) and they panic when they hear new lexical items because they think they need to understand every word. One final problem, and this is probably the most important of all, is that they don't even recognise words which are part of their active vocabulary when these occur in a stream of natural speech.

These were the factors uppermost in my mind when I began devising exercises to accompany the authentic listening texts I have been recording over the past two years. I now have nearly 90 recordings of native and non-native speakers from all over the British Isles, Canada, the USA, Germany, Japan, the Czech Republic, Pakistan and many other countries. In exploiting these recordings I have taken a theme, such as 'A typical day', and then selected speakers for different levels, depending on their speed of delivery, their accent and the complexity of the language they used.

Although I provide standard listening comprehension exercises and transcripts, the main focus is on what I term 'pure listening exercises' which focus exclusively on listening training. These include dictations and gapped dictations, where I cut and paste various short utterances in the text, focusing particularly on where assimilation and linking has occurred with lexis which is almost certainly in the active vocabulary of students at that level. I also take words which the speaker has uttered and add other words to form minimal pair exercises of various types. These are much more meaningful when the sounds they focus on were used in context by the real people they have been listening to. In other exercises I remove the final word in an utterance and ask the students to guess what it is likely to be as a way of encouraging them to think ahead when listening and to realise how accurately they can predict what comes next. Students hear the speaker say, 'I walk to the bus _____' and they have to guess the next word. Any which are logical are considered correct. Later they hear for themselves the actual words the speaker used.

A particularly useful exercise is one where students mark sentence stress in various short extracts from the texts. This draws their attention to how much we use stress of content words in English to convey meaning, something which students are frequently unaware of initially, but which can have an enormous impact on their ability to listen effectively. Other exercises focus on standard intonation patterns such as the British English fall at the end of statements, where students are asked to mark where the speaker's voice begins to fall (or rise in the case of the recordings I've made of British teenagers and Canadians and Australians).

I concluded my talk by playing a selection of extracts from these new materials I have devised to demonstrate how the same theme can be exploited at different levels depending on the speakers. I also provided examples of the listening exercises I have devised and played the accompanying tracks.

Email: sthorn@clara.net

2.5 A collaborative learning approach to listening

Anthony Green   *University of Bari, Italy*

Why was listening the least discussed skill at major conferences? Perhaps my experiences could be of interest to the community … With a class of 18 and only 9 working PCs, I had had to assign two students to each.

My premise was that the primary need in L2 listening is decoding the sounds. My students often claim to use luck and logic more than their ears when answering listening comprehension questions, and often ask me to tell them the actual words. They often refuse to believe me, but believe a transcript (grr!).

I had often tried getting students to transcribe extracts onto paper, but on reaching their threshold, the intensive nature of the exercise and technological limitations (tape recorder under teacher's control, poor acoustics, etc.) made it a difficult classroom task, leading to student frustration at their lack of progress and my annoyance at not meeting their needs.

This frustration holds the key to better listening solutions. How often as L2 learners have we experienced the same frustration with listening, always so much more difficult than reading? How often students want to avoid losing face, and are even willing to forego a learning experience in order to avoid humiliation, especially in front of the teacher! I aimed to put my audience into that same affective situation, to encourage them to face their fears and find a tool to overcome them... Would they be able to overcome that fear in the short time at our disposal?

VOICEbook technology hands control of the listening to students, who listen first extensively and then seek to transcribe what they have heard, getting immediate feedback. Interestingly, if they work at an *i* + 1 level, they spend under 20% of their time on the 60–70% they find easy to understand (little learning goes on here), while 80% is spent on training their ear and improving decoding skills. (All the learning is happening here.) Decoding skills improve when they find words they cannot identify; once transcription becomes impossible, they use various levels of help, from a definition for each guessed or blank word, down to letter level. This enables them in effect to create their own learning pathways, as no two users have the same problems; indeed teacher-led listening is fraught with difficulties as a learning experience since classes are invariably heterogeneous in terms of listening skills, and everyone hears something different. Collaborative learning is not usually associated with listening, but when my students worked in pairs, and created their own learning pathways, I was astounded to watch them all begin metalinguistic discussion!

Could I replicate this behaviour on stage at IATEFL? I decided to begin by striking fear into the hearts of my audience, threatening to choose 'volunteer learners' at the end of the session. After illustrating the system, I invited two whose Spanish reading skills were better than their listening skills to face up to their fears. They set about transcribing a phrase from the VOICEbook '*Mi perro Pelusa*' with what for me was alarming ease (that 20% of time spent completing 60–70% of a transcription). They finally met their match with the three words '*aunque a Joaquin*', which before you start feeling superior are very simple to read, but here very difficult to understand orally. So our plucky volunteers began metalinguistic discussions; 'He's his best friend, so there must be something like "*a quién*"—is that good Spanish? Let's try it', only to realise after various attempts that it was a proper name, Joaquin, a major character they would have completely overlooked in a traditional listening context. Seeing the unexpected difficulties surrounding this name (so easy on the eye, so hard on the ear) proved to be the audience's 'a-ha' moment; the decoding premise suddenly made sense. I wiped the sweat from my brow: the fear had been dispelled, and their mistakes (i.e. their learning opportunities, often sources of unresolved frustration in a traditional learning context) had been rewarded by their collaborative metalinguistic approach. Listening 'comprehension' exercises traditionally provide few learning opportunities, and mistakes are punished by low marks (many listening exercises are oddly enough more like tests), whereas students are rewarded for right answers which require no effort! Such an inverted reward system is paradoxical, and yet that is the schema that many listening exercises are based on.

By the way, the complete phrase was, '*Es más, lo considero mi mejor amigo, aunque a Joaquín, mi compañero de clase, no le gusta mucho la idea de ser suplantado por un perro.*'

Email: anthony@voicebook.com

2.6 Writing—a neglected skill?

Audur Torfadottir *Iceland University of Education, Reykjavik, Iceland*

Introduction

This paper presents the results of a study on the writing skills of Icelandic learners of English. The data was based on a sample from the standardised national examination held at the end of compulsory schooling when learners are fifteen and have had four years of English. According to the objectives of the national curriculum for English learners should have reached a stage where they can, among other things:

- write a connected text about a familiar subject and divide it into paragraphs,
- use the most common connectives and transitional words and phrases.

The study

In the part of the study presented here, the focus was on discourse knowledge, in particular the use of transitional words and phrases. The textbooks currently used present writing skills in a systematic way, gradually introducing the most common connectives, transitional words and phrases.

The sample, consisting of eighty pupils, was divided into four different ability groups of equal size on the basis of test scores in the writing component of the national examination.

- Group 1:   10–12 points out of 12
- Group 2:   8–9 points out of 12
- Group 3:   6–7 points out of 12
- Group 4:   2–5 points out of 12

The writing task in question consisted of a picture sequence and was supposed to form a short narrative. Pupils were instructed to write 100 words in the past tense. For learners at this age, most of them heading for upper secondary or grammar school, this is a rather simple task, keeping in mind the objectives of the curriculum. The texts varied in length from 69 to 258 words, with an average of 130 running words.

Results

The following tables present the pupils' use of connectives, transitional words and phrases.

	Group 1	**Group 2**	**Group 3**	**Group 4**
first, at first		2		
next	3			
then	12	7	8	14
next	3			
later	1	1	3	
afterwards	1			
finally	1	1	2	2

Table 2.6.1: Words indicating time sequence

	Group 1	**Group 2**	**Group 3**	**Group 4**
and	82	70	77	98
but	21	15	15	14
however				1
nevertheless	1			

Table 2.6.2: Words indicating addition and contrast:

	Group 1	**Group 2**	**Group 3**	**Group 4**
because	3	6	3	11
so	5	22	8	7
since	2			
if	8	8	11	6

Table 2.6.3: Words indicating cause and effect and condition

Judging from the sample used in this study considerable weakness in the pupils' writing was revealed. The use of transitional words and phrases was limited, in particular the use of words indicating time sequence, considering the type of text in question. Contrary to what was to be expected, there was no striking difference between Groups 1 and 4 in this respect. The majority of the texts therefore lacked cohesion as well as coherence.

It is hardly realistic to expect perfection at this stage, but given the fact that pupils in Iceland acquire a lot of English outside school and given their strong motivation to learn English, they should have done better in their writing. It should also be kept in mind that the textbooks most widely used deal with writing in a systematic way.

Conclusion

The study raises a lot of questions about the place of writing in language teaching. If there ever was need for good writing skills in English it is nowadays with increasing global communication. It is important to teach students how to write in a foreign language, but it is equally important to consider writing as a signifant tool for learning a language. Through writing students have to organise their thoughts. Writing is thus a good way to integrate language learning and thinking. Writing increases the awareness of the structure of the language and can no doubt improve reading comprehension, just as reading can contribute to better writing.

There has been considerable emphasis on grammar at the sentence level in the teaching of English in Iceland and this may be reflected in the pupils' general lack of organising skills in their writing. It might therefore be a good idea to keep the following in mind:

- less focus on traditional sentence-based grammar; more on discourse grammar,
- less focus on the sentence as a unit; more on the text as a whole,
- writing as communication,
- writing for a purpose,
- integration of thinking and writing skills,
- integration of reading and writing,
- process writing and reading journals,
- a healthy balance between creative writing and more structured writing.

Email: audurt@khi.is

2.7 Symposium on academic writing

Convenor: Edward de Chazal *University College, London, UK*

The academic writing symposium offered four talks which analysed and described several approaches and issues within the teaching of academic writing in a tertiary context. The first talk addressed universal issues within academic writing, while the other three were based on research within specific academic contexts of universities in England, Saudi Arabia and Australia. The audience comprised teachers of writing within various contexts including secondary and tertiary, leading to a range of examinations from local assessments to IELTS. As a warmer, the convenor asked the participants to identify the greatest challenges facing learners in academic writing in English. These included, among others, incorporating source material, structuring the text, and a number of language considerations, particularly style. Usefully, several of the challenges identified were explored during the symposium.

Edward de Chazal (*The Language Centre, University College, London*) opened the talks phase of the symposium by presenting his work on the 'adverbial cycle' in academic writing: meaning, function and form. Initially the participants rated linguistically a text written by an advanced student. Most rated it highly in terms of accuracy and sophistication. A key characteristic of the text was the very high incidence of adverbials which contributed to these effects and the sense of flow. Examples ranged from widely-used items, typically simple adverbs, such as 'nowadays' and 'moreover' to more complex structures: 'due to the expansion of urbanisation'; 'in terms of psychological and mental health'; and 'such as the influence of media and friends'. The latter include examples of prepositional phrases, which are the most frequent exponents of adverbials, headed in these examples by complex prepositions ('such as', 'in terms of'). De Chazal argued that the text is a successful example of the strategic incorporation of adverbials in academic writing. To achieve such success he proposed a three-stage cycle for expressing key meanings, based on the semantic organising principles of Biber *et al.*'s (1999) *Longman Grammar of Spoken and Written English*. There are three semantic areas: circumstance, for example condition and result; stance, which explicitly expresses the writer's attitude to the material expressed in the clause; and linking, which supports cohesion and signposting needs. These are expressed through adverbials as phrase- and clause-based structures. Uniquely among clause elements the adverbial is syntactically optional, thus an efficient way of including target meanings without changing the underlying sentence structure. The writer can select an appropriate form from the toolkit of structural items and generate their own language based on the given prototypical patterns, thereby meeting their semantic needs.

Amna Yousef (*College of Education Almajmah, Saudi Arabia*) focused on her local context, discussing the impact of peer collaborative revision on college students' essays. She presented the results of her study, which aimed to determine whether it is feasible to pursue peer collaboration in the college writing course. There were two main focuses: the incorporation of collaborative revisions in final versions; and the integration of peer comments in subsequent individual writing.

Yousef presented her study in which 24 students of intermediate level divided into six groups participated in peer reviews in a writing course. During the collaborative revision stage the students revised each others' drafts, based on different language aspects. Students interacted by asking and answering questions, offering explanations and suggestions, correcting language, and examining content and organisation. Each student draft formed the basis of analysis. This analysis revealed that the students in the study incorporated in their final versions the majority of the revisions arising from the collaborative sessions. A few students, however, opted to ignore their peers' suggestions and developed their own individual revisions. Analysis also showed that students focused mainly on linguistic accuracy rather than content and organisation. Some participants benefited from the group discussions by apparently internalising peer suggestions and integrating them into subsequent texts.

The focus of the following talk moved to England with **Dr Alejandro Armellini**, (*School of Education, University of Manchester*). He presented a practical approach to developing Chinese graduate students' writing. This presentation addressed some of the challenges in the area of academic writing faced by Chinese students on Manchester's MA in Educational Technology and TESOL. These students are English language teachers with a minimum of three years' teaching experience. Data collected from the 2004–2005 cohort suggest that prioritising, providing evidence of critical analysis, synthesising and the programme's demands for quality are among the main factors contributing to these students' anxiety and difficulty in producing academically sound assignments and dissertations. Lack of training in academic writing is also highlighted as a key issue. These difficulties are further emphasised by the students' overestimation of their own English language proficiency and what they term 'influence of oriental ideologies'.

The data also suggests that as the programme unfolds, academic writing improvement correlates with enhanced reading skills, regular interactions with tutors, peer reviews and the critical analysis of 'good models'. Pre-sessional courses, the systematic use of digital resources designed for the improvement of academic writing and general exposure to an active academic environment are also mentioned as contributing factors for improvement. However, the most significant difference appears to have been made by the iterative, constructive, formative feedback provision process. In other words, the regular, focused, written interactions with tutors offered the most valuable contribution in terms of these students' enhancement of their academic writing skills. The following quotation illustrates this:

> I've benefited significantly from the insightful feedback from course tutors who read my assignments. The dissertation writing process, with a constant interaction between the supervisor's prompts, critique and detailed comments and my follow-up revision, provided me with a fabulous opportunity for academic writing improvement.

The symposium concluded with **Dr Lindy Woodrow** (*University of Sydney, Australia*) who offered an ethnographic perspective on the teaching of academic writing for graduates. Her talk described a project to address the academic writing needs of graduate students at the University of Sydney. The talk focused on a graduate unit for credit in academic writing aimed at international and non-English speaking background students (NESBs) developed at the University of Sydney.

First she described the background to the project. The need for this emerged from the diversification of the student body and the apparent mismatch of student and academic staff expectations concerning academic tasks. She then talked about the theoretical rationale for the graduate unit for credit 'English in Academic Settings'. The unit is informed by a socio-literate approach to writing. Relevant issues in academic literacies, genre and academic discourse communities were briefly outlined.

'English in Academic Settings' combines both theoretical and practical approaches to academic writing. This dual focus was required because a skills-alone course was not acceptable as a graduate unit to the university's academic board. She proceeded to describe the course in more detail with a course outline. The most significant aspect of this course is the notion of ethnography of writing whereby students are trained to conduct research as insiders upon their own required writing tasks. She talked about student evaluation of the course, which was largely positive. She also referred to the need to address the disparity of levels of tolerance amongst academic staff concerning academic writing of NESBs. Finally, she talked about a future academic writing unit to be offered in 2007 focusing on thesis and dissertation writing.

Email: e.dechazal@ucl.ac.uk

3 Form, meaning and use

This chapter focuses on the teaching of language systems, including grammar and vocabulary. In his plenary **Michael Swan** appeals for well-balanced language-teaching programmes which he defines as requiring extensive, intensive and analysed input and output stages. Far too often, he argues, one of the important elements is missing. He goes on to explain how to link intensive input and output effectively by means of a concrete teaching example. He then draws our attention to practical, cultural and theoretical considerations that sometimes militate against well-balanced teaching and ends by advising us to take care to choose language teaching routes that will lead the learners towards knowledge of the target language.

The next two papers are also concerned with appropriate ways to introduce and practise language. **Joanne Collie and Hans Mol** recommend presenting grammar in use, inviting learners to ask questions that lead to discovery of patterns and rules. Through a workshop example of controlled practice in an unfamiliar target language they illustrate how learners can become aware of the primacy of lexis for communication at elementary level. **Maria Estling Vannestål** reports on a first-term university English grammar course. Her project aims to increase students' awareness of English grammar in authentic use with the help of corpus exercises, to help them interact more with each other and to enable them to assume more responsibility for their own learning.

Moving from grammar to lexis, **Birgit Winkler** reviews dictionaries, especially the many useful features of CD-ROM dictionaries. **Adam Simpson** describes the process of developing a vocabulary syllabus based on his university's coursebook series. He enumerates and comments on the stages of his project from conception, through data gathering, the creation of materials, classroom use and evaluation. He thus provides a possible blueprint for others who would like to develop a vocabulary syllabus for a specific context. Both **Andreja Kovacic** and **Tilly Harrison** explore ways of helping university students to improve their vocabulary. Andreja Kovacic introduces her work with information technology (IT) students on the IT lexicon; she gets them to study multiple lexical relationships between subsets of technical vocabulary. Tilly Harrison got her Chinese undergraduates studying in the UK to record new words on a wiki (a web page which anyone can edit) together with a definition, context and mnemonic linking the English word to some Chinese words. Through their joint wiki the students were able to find out what their peers were reading, to learn new words from classmates and to access the ready-made mnemonics in their own language.

3.1 Plenary: Two out of three ain't enough—the essential ingredients of a language course

Michael Swan *Freelance and Visiting Professor, St. Mary's College, University of Surrey, UK*

It's all very complicated

Looking over the programme at the beginning of an IATEFL conference, one can easily experience two rather contradictory reactions. First of all, sheer gratitude. Such an occasion offers us a remarkable opportunity to meet colleagues, exchange ideas and extend our professional knowledge. Annual conferences don't arrange themselves, and we owe a considerable debt to the many people whose work, past and present, has made this kind of event possible.

A second, equally valid, reaction is bewilderment. Titles of sessions on this year's programme included references to the following topics, among many others:

anxiety, CALL, classroom research, collaborative learning, consciousness-raising, corpus, critical discourse analysis, critical reading, cultural awareness, developing teacher reflection, ELF, innovation management, interactivity, intercultural competence, internet, IT, kinaesthetic learners, learner differences, learner independence, learner preferences, learner training, learner's self-concept, metaphor, motivation, multiple intelligences, negotiated interaction, new technologies, pragmatics, prefabs, professional development, reflective practice, scaffolding, strategy training, teacher's role, ...

(And if I told you that there was a seminar on 'multiple kinaesthetic interactive classroom discourse strategy development', you might have to think for a moment before you could be quite sure I was making it up.) It is easy to see how a young teacher, attending IATEFL for the first time, can feel daunted and discouraged: 'If I need to know about all this in order to be a good English teacher, how am I ever going to manage it?'

When I started in ELT, you had to know how to teach grammar, pronunciation, vocabulary and the 'four skills'. We have come a very long way since then, and this is all to the good; but there really is an awful lot to know about. The landscape has become extremely complicated, and we don't seem to have much in the way of maps—it is not nearly as easy as it used to be to see where we are going and how to get there. Does this matter? Perhaps not. Should we, in the spirit of the age, avoid getting hung up on product, and decide that it is the process which is important—so that it is enough to choose roads that look interesting, and go where they take us? To travel hopefully, Stevenson said, is a better thing than to arrive. This is certainly the view of more than one influential scholar in the field. Kumaravidevelu tells us (2006: 195) that according to the principles of 'Exploratory Practice' developed by Allwright and others, 'the quality of life in the language classroom is much more important than instructional efficiency'. And Ellis, arguing for a full-scale task-based approach to language teaching, says that the blurring of the distinction between syllabus and methodology is an 'attractive feature' of task-based work, and that a central tenet of the approach is arguably the idea that 'no attempt is made to specify what learners will learn, only how they will learn' (2003: 30–1).

I believe that this attitude is profoundly mistaken. The world is full of language learners who travel hopefully without arriving, and these learners are not generally pleased. Language learning and teaching cost time, effort and money, and it is reasonable to expect a product—knowledge of a language—as a result. A language course should, therefore, contain the essential elements which will make this result possible. What are these elements? The topics listed above may all contribute usefully to more effective learning and teaching, but they are not in themselves constitutive of a language course. We need to know what are the fundamental components that actually make language teaching work.

Language teaching takes place, of course, in a vast variety of contexts, and there are very great differences between these. One thing that is common to all situations, though, is that teaching and learning can fail—things can go wrong. Essentially, this can happen for three reasons. One is that teachers and learners may simply be working under impossible circumstances: there may be far too little time for effective teaching, or classes may be dominated by undisciplined students who are determined not to learn. A second reason for failure is that teachers may just not be doing things right: the methodology may be so inappropriate, or the quality of the teaching so poor, that no significant learning is possible. Thirdly—and this is what I want to focus on—teachers may not be doing the right things.

What are these right things? In what follows, I shall offer a suggested answer to this question—a map, so to speak, showing what I think are the main roads through the complicated language-teaching terrain. I must stress that this is a personal view, not based on empirical research, and scarcely to be dignified with the name of 'theory'. It does, however, derive from many years of practical involvement in, and thought about, language teaching.

Three elements

Language learners need *extensive input*. Children learning their mother tongues are immersed in a bath of language, some of it roughly attuned to their level of development, much of it not. Without this element, it is unlikely that they would succeed in acquiring language. Second-language learners, similarly, must have extensive input—they need to be exposed to quantities of spoken and written language, authentic or not too tidied up, for their unconscious acquisition processes to work on.

Equally, learners need *intensive input*—small samples of language which can be assimilated, memorised, analysed unconsciously, and/or used as templates for future production. Children instinctively seek this kind of input, and their caretakers instinctively provide it, in the form of nursery rhymes, songs and stories, which—children insist—must always be repeated in exactly the same words. Daily routines also provide children with intensive samples of language—the little scripts that are repeated at mealtimes, bathtime, bedtime and so on. Adult second-language learners are no different in principle: they too need intensive engagement with small samples of language which they can internalise, process, make their own and use as bases for their own production. (For a fascinating discussion of this element of language acquisition and use, see Cook 2000.)

A third kind of input is what one might call *analysed*: information about the workings of particular aspects of the language, presented implicitly or explicitly. As far as first-language acquisition is concerned, this is perhaps of less importance: children naturally pick up grammar and pronunciation without being told anything about the workings of the very complex systems involved, and corrective feedback generally has little effect. (On the other hand, children are very conscious of their need for explanations of vocabulary—English-speaking children learn something like eight new words a day—and they very often ask for explicit information about words: 'What's a …?'; 'What's that?'; 'What does … mean?'.) While the value of analysed input to adult second-language learners has become controversial, it seems likely that it is helpful or necessary for at least some aspects of language. Since adult learners are past the critical period when a perfect command of a language can be acquired naturally and unconsciously, and since instructed second-language learners have only a fraction of the input that is available to child first-language learners, the deliberate teaching of regularities helps to compensate for the inadequacy of naturalistic exposure.

Input, of course, is only half the story. By and large, people seem to learn best what they use most. Children produce quantities of extensive output, activating what they have taken in by, in many cases, chattering non-stop. They also recycle the intensive input they have received, repeating their stories, nursery rhymes and so on, and speaking their lines in the recurrent daily scripts of childhood life. Some children, at least, also seem to produce certain kinds of analysed output, rehearsing and trying out variations on structures that they have been exposed to, like more formal language learners doing 'pattern practice' (Weir 1970).

Adults, of course, also need opportunities to produce all three kinds of output. They must have the chance to engage in extensive, 'free' speech and writing; they must be able to do controlled practice in which they recycle the intensive input that they have more or less internalised (and thus complete the process of internalisation);

and they need to practise the analysed patterns and language items that have been presented to them, so that they have some chance of carrying them over into spontaneous fluent production.

A properly-balanced language-teaching programme, then, has three ingredients—extensive, intensive and analysed—at both input and output stages. All three ingredients are important. (See Table 3.1.1.) A song by Meatloaf has the chorus:

I want you
I need you
but there ain't no way I'm ever going to love you.
Now don't be sad
'cause two out of three ain't bad.

Leaving aside the question of whether Meatloaf's addressee is comfortable with this reduced offering, one thing is certain: in language teaching, two out of three ain't enough.

Input	Extensive	Intensive	Analysed
	• books, magazines, etc. • speech	• spoken or written texts studied in detail • material learnt by heart	• rules, examples, lists
Output	Extensive	Intensive	Analysed
	• free writing • free speaking	• controlled speaking or writing reusing learnt material.	• exercises

Table 3.1.1: A balanced programme

Gaps in courses

It is instructive to look at some typical language teaching approaches (discussed here in rather stereotypical versions) to see how well they satisfy this principle. Nearly always, something is missing.

One formula, traditional but still very common in various guises round the world, is a course-type that relies heavily on teacher-fronted text study, often coursebook-based. (Textbooks, as the name implies, tend to be disturbingly text-heavy.) This approach is strong on 'intensive' input (though I shall suggest below that this is often pseudo-intensive); analysed input also typically gets good coverage, at least as regards grammar; extensive input is usually weak or completely lacking. As far as intensive output is concerned, the input from text study is not generally recycled very efficiently—often, all that the learners do with it is to answer a few so-called 'comprehension' questions. Analysed output is common, in the form of grammar exercises. There is often little or no extensive output.

Although we like to feel that we have moved on from the methods of a century or so ago, there are actually close structural resemblances between a modern text-heavy course and a grammar-translation approach (though the methodology is somewhat different). Similarly, the audiolingual approach that was popular a few decades ago, revolutionary though it was felt to be, differed mainly in the type of text that was used (spoken rather than written), and in the methodology of grammar teaching; the balance of ingredients was not very different. Revolutions do not always change the underlying structure of things very much. (See Table 3.1.2.)

Input	Extensive	Intensive	Analysed
	(readers?)	written texts studied more or less in detail ('listening' material?)	grammar rules and examples
Output	Extensive	Intensive	Analysed
	(occasional free composition and/or conversation practice?)	(answers to 'comprehension' questions)	grammar exercises and tests

Table 3.1.2: The text-heavy formula

Heavily 'communicative' courses do have a rather different kind of structure, but again, there are problems of coverage and balance. Typically, they are much stronger than more 'traditional' course types on output. On the other hand, there may be little extensive input, and far less analysed input or output than in 'traditional' courses—this element may be limited to studying and practising the language of particular communicative functions ('apologising', 'eliciting personal information', 'inviting', 'enquiring about timetables' and so on). (See Table 3.1.3.)

Input	Extensive	Intensive	Analysed
	• (written material?) • (recorded speech?)	• input material for communicative activities • 'listening' texts	• (lists of functional language?)
Output	Extensive	Intensive	Analysed
	• discussion • role play	• communicative activities	('functional' practice?)

Table 3.1.3: One kind of 'communicative' course

Some approaches—what one might call the Atkins Diets of language teaching—simply leave out most of the ingredients. One extreme case is the kind of course (if it was ever put into practice) recommended by scholars such as Stephen Krashen a

Chapter 3: Form, meaning and use

couple of decades ago. The basic principle was that 'comprehensible input' was all that was needed for successful acquisition. If this was provided, output would take care of itself. 'Theoretically, speaking and writing are not essential to acquisition. One can acquire 'competence' in a second language, or a first language, without ever producing it' (Krashen 1981: 107–8). Furthermore, analysed input such as grammar rules was said to be useless, since (it was claimed) it had no effect on acquisition, and would not carry over into spontaneous production. While the 'input is all' line of thought was greatly consoling to teachers who had trouble getting output from their learners (they no longer needed to try), it can scarcely have benefited the students of any teachers who took it seriously. (See Table 3.1.4.)

Input	Extensive	Intensive	Analysed
	• written material • recorded speech	• written material • recorded speech	
Output	Extensive	Intensive	Analysed

Table 3.1.4: 'Comprehensible input is all'

At the other extreme, what one might call the hard-core task-based approach, recommended by some contemporary researchers, puts almost all the emphasis on extensive output, to which everything else is subordinated. (See Table 3.1.5.)

Input	Extensive	Intensive	Analysed
	(pre-task reading/ listening?)		incidental focus on form during task performance
Output	Extensive	Intensive	Analysed
	task performance	(planned task performance) (task repetition)	

Table 3.1.5: Hard-core task-based

Balance

While a normal language course must, I believe, contain all three elements, they do not of course need to occur in equal proportions: the appropriate balance will depend on the learners' level, their purposes and their learning context. In particular, if students are learning a language in the country where it is spoken, or if other parts of their education are in the target language, extensive input and perhaps output may be taken care of outside the language course. And analysed input and output are likely to be less appropriate or necessary for younger learners. But in general terms, in my view, these criteria apply; so that if students fail to learn, it may simply be because their course is not doing all the right things. It is therefore, worth checking over the menu that our materials, activities and syllabuses are offering to our students. Do the ingredients—text-study, grammar, dictation, comprehension, communicative tasks or whatever—add up to a balanced diet, or are essential elements missing? As in other areas of life, it is important to look not only at what we are doing, but at what we are not doing.

A common weakness: pseudo-intensive work

For successful language teaching, I believe that it is essential to link intensive input and output effectively. The intensive element works (or should work) like this:

1. Students engage with a sample of language—generally a short spoken or written text of some kind.
2. They work hard enough on this sample to make some of the language their own: words, expressions and structures stick in their minds; perhaps whole stretches of the text are even memorised (as when a dialogue is learnt by heart).
3. Then their acquisition of the new input is consolidated by output work—by using what they have learnt, they fix it in their memories and make it available for future use.

What happens in classrooms, all too often, is not quite like that. Briefly: the 'intensive' input isn't really intensive, and the intensive output doesn't really happen. One common version of this pseudo-intensive cycle involves the kind of lesson that we have all seen, and perhaps given, where the teacher uses a text as the basis for a kind of free-association fireworks display. He or she comments on one word, expression or structure after another, elicits synonyms and antonyms, pursues ideas sparked off by the text, perhaps gets the students to read aloud or translate bits, and so on and so on. Meanwhile the students—or at least, the conscientious ones—write down hundreds of pieces of new information in those overfilled notebooks that someone once memorably called 'word cemeteries'. What happens next? The students answer some so-called 'comprehension questions' (what exactly are these for?), and then perhaps go away to write a homework on a topic distantly related (or even not at all related) to that of the text. At the end of the cycle the students have been given much too much input, have engaged with it too superficially for much of it to be assimilated, and have used (and therefore consolidated) little or none of it. They have been taught—inefficiently—one lot of language, and then asked to produce a substantially different lot.

How to get it right

It is not actually very difficult to link intensive input and output more constructively: it just needs a clear understanding of how texts can be used effectively for language teaching. There are all sorts of possible approaches—the key technique is to select a relatively small text (spoken or written) that contains some useful language, to work over it quite thoroughly (so that students are at least halfway to knowing it by heart), and to give them an activity in which they can reuse the material interestingly. Here is one way of doing it with a lower-level class:

- Take a story or other text of perhaps 200 words.
- Read it to the class, with explanations where necessary.
- Ask what they can remember.
- Read it again and see how much more they can recall.
- Hand out the text/get them to open their books.
- Go through the text explaining and answering questions where necessary, but concentrating particularly on a relatively small number of useful language points (perhaps 8–12) which the students don't yet have an active command of.
- Tell them to note and learn these points.
- Ask them to choose for themselves a few other words, expressions or structures that they think it would be useful to learn.
- Get them to close their books or put away the text, and ask recall questions (*not* 'comprehension questions'), designed specifically to get them to say or write the words and expressions picked out for learning.
- Finally, set a written homework in which they are expected to use most of the new material, but in their own way. (For instance, ask them to tell the story they have studied in the form of a letter written by one of the characters in it; or to write about a similar incident from their own experience.)

There are plenty of other ways of achieving this level of close engagement with input material, followed by creative output using what has been learnt. Students can work on a dialogue, and then script and perform (or improvise) new dialogues on a similar theme. One class I heard about hijacked the whole of their boring textbook, rewriting the stories and dialogues with added elements (a pregnancy, an explosion, an arrest, a lottery win, alien invaders, …) to make them more interesting, and thus using what they had learnt in highly original and motivating ways. What is essential is that students should, little by little, build up a repertoire of key vocabulary and structures that they have made their own by working on them intensively and reusing them in this way. Compared with the typical 'text study—comprehension questions —free writing' cycle, the crucial difference is that learners do *more* with *less*, so that they really do learn and remember what they take in, instead of forgetting most of it before the lesson is over.

Why the gaps?

If a language course lacks some of the essential ingredients, this may be for several possible reasons. One is purely practical: in many teaching situations round the world, it can be hard to provide extensive input. There isn't time in class for students to do extensive reading; it may not be possible to get them to do it out of class; good extensive listening materials may be in short supply; a non-native-speaking teacher may not feel confident in his or her ability to compensate for this by talking freely to the class. Fortunately, the internet is making it much easier for learners to obtain interesting and motivating forms of exposure to authentic input, and this is likely to improve language-learning worldwide.

A second reason may be cultural. In countries where the educational tradition favours authoritarian teacher-fronted presentation and a traditional transmission model of education, there is likely to be a strong emphasis on input and a correspondingly reduced emphasis on learner output. And if public self-expression is discouraged, as it is in some cultures, it may be particularly hard to get students to recycle input material creatively in personalised communicative activities. Equally, in strongly rule-governed societies, the rule-based part of language—grammar—tends to be highly valued and to play a dominant role, taking away time from other important components.

Theoretical fashions can also push language teaching towards extreme positions where important components are sidelined or dropped altogether. Contemporary theory is in fact fairly hostile to the kind of intensive input-output work discussed above. The theoretical preference today is emphatically for learner-centred models, with extensive communicative output being highly valued. Intensive output, deliberately reusing what has been taught, is condemned as being unoriginal, not properly communicative, mere 'regurgitation' of other people's language. But teacher-controlled input-output work has a key place in language teaching, alongside other types of activity. You cannot teach by eliciting what is not there, and the best way of making sure that new language is acquired is, very precisely, to give learners other people's language (as we have to—they can't make the language up for themselves) and to help them to make it their own as they use it for personal and creative purposes.

Changes in theoretical or pedagogic fashion often come about because of disillusionment: our teaching doesn't seem to be getting very good results, and the temptation is to drop what we are doing and look for alternatives. But this may not bring about any net gain. If we are doing too much formal input and not enough communicative output, the solution is to balance things up, not to move to a position where we are doing too much communicative output and not enough formal input. This is to act like a man who, feeling cold, puts on a sweater and then takes his trousers off. We need to face the sobering fact that language teaching won't usually get very good results. Languages are hard to learn, and there is never enough time to teach them properly. In particular, the depressing gulf between successful controlled classroom practice and correct spontaneous use—the carry-over problem—will always to some extent be with us. But we can at least optimise our work, so as to get the best results we can under the circumstances. This means, among other things, making sure that our courses have all the key ingredients. We need in particular to beware of miracle solutions, and of packages with labels like 'The X Approach' or 'The Y Method'. Such approaches are nearly always subtractive as well as additive, putting a great deal of emphasis on one or other ingredient of language teaching while neglecting others.

Conclusion

I began by claiming that our professional landscape has become very complex, offering a bewildering variety of features for our attention. I have suggested that there are, however, main roads through this complicated terrain. If we keep to these roads most of the time, we will be better placed to make useful side trips to benefit from the many interesting and instructive features that can be found along the way, without getting totally distracted and disoriented as we do so. In this way, we can perhaps not only travel hopefully, but also arrive.

References

Cook, G. 2000. *Language Play, Language Learning*. Oxford: Oxford University Press.
Ellis, R. 2003. *Task-based Language Learning and Teaching*. Oxford: Oxford University Press.
Krashen, S. *Second Language Acquisition and Second Language Learning*. Oxford: Pergamon.
Kumaravadivelu, B. 2006. *Understanding Language Teaching: From Method to Postmethod*. London: Lawrence Erlbaum Associates.
Weir, R. H. 1970. *Language in the Crib*. The Hague: Mouton.

3.2 Easing your way into grammar

Joanne Collie *University of Warwick, UK*
and Hans Mol *Southern Cross Connexxions, Australia*

The workshop began by our exploring some of the things that had been said about grammar in the preceding days of the conference, often contradictory statements such as:

'Grammar has no psychological validity.'

'It's a skeleton in the closet that needs to be re-interred.'

'Without grammar, there is only meaning-impoverished instruction.'

'Planting seeds doesn't guarantee that they grow—not planting them pretty well guarantees that they don't.'

'To boldly go … no one's going to die of a split infinitive.'

'People want to know how it works.'

'It's a beautiful set of ideas that will always remain out of use.'

We then explained the main aim of the workshop, which was to experiment with a type of grammar that takes the learner's questions as its starting point, approaches language structures through functions, invites reflection on the native language, and makes grammar come alive in communicative settings. Our belief is that students speaking and writing in English, at any level, will employ strategies that enable them to communicate successfully with others, and that building upon these strategies is an effective and motivating way of extending their language mastery.

We began by introducing ourselves to the audience in our own native languages, French and Dutch. The short dialogues of introduction were displayed, and participants asked to mingle and introduce each other, using one language not familiar to them. They then discussed their experience, wrote down and reported one or two questions that had occurred to them when they actually used their new language. Queries for the French dialogue focused on the different forms used—*'tu'* or *'vous'*—and on word order; for Dutch, the difference between *'dit'* and *'dat'* and the singular/plural forms of the *verbs*.

We then explained the rationale underlying our view of a fruitful way forward from this initial position.

Our aims were: to empower learners, to provide extra practice, and to produce clear, meaningful principles. The teacher's role would be to present examples, invite questions, guide deduction, and help reflection. The learners' tasks would be to recognise structures and patterns, guess how the language works, practise and produce meaningful chunks.

A sequenced method would consist of:

- presentation, based upon varied contexts and inviting questions,
- reflection and discovery, deducing the way language works,
- controlled practice,
- homework and consolidation, and
- presentation of a 'rule book' outlining rules in simple language.

An example was displayed of a presentation, based on a simple dialogue for beginners, in which children talked about their party.

The second activity was an illustration of controlled practice (or, in the words of Herbert Puchta, 'practice to control'). We divided participants into two groups, one consisting of people who did not know Dutch. The groups heard a short dictation which practised the forms 'there is' and 'there are' in either English and Dutch. Here is the Dutch:

Welkom op mijn feestje!
Dit is onze woonkamer. Hier houd ik mijn feestje.
Er is een grote tafel.
Er zijn vier stoelen.
Er staat een televisie op de vloer.
Er staat een computer op de tafel.
Er zijn twee lampen.
Vind je mijn huis leuk?

Participants were asked to draw the room and its objects. They then rejoined their first partners, exchanged drawings, and described the rooms in English or Dutch. In this part of the exercise, many participants asked questions about the forms that they should use. When a pair demonstrated their conversation to the whole group, however, it was obvious that the actual structures '*Er is ...*', '*Er zijn ...*' and '*Er staat ...*' were not used, just the vocabulary items which had been learned. This was quite a vivid demonstration of the fact that whereas vocabulary is essential for communication, often at this elementary level grammar is not. Awareness of that fact was, participants agreed, useful for learners and could lead to a more autonomous and learner-oriented grasp of the way languages work.

Finally, a questions-and-answers session rounded off the workshop. Participants expressed interest in their own experience of working with a different language and comparing it to their own. There was also discussion of possible classroom adaptations of the method used.

Email: mail@jmacollie.co.uk
connexxions@bigpond.com

3.3 Language corpora and peer teaching in an English grammar course

Maria Estling Vannestål *Växjö University, Växjö, Sweden*

Computerised language corpora, i.e. large collections of authentic texts which can be accessed by means of so-called concordancing programs, have been used in linguistic research for several decades. In recent years, teachers have also started appreciating their potential as a tool for learning a foreign language. In Sweden, however, corpora have mainly been used by university students doing research for their third- or fourth-term papers. Furthermore, there have been few empirical studies actually evaluating the outcome of using corpora in language learning. The present pedagogical project, which is financed by the Swedish Council for Higher Education, combines the use of language corpora and peer teaching in a first-term English grammar course and contains a substantial evaluation component.

The background of the project is that many students have negative attitudes towards grammar, and that they often have trouble both with understanding grammatical principles and with applying these to their own usage. In the project we hope to increase the students' awareness of the fact that English grammar is more than a set of rules in a book (authentic language in the corpus), to help them interact more with each other (the peer-teaching model) and the material they work with (the corpus work), and to enable them to assume more responsibility for their own learning. The project ideas are thus based on several different theories of language learning—the benefits of authentic material, interaction, peer teaching, exploratory learning—all of which have the same goals: enhanced student motivation and deeper learning.

The work is carried out in the following manner: between classes, the students (in pairs) explore areas in grammar which tend to be problematic with the help of corpus exercises that have been prepared within the project. These exercises deal with, for instance, subject–verb agreement and the use of articles, and the students extract grammatical patterns based on examples from the corpus. They use a free online version of one of the largest corpora, the Cobuild corpus, which includes 55 million words of spoken and written British and American English. The corpus can be accessed at: http://www.collins.co.uk/Corpus/CorpusSearch.aspx.

Since the corpus is free of charge and available to all, the students get a tool that can be used for lifelong learning, whenever they write English texts in the future. Peer teaching is also an important aspect of the project. In the classroom students take turns at 'teaching' each other, based on their experiences in front of the computers, with the underlying assumption that you learn more when having to explain things to someone else.

At the time of this interim report, the corpus work has been tried out for one semester. We are in the middle of the evaluation process, which consists of comparing the corpus group with a control group as regards attitudes before and after the course, and their results in the final tests (a grammar test and an essay test). Some insights have been gained already. First, we have realized how extremely important it is to give the students a thorough introduction to the use of corpora. The two two-hour classes devoted to the introduction to corpora turned out to be insufficient, and it seems that the students need more supervision than expected before they can start working with corpus exercises on their own, especially weak learners. Second, it is crucial to make the students understand how to find grammatical patterns in the lists of example sentences from the corpus that they can see on the screen (going beyond the mere counting of examples). Third, it is vital that the exercise instructions should be easy to understand, since the students are supposed to work with the corpus between classes. Finally, we would like to focus more on making the students aware of how they can use the corpus independently when writing texts in English.

Here are also a few voices from the student group, taken from their mid-term evaluation:

'More fun to work with corpora …'

'I actually use the corpus to look up things for my essay writing, not just for the exercises …'

'A bit tricky at the beginning but good when you understand how it works …'

'Feels like just a lot of counting …'

Anyone interested in the project can read more about it, find references to useful literature and web links and download our exercise material at http://www.vxu.se/hum/utb/amnen/engelska/kig/.

Email: maria.estling-vannestal@vxu.se

3.4 Discover your dictionary: book, CD-ROM, online

Birgit Winkler *Fh. Joanneum, Graz, Austria*

The presentation aimed to increase dictionary awareness among teachers and students of English. First, information in book dictionaries was exemplified through a guide in one of the five major English learners' dictionaries that are currently available for advanced level. Now included in most dictionaries, such guides are meant to help users find and interpret dictionary information. Workbooks offering various activities to enhance dictionary skills are also available.

The focus of my presentation was, however, on CD-ROM dictionaries as they provide more information than their printed or online counterparts. The online versions of the Longman, the Oxford and Cambridge dictionaries—Cambridge was the first to offer Internet dictionaries gratis—are especially easy to access: users can enter search words and are then offered the same information as in the respective book. (See http://dictionary.cambridge.org, http://www.longman.com/ldoce and http://www.oup.com/elt/catalogue/teachersites/oald7 .) All the websites offer further features, for example, online activities, resources for teachers and students, word/idiom of the week/month and corpus information.

The latest editions of the following CD-ROM dictionaries were explored:

The Cambridge Advanced Learner's Dictionary on CD-ROM (2005: *CALD*);
Collins COBUILD Advanced Learner's English Dictionary (2003: *CC*);
The Longman Dictionary of Contemporary English (2005: *LDOCE*);
The Macmillan English Dictionary for Advanced Learners on CD-ROM (2002: *MED*);
The Oxford Advanced Learner's Compass (2005: *OALC*).

Compared with their antecedents—the first English learner's dictionary on CD-ROM came out in 1992—current editions are significantly user-friendlier due to a number of changes in content and presentation, which is true for learner's dictionaries in general. In computer-related tasks, for example, searching the Internet or writing emails or other texts, CD-ROM dictionaries can be very useful as they offer further search options and include more materials (for example, additional books and practice materials).

The CD-ROM dictionaries presented here are somewhat similar: all of them contain A–Z lists and pronunciation (British and American English—apart from *CC*, which additionally presents pronunciation of derived forms, however); pronunciation practice facilities (where users need to compare their version with the dictionary one, though); print/copy functions and an option to change settings (for example, font size, automatic displays). The five CD-ROM dictionaries also offer a guided tour or at least a help facility, which can be studied to understand better what information is included, how it is presented and what searches can be conducted. (*CALD* has a 'talking' guide.)

Frequency information is now provided as a standard feature of learners' dictionaries: each of them is based on a corpus. Usually three levels for the 3000 most commonly used words are indicated: *CALD* uses 'E' for essential, 'I' for improver and 'A' for advanced; *MED* employs */**/***; CC has diamonds ♦/♦♦/♦♦♦; *OALC* uses a key-symbol for the Oxford 3000 list, Longman indicates levels 1–3 for S (spoken) and W (written) English.

Pictures/illustrations are available in four of the five CD-ROM dictionaries. *CC*, however, which also has no pictures in its book dictionary either, contains a vast reference tool—the Wordbank—presenting a myriad of authentic sentences from the Bank of English. A supplementary user-defined dictionary has also been added. A similar feature is offered in *MED* as 'Notebook'. Exercises (grammar, vocabulary, culture, listening or exam practice) are part of *CALD*, *OALC* and *LDOCE*.

Additional cultural information can be found in *OALC*, which includes *The Oxford Guide to British and American Culture*. Extra grammatical details in *LDOCE* comprise the *Longman Essential Grammar*. This CD-ROM dictionary's special attraction is that spoken examples are included.

Some help with grammar and spelling mistakes can be found in *OALC* (a new feature called 'Oxford Know-how'); the sound search facility in *MED*; and the 'Writing Assistant' as part of *LDOCE*. *LDOCE* and *OALC* also allow the dictionary to shrink to the size of a pop-up screen-window, allowing users to access dictionary information from other applications such as word-processor, Internet or email. Assistance when reading and writing on the computer is also provided by *CALD* ('QUICKfind' and 'SUPERwrite') and OALC (the Oxford Genie).

Advanced searches can also be carried out with the help of Boolean operators (AND, OR, NOT) or wildcards (*) (not in *CC*). Some search filters, for example, for frequency, part of speech, grammar, usage, region or topic are offered too (*CALD*; *LDOCE*; *MED*: 'SmartSearch'; *OALC*). Synonyms can be found in *CALD* (smart thesaurus), in *CC* and *LDOCE* (*Longman Language Activator*). *OALC* provides information on related words through the 'Wordfinder'. A completely new feature for learners' dictionaries is word origin, included in *OALC* and *LDOCE*.

User studies should allow further insight into the actual use of these CD-ROM dictionaries.

Email: wbaustria@yahoo.co.uk

3.5 How we made an academic vocabulary syllabus

Adam J. Simpson   *Sabancı University, Turkey*

The process of developing a vocabulary syllabus based on Sabancı University's *Beyond the Boundaries* coursebook series was undertaken with two major considerations in mind: the needs of the learners within the university environment, and the constraints created by developing a syllabus based on the descriptors set out in the *Common European Framework of Reference for Languages* (*CEFR*). After establishing the aims and objectives of the vocabulary syllabus with regard to the needs of our students and the *CEFR*, it was necessary to consider how this project would fit into the language school's overall syllabus.

The presentation's first main section was an analysis of the stages the project went through in collecting and analysing data, with reference to such tools as frequency analysis, vocabulary profiling and concordance. Practical examples from the work were shown, with participants being asked to undertake the role of students for the analysis of a text in which only a small part of the vocabulary was known to them. Also described was how this analysis led to the development of lists of lexical items, and then on to the creation of mini-dictionaries for each coursebook unit, which were given the name vocabulary 'companions'. The audience were not only made aware of all of the tools used in the process of analysis, but were shown how these enabled the project to fullfil *CEFR* requirements in terms of selection and ordering of vocabulary items.

Next was a description of how these lists and companions were used as a classroom resource, along with the other materials developed to exploit these resources, and the subsequent washback effects on the school's vocabulary assessment. Again, practical examples were shown to enable the participants to conceptualise the process of taking students on the path to knowing a word, from first encounter to effective productive use. This was made possible by listing the descriptors used in the syllabus documents, namely; Stage One—*First encounters* (at which stage the students would first come into contact with the vocabulary item); Stage Two—*Getting to know the word* (where the students' knowledge of the word (preposition/grammatical structure used with the item, etc.) was developed); and Stage Three—*Using the word* (production of the word at sentence level). A fourth level, Stage Zero, which focused on learner training materials, was also included in order to further satisfy the *CEFR* guidelines. These stages were exemplified with some of the documents used in classroom teaching. An example of a Stage One would be one in which the student was required to choose a correct definition of a word from a contextualised sentence, with the aim of giving the learner an entry point to understanding the word. At Stage Two, the activities addressed such issues as collocations, usage restrictions and other elements relating to word usage, necessitating that students develop a deeper level of understanding. Stage Three activities created need for students to use vocabulary productively. The activities required the learners to complete such tasks as making sentences from prompts. One of the fears of using a relatively small corpus (250,000 words), that the amount of data available to develop linguistic competence would be insufficient, was highlighted. This issue was addressed in the development of Stage Zero activities, for learner training. A typical activity was to assign particular lexical items to groups of students and have them research that word on the Internet. By searching using the lexical item as the keyword, a list of headlines was shown, from which collocations could be observed; these collocations were then used by students to prepare materials to share with their friends.

Finally, the presentation highlighted the process of evaluation. Two forms of feedback were received. Firstly, semi-formal teacher feedback, from which three main issues became evident: the number of unit-specific items was considered too high, there was insufficient recycling of essential vocabulary, and further assessment practice was required for students to measure progress. The consequences of these comments were as follows: unit specific vocabulary was revised and the number of items reduced; vocabulary was recycled to a greater extent across levels (words presented at lower levels were generally presented again at higher levels); and quizzes were prepared for each unit. Students were also asked for their feedback in the form of group interviews, and samples were taken from students at all levels of proficiency. The main themes were that the materials had to be 'fun' and that assessment was necessary to motivate them.

Email: adams@sabanciuniv.edu

3.6 What's in a name? Plotting lexical relationships in computer English

Andreja Kovacic *Faculty of Organization and Informatics, Varazdin, Croatia*

The ever-changing context of information technology (IT) presupposes an equally dynamic linguistic environment in which new items are constantly created for the new concepts to be encoded. Apart from the abstract nature of these concepts, it is the very features of this new jargon—as well as the rate (Crystal 2002) at which it is being expanded—that make it difficult to absorb in a structured way. Therefore, the question of whether the new jargon used by a growing number of computer users is user-friendly, is one that often gives rise to controversy among IT jargon experts. (Meyer 2002; Woltjer 1981).

The apparent fuzziness (Crystal 1995) is primarily accounted for by the following: the abundance of terms, the high proportion of lexemes borrowed from general English when compared to proportion of lexemes existing solely in the IT context (Raguzzoni 2006) and the semantic overlapping resulting from such lexical productivity. The latter constitutes one of the idiosyncrasies of IT nomenclature, namely a high occurrence of synonymy (multiple signs for one concept) and polysemy (multiple meanings of one sign), as well as stylistic variations, all of which interfere with the basic requirement of any scientific or technical jargon: its pragmatic nature.

Decoding a particular lexical item pertaining to this complex geography inevitably implies disambiguating the numerous instances of polysemy by putting the words in context and looking at procedures in which new items are produced. When it comes to lexical production, apart from standard mechanisms of wordbuilding (affixation, clipping, blending), the issue of the arbitrariness needs to be highlighted. Namely, although arbitrariness is an inherent property of language (Yule 1996), which means that content and forms are mutually unrelated, there are numerous cases in IT jargon in which the sign is transparent owing to its etymology or metaphorical meaning.

The importance of context arises not only from the fact that language itself is a system—so while trying to identify each unit pertaining to the system, their interrelations should be taken into consideration as well (Lyons 1977)—but also from the fact that our very experience of the world is stored in 'schemata' (Khairi 1993; Rumelhart 1980) of related concepts in the human memory. The whole is therefore crucial to understanding any part belonging to it.

Semantic analysis is a major resource for establishing the relationship between interrelated terms. If we conceive of lexical items as 'being related along two intersecting dimensions' (Crystal 1995), then on the vertical dimension the following (paradigmatic) relationships can be established: synonymy, antonymy, hyponymy, part-whole relationships, etc. The most significant type of syntagmatic relationships existing between adjacent elements on the vertical dimension is collocation. Thus the presence of other items existing around the item to be defined helps identify the meaning of the item more accurately.

Visualisation of the underlying lexical structure of IT jargon is facilitated by a graphic approach. Vocabulary exercises including lists, tables, diagrams, and mind maps (Buzan 2002) are designed in a way to motivate students (mature tertiary-level language learners) to use their linguistic and extralinguistic assets (knowledge of the subject matter, familiarity with data structure and abstract concepts used for classifying information). Further contextualization is achieved through the very choice of method (Williams 2005); IT students will be familiar with basic data structure, involving 'trees', 'nodes' and 'links' from fields such as networking, Internet, hyperlinks, (in)compatibility, mathematical sets and subsets, etc. Other, psychological concepts incorporated into such an approach to teaching vocabulary are multiple intelligences theory (Gardner 1993) and *gestalt* or closure (Buzan 2003).

Consider an example of multi-layered mind maps on IT terms comprising numerical expressions:

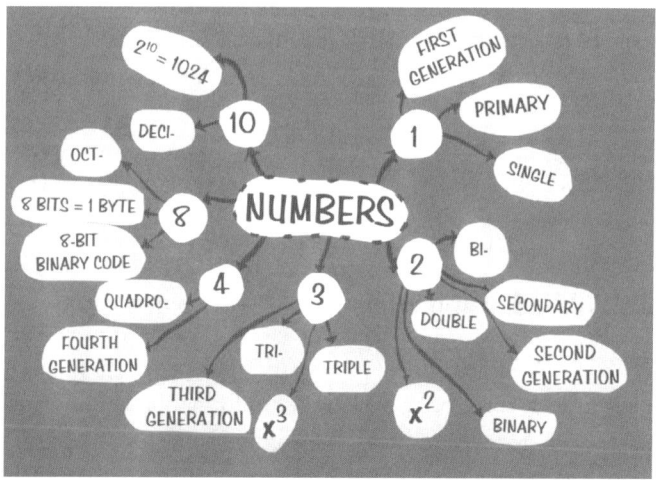

Figure 3.6.1: Mind map 1

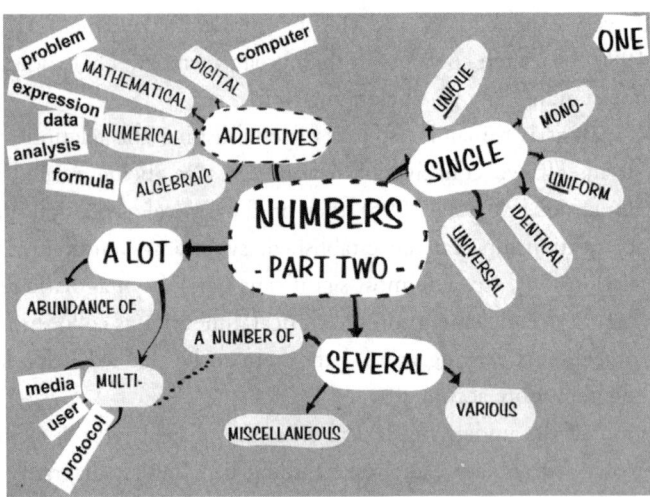

Figure 3.6.2: Mind map 2

The idea underpinning this approach is twofold: to make the students aware of the existence of multiple lexical relationships between subsets of technical vocabulary; and to empower them to build their own associative hyperlinks between new and familiar lexical items. In this way they do not necessarily learn more words, but they learn them better—the vocabulary they can handle ends up being a much more transparent, solid and viable structure, which in turn may even lead to a better understanding of the subject matter itself. Thus dealing with the IT *lexicon,* rather than *lexemes,* through engaging in contrastive explanation is not only more efficient, but also more fruitful for the teacher and more rewarding for the student, and 'most importantly of all, reflects the real nature of language.' (Hill and Lewis 1992:101).

Email: andreja.kovacic@foi.hr

Reference

Hill, J. and M. Lewis. 1992. *Practical Techniques for Language Teaching.* Hove: Language Teaching Publications.

3.7 Totally Wiki-ed: using Wikis in EAP—a swapshop

Tilly Harrison   *University of Warwick, Coventry UK*

The session began with some basic background information about wikis since these are still new enough to need explanation (unlike, perhaps 'blogs' or 'discussion boards'). A wiki is a web page which anyone can edit. The procedure for editing the page is usually intuitive—either 'Edit Page' or double click or something equally simple. All previous changes are saved so the history of editing of a page is recoverable and any disasters (or malicious use) can be rectified.

The largest and most famous wiki is Wikipedia—a vast repository of free-access knowledge which is constantly improved and added to. But many other humbler wiki sites also exist and are offered free. The talk was essentially about how such free wiki facilities can be harnessed in teaching English for Academic Purposes. I had hoped other wiki users would share their experiences and ideas but there were rather few of these and in the end people were keen to learn about my project.

I saw a potential use for wikis with a particular group of students I teach—an undergraduate degree programme for Chinese students at the University of Warwick. Within the context of their Advanced Language Skills module, I introduced this project as a way of helping them improve their academic vocabulary. Every week each student was asked to provide one word from their week's required reading, including the full context sentence and the source reference, and a relevant definition from a good dictionary. They also had to think of a way to remember the word using the way it sounds in Chinese to link words from Chinese into a 'story' which includes the meaning of the English word. Students then added their words to the wiki page for that week.

The following figures show what one week's page looks like (Figure 3.7.1) and what one student's contribution was for that week (Figure 3.7.2). These and all the words added by the students can be seen on the following web site:

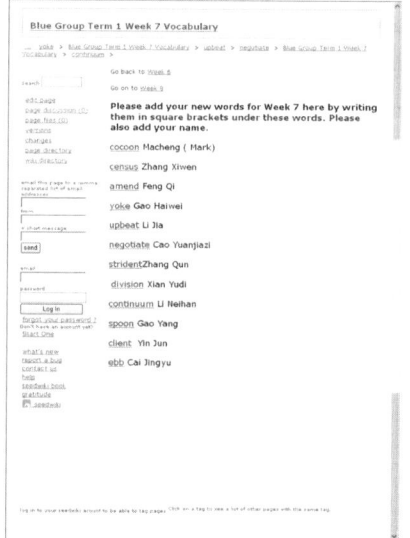

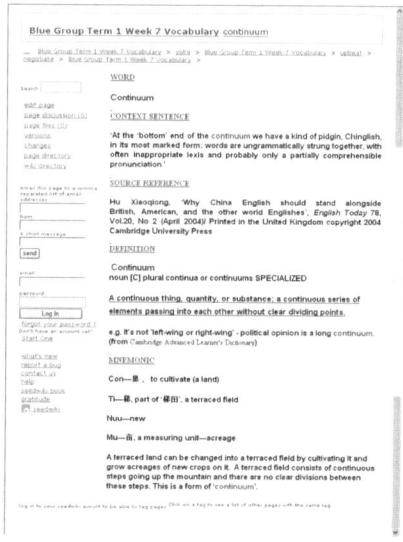

Figure 3.7.1: An example week's vocabulary list

Figure 3.7.2: An example of a student's entry for her word

http://www.seedwiki.com/wiki/blue_group_term_1_week_7_vocabulary/blue_groupterm_1_week_7_vocabulary

Why should a wiki be useful for this exercise? Firstly it is a shared space and wikis are ideal for allowing expression of something that benefits the community of users. Students could see the advantage of having an instant vocabulary list to work on every week. They were able to find out what others were reading, and learn new words from classmates, with ready-made mnemonics in their own language.

Student comments

> Every time when I put my word on line I saw others' words. It interested me to have a look and I tried to remember. It made me think very carefully when I was reading. I needed to think which word was suitable not only for me, but also for others.

> I can edit the webpage and add images as if it is my website. It provides a platform for us to exchange and share words. ... To some extent, I think this is also a team work. In other words every time each of us add new vocabulary on the website it actually is a way of helping others to expand their vocabularies.

> Our pages could be changed by any other people. I think it is very bad.

This project was individual enough to allow each student to contribute at the level of their interest, ability or motivation. This tended to vary, and although all the students thought it was a project that should continue for future students, some confessed that they had found it a burden and rarely looked at the site. Just as discussion lists and blogs have variable uptake in any given group of users, so wikis have their enthusiasts and reluctant users. It is the teacher's job to find educationally sound, motivating tasks which best use this freely available technology. To that end I finished the session recommending two excellent resources from Edwiki.org, a check list for motivational status of any given wiki task (http://edwiki.org/mw/index.php/Motivational_Analysis_Form) and a taxonomy of educational wiki types (http://edwiki.org/mw/index.php/Design_Patterns_for_EduWikis.) and called on the participants to join me in experimenting and share their ideas by e-mail.

The handout is available at: http://www.iateflcompsig.org.uk/conference2006.

Email: Tilly.Harrison@warwick.ac.uk

4 Classroom interactions

Teachers' interactions with their pupils are the theme of the first four summaries in this chapter. **Zehang Chen** investigates the nature and quality of classroom interaction in the primary classroom in an EFL context with non-native-speaker teachers. Zehang Chen concludes that teacher–student interactions offer few opportunities for pupils to use language in a creative way since most of the output is highly controlled. **Qiang Wang**, also looking at the Chinese context, considers the perceptions and practices of primary teachers regarding the concept of learner-centredness. She notes that some Chinese teachers have adopted learner-centred methods and techniques, but that, among other factors, lack of support from parents and the school authorities together with large classes and a heavy workload hinder full implementation of the approach. The contributions from both **Habsah Hussin** and **Linda Taylor and Shan Fu** are concerned with teachers' classroom language, with regard to, respectively, their questioning techniques and teacher feedback on students' responses. Habsah Hussin conducted a qualitative study at a secondary school in Malaysia on teachers' questions. The local curriculum stipulates questioning techniques that arouse learners' curiosity and train their thinking skills, but the study indicated that the techniques actually employed were not likely to achieve those aims. Linda Taylor and Shan Fu studied teachers' use of language to create and maintain positive affect through rapport. The research with native-speaker teachers of English revealed the use of praise, playful repartee and self-disclosure in feedback responses as significant in promoting positive affect. The study of non-native-speaker English teachers, however, revealed little use of such discoursal feedback, with the teachers reporting that they lacked training in teacher talk, and that they viewed their own perceived level of language proficiency as a barrier to communication and a threat to teacher authority.

Diego Rascón's study sheds light on the teaching of a group of eight cross-curricular issues within the primary English classroom at schools in an Andalusian city. He discusses a number of factors including how difficult it is for teachers to deal with the issues, how much they rely on published materials for cross-curricular teaching and whether they make use of information technology when working across the curriculum. Staying with the primary level, **Irma-Kaarina Ghosn** examines foreign language literacy development in young learners. She compared the reading comprehension levels of pupils who were taught English through ELT courses with those who learned English through reading scheme materials intended for native-

English-speaking children. **Andrew Wright**'s report, the last in this chapter, presents ideas for teachers of all age groups. He suggests ways of transforming language practice activities into communicative activities through the notions of 'challenge and invitation'.

4.1 The nature and quality of classroom interaction in the primary classroom—three case studies

Zehang Chen *Beijing Normal University, China*

Introduction

In the past forty years there has been an increasing recognition that successful language learning depends, to a large extend, on dynamic interactions between the teacher and students. Allwright (1984:159) considers the term 'interaction' not just as 'an aspect of "modern" language teaching methods, but as the fundamental fact of classroom pedagogy'. In other words, interaction is undoubtedly the most crucial aspect of classroom teaching.

Most previous studies have been conducted within an ESL context and the teachers were mostly native speakers. Few studies have addressed the nature and quality of classroom interaction in the primary classroom in an EFL context with teachers who are non-native speakers. The study described below hopes to contribute to these areas.

The study

The subjects in the study were three primary school English teachers and their pupils. All of the teachers in this study had a BA degree and over 10 years' teaching experience. There were about 30 pupils in each class.

Lessons were video-taped on a weekly basis from the beginning of the semester and they became the main source of data for this study. Among them, four lessons (one from each month) of each teacher were randomly selected and transcribed.

General findings

The transcripts of the 12 video-taped lessons were carefully examined and analysed. The results are presented from three aspects:

1. The nature of classroom interaction

In the observed lessons, classroom interaction was still a typical teacher-fronted interaction. This pattern occupies 90 per cent of all the interaction patterns on average.

a. The teacher's 'interactional' adjustments

The most commonly used strategies by teachers to modify their input were to repeat their own utterances, to simplify their questions, to set an example or to switch to Chinese. From the beginning to the end of that semester, self-repetition and repetition of pupils' utterances were the two outstanding features in the classroom interaction. Another prominent phenomenon was that teachers used very few confirmation checks and clarification checks, which reduced pupils' chances of repairing their utterances.

Research by Shatz (1982) has shown that 'only about 4 per cent of all children's errors are explicitly corrected by parents'. In these lessons, about 53 per cent of the errors were explicitly corrected, 33 per cent of them were repaired and expanded by the teachers and 14 per cent of them were ignored. This means most of the output modification served the purpose of producing accurate language. The different attitudes towards error treatment in a pedagogical context and the natural context are astonishing.

b. The tasks and the breakdown in interaction

Teachers used far more questions requiring object identification at both the beginning and the end of the semester. There were also more closed questions than open questions. What's more, they often gave translations after the English instructions. As a result, little communication breakdown could be observed.

c. The pupils' 'interactional' behaviours

The results show that pupils were so willing to please their teacher that they seldom missed a turn even though their answers might not be correct. Language like, 'Pardon', 'Could you say that again' and 'Sorry, I don't know' needs to be taught at an early stage.

2. The quality of interaction

The quality of teacher–student(s) interaction plays a vital role in supporting pupils' language development. Walsh (2002) identifies a number of features which either help to construct learning potential or obstruct it. The following are the obstructive features:

1. The teacher completes the turn for the student,
2. The teacher interrupts the student's turn in order to correct,
3. No negotiation of meaning is detectable via clarification requests, confirmation checks,
4. The teacher echoes the student response even if it is correct,
5. IRF (initiate–response–feedback) turn-taking structure as the predominant discourse pattern.

Unfortunately, all these five obstructive features were quite common in the 12 lessons.

3. The role of interactional features in pupils' language development

The transcripts of the recordings from September to December were examined to identify 'creative' utterances produced by pupils. In summary, it is apparent that in the English classes at beginner level in this study, teacher–student(s) interaction did not encourage or offer many opportunities for pupils to use language in a creative way since most of the output was highly controlled.

Conclusion

The present study tries to provide a clear picture of interaction in the first grade of primary schools. However, the cases reported here cannot represent the whole picture of primary school teachers and pupils in China. The findings are informative rather than prescriptive because they are not eligible for generalization.

Email: chenzehang@yahoo.com

4.2 Teacher-centred or learner-centred—does it have to be a dichotomy?

Qiang Wang *University of Warwick, UK/Beijing Normal University, China*

Learner-centredness (LC) has been a robust word in the field of education for a long time. Its origin can be traced back to over 2000 years ago (Entwistle 1970; Brodie Lelliott, and Davis, 2002). In the last 20 to 30 years the term has come to occur with increasing frequency in books and articles on language teaching (Tudor 1996) as opposed to teacher-centred (TC) or traditional ways of language teaching. However, LC has been interpreted differently by different people in different contexts (Entwistle 1970; Tudor 1996; Chung and Walsh 2000). In China, LC has been explicitly promoted in the 21st century national curriculum innovation in all school subjects including English in basic education, initiating a paradigm shift from the traditional teacher-dominated didactic mode of teaching into a more learner-oriented, experience-based, problem solving mode of teaching.

With the awareness that many of the indicators in the current use of LC are derived from Western notions of good practice and that there is a considerable degree of confusion in the literature as to what the term 'learner-centredness' should be taken to mean (Entwistle 1970; Tudor 1996), the study on which I report aimed to investigate both the perceptions and practices of Chinese primary teachers regarding the concept in English language teaching in the process of curriculum change. The main research questions included: What are Chinese teachers' perceptions and reported practices regarding LC in the context of primary English in China? What does generally accepted good practice reveal about LC in classrooms? How do the teachers perceive their own teaching approaches: teacher-centred or learner-centred?

The research used a mixed mode of methods combining quantitative (a large scale questionnaire survey) and qualitative (classroom observations to explore answers to the above questions). 1000 valid questionnaires were collected anonymously from seven different regions and 18 classroom observations were carried out on recommended good teachers from 5 cities in China. The following are the main findings:

- The primary ELT profession in China is a young one, composed largely of females (92.5 per cent), holding different educational degrees and teaching in diversified contexts.
- An overwhelming majority of teachers welcome the idea of LC and see its importance in and relevance to improving primary English language teaching.
- Both teachers' beliefs in and reported practices of language teaching are largely in line with the ideology of LC. At the same time, many teachers stress the importance of teaching the basics and express concerns for discipline. As far as teaching approaches are concerned, teachers in the survey preferred the middle path. They saw themselves as playing both LC and TC roles.
- Classroom observations of good teaching show that these teachers adopt a blending of methods/techniques drawn from both LC and TC, characterized by a large proportion of time (80 to 90 per cent) spent on teacher-led whole-class teaching with a variety of activities and a much smaller proportion of time on group/pair/individual work (between 10 and 20 per cent). Whole-class activities include TPR, songs and chants, games and competitions, stories, role-plays, pair/group work, etc., along with quite a lot of repetitions, imitations, spelling, reading aloud, questions and answers. The teacher is in control almost all the time, carefully shaping learning and children were seen to be motivated and active in participation.
- There exists some confusion as to what LC is taken to mean. To quite a number of teachers, it means teachers giving up control completely and pupils doing whatever they want to do.
- Main factors that were seen as hindering the implementation of LC include school administrative systems and lack of organisational support, lack of parental support, large classes, heavy workload, young age of children, teachers' personal capabilities, and the testing system.

To conclude, it seems that viewing teaching approaches as a dichotomy with LC and TC at each end is a very simplistic way of describing teaching. Teaching is a far more complicated process and its approach is often neither TC nor LC but perhaps a fluid and dynamic process between the two ends determined by many factors including social, cultural, economical, educational and personal. Teaching is rather a process in which teachers have to make compromises between caring for children's affective needs and helping them to achieve standards for learning in a specific context. The way out is to go beyond the dichotomized thinking of either/or categories by emphasising what is the most desirable and possible in the context and to develop practical and enabling pedagogies to support teachers in order to help all learners to reach the highest possible standards both academically and affectively.

Email: wang_qiang99@yahoo.com

References

Chung, S. and D. J. Walsh. 2000. 'Unpacking child-centredness: a history of meanings'. *Journal of Curriculum Studies* 32: 215–34.

Entwistle, H. 1970. *Child-centred Education*. London: Methuen and Co Ltd.

Tudor, I. 1996. *Learner-centredness as Language Education*. Cambridge: Cambridge University Press.

4.3 Classroom questioning in Malaysia: mismatch of expectations and realities?

Habsah Hussin *Universiti Malaysia Sabah, Kota Kinabalu, Malaysia*

Questioning is the key technique in most teaching and a central aspect of any classroom interaction as it serves so many functions. Effective questioning by the teacher focuses students' attention on understanding lesson content, arouses their curiosity, motivates them to seek out new knowledge and raises their thinking ability. However, although questioning is acknowledged as part of the staple diet of classroom interaction, skilful questioning does not always happen, even among teachers with considerable experience in teaching. Teachers' lack of awareness of questioning techniques and poor questioning skills may lead them to use questions in ways that prevent their students from reaping the benefits of questioning.

In this presentation, I discussed a small segment of the findings from an in-depth qualitative study on this issue, which I conducted at a secondary school in Malaysia, and the implications of the findings when there is a mismatch between the expectations of questioning as stipulated in the curriculum, and the realities of teachers' ways of posing questions in the classroom.

Policy makers are concerned with long term goals of education (to provide learners with a holistic education, to help them develop into thinking individuals and to prepare them to meet the challenges of the real world). Teachers, on the other hand, due to their knowledge and beliefs, may be more concerned with short-term goals. This concern can affect their classroom practice and may be in contradiction with national aspirations. For instance, teachers' knowledge that the education system in Malaysia is very much examination oriented has made them gear their questions to the examination format. Most of the questions they pose are at a factual level since, according to the teachers interviewed, '50 per cent of the questions in national examinations are at factual level'. Their belief that their students' performance reflects their effectiveness as teachers has led them to pose questions in this way, to ensure that 'all students (even the weak ones) pass the exam'.

While questioning according to the examination format will give students exposure to, and preparation for examination questions, this type of instruction will not improve students' level of thinking because they are trained only in how to answer the expected and not in thinking out the answer themselves. Even those who score high marks may be involved in rote learning as they have become adept at answering questions and memorizing facts. Similarly, while factual questions do have a place in the language classroom, overuse of this type of question is detrimental for student progress towards higher-level thinking and for learning 'how to learn' because their teachers have been teaching them 'what to learn'.

Teachers do not realise that their techniques may affect the quality of their questions. For example, a high-level question with possible multiple answers may become a low-level question when a teacher accepts one answer only and then moves on to the next question. Besides narrowing the perspective for the question, the rest of the class is not challenged to think in order to give other answers to the same question. Teachers who have the tendency to answer their own questions actually deny their students the opportunity to share ideas with the class and thus turn these questions into pseudo-questions. In the long run, students may become passive learners because in reality they are mere spectators who are not involved in the learning process; the teacher dominates the classroom interaction. A teacher believes that she is helping her students by elaborating on their answers, 'modelling the answer' for them, without realising that in doing so, she undermines her students' confidence in answering her questions and stifles their creativity. Teachers' preference for posing questions spontaneously may make them pose a series of 'rapid-fire' questions to their students which succeed only in confusing the students because they are uncertain as to which question they are expected to respond to.

Teachers' techniques of questioning as delineated here clearly indicate the mismatch between what is stipulated in the curriculum and its expectations of teachers and the realities of teachers' questioning practice. Since questioning is the most frequently used instructional strategy in the classroom and has a great influence on students' learning, teachers need to plan their questioning carefully. Therefore, teachers need to be made aware of the weakness(es) in their current practice of questioning in order to improve their question-posing techniques. This would enable their students to reap the maximum benefits from their questioning.

Email: hbh_hussin@yahoo.co.uk

4.4 Aspects of teachers' feedback on students' contributions in class

Linda Taylor and Shan Fu *Nottingham Trent University, UK*

The starting point for this paper was our attempt to understand notions of 'effectiveness', 'competence' and 'appropriateness' for teachers working in the context of communicative language teaching, in which classes are viewed as interactive learning communities. These three aspects of teacher behaviour can be observed through what teachers do and say in their classes. Our position is that the content of teacher training courses currently emphasises 'doing' over 'saying', i.e. it prioritises applying a set of techniques and procedures over creating purposeful interaction during which learning takes place.

We focused on functions of spoken English that teachers use in class, and more specifically on how teachers use language to create and maintain positive affect through rapport. We used classroom data to do this. Linda Taylor's research, based on 22 audio-recorded EFL lessons from multilingual groups studying in the UK with native-English-speaking teachers, revealed the use of praise, playful repartee and self-disclosure as being significant in promoting positive affect. These three aspects were evidenced most clearly in teacher feedback on students' responses, i.e. in the follow-up, or 'F-move' (Cullen 2002).

In the traditional classroom, the F-move typically acknowledges and evaluates the student's response, for example:

Teacher initiation	So who can tell me the capital city of Belarus?
Student response	It's Minsk, Sir.
Teacher follow up	Minsk. That's right. [acknowledgement] Good. [evaluation]

In naturally occurring conversation, acknowledgment is often followed, not by evaluation, but by a comment that may encode social, cultural or affective meaning (McCarthy 1998), for example:

Speaker A initiation	What's the capital of Belarus again?
Speaker B response	It's Minsk.
Speaker A follow up	Oh that's right. I knew it began with 'm'.

Some teachers in our research data adopted F-moves akin to those used in general conversation. 'Discoursal' feedback like this is not evaluative, but aims to develop a dialogue between teacher and class by 'picking up students' contributions and incorporating them into the flow of discourse' (Mercer 1995).

Shan Fu's research involved a comparison of five adult EFL classes taught in the UK by native-English-speaking teachers (NSTs) with five adult EFL classes taught in China by Chinese-speaking teachers of English (NNSTs). She noted five different strategies for providing discoursal feedback being used in her data. These were: *repetition*, *elaboration*, *comment* (Cullen 1998), *further information*, and *self-disclosure*. These strategies are exemplified in the following classroom extracts:

Teacher initiation	Now suppose you were in the plane that would crash, what would you do?
Student response	I will shout.
Teacher follow up	You will shout. [repetition] Aagh! [elaboration] I don't know if Heaven will hear you. [comment]

(Cullen 1998)

Teacher initiation	What do people wear in funerals, red or black?
Student response	White.
Teacher follow up	After the queen mother died, do you know the Queen Mother? She was a very old lady. We had an official mourning. We didn't have to wear black. [further information] I'm shocked she was dead. [self-disclosure]

Shan Fu found that the NSTs in her data picked up learners' contributions and made use of the learning opportunities these created. The NNSTs rarely gave discoursal feedback, but moved the lesson on with 'OK', 'Good', 'All right', 'Any other ideas?' The grid (Table 4.4.1, page 76) shows Shan Fu's findings, where 'yes' indicates presence of the strategy concerned, 'no' indicates absence of the strategy.

When interviewed about their use of the F-move, the NSTs in Nancy's study revealed that they saw communication as central to English Language Teaching, and congruent with the use of discoursal feedback. These NSTs also mentioned their concern with affective factors, such as self-esteem and anxiety. The NNSTs explained that they lacked training in the domain of teacher talk, and viewed their own perceived level of language proficiency both as a barrier to communication and as a threat to teacher authority in class. They also mentioned constraints of time, class size and examination requirements as factors affecting their use of feedback strategies.

Email: linda.taylor@ntu.ac.uk
happygirlenglish@hotmail.com

	Repetition	Elaboration	Further information	Comment	Self-discipline
NST1	yes	yes	yes	yes	yes
NST2	yes	yes	yes	yes	yes
NST3	yes	no	yes	yes	yes
NST4	yes	yes	no	yes	yes
NST5	yes	no	yes	yes	yes
NNST1	no	no	no	no	no
NNST2	no	no	no	no	no
NNST3	no	no	no	no	no
NNST4	no	no	no	no	no
NNST5	no	no	no	yes	no

Table 4.4.1: Types of feedback—NSTs and NNSTs compared

4.5 Spanish cross-curricular issues and English teaching at some Andalusian schools

Diego Rascón   *University of Jaén, Jaén, Spain*

Introduction

Not only in the Andalusian primary education curriculum, but also in the Spanish one (to which all Autonomous Communities must stick), it is stated that a group of eight cross-curricular issues must be dealt with in all subjects throughout the whole educational period. The study described below tries to shed light on their teaching within the English classroom at some schools in the inland Andalusian city of Jaén.

Hypotheses

- Cross-curricular issues (CCI) are not dealt with in the English classroom as much as they should be.
- Teachers find it difficult to deal with cross-curricular issues in the English classroom.
- Teachers rely almost totally on published materials for CCI teaching.
- CCI are rarely covered by means of IT.

The sample and procedure

The study was carried out in 28 of the 32 schools in Jaén. 757 students and 32 teachers participateducation The subjects under study were in the 5th or 6th years of primary education

Schools were first visited in December 2005 and January 2006 to obtain data from pupils by means of questionnaires and then in January and February 2006 to collect the questionnaires that had been handed to teachers on the previous visit.

Data analysis

Results from pupils' questionnaires can be clearly shown by means of Table 4.5.1:

CCI	Always	Often	Few times	Never	N/A
Peace education	19,8	34,2	30,1	15,3	0,5
Health education	23,2	32,1	28,9	15,1	0,7
Environmental education	22,2	34,6	26,6	15,5	1,2
Gender education	34,9	18,2	17,4	28,5	0,9
Sex education	7,3	9,4	19,8	61,6	2,0
Moral and civic education	39,1	27,3	20,7	11,1	1,7
Road safety education	11,5	19,9	25,5	40,8	2,2
Consumer education	11,8	24,2	26,7	35,0	2,4

Table 4.5.1: Percentage of students reporting how frequently each CCI is taught in their English classroom

On the other hand, the teachers' questionnaires consisted of many questions. One had to do with giving a definition of CCI. Surprisingly, only 26.7 per cent of teachers gave a correct or partly correct answer. To the question, 'Should CCI be integrated in the English classroom?' a hundred percent of teachers responded 'yes'. 93.3 per cent of them said that CCI can be taught at the same time as English language and culture. The question, 'How do you find integrating the CCI into the English classroom, easy or difficult?' also prompted many positive answers, 83.3 per cent of the total.

Nevertheless, only 40 per cent, 37.9 per cent and 11.1 per cent of teachers stated having been sufficiently trained to teach CCI, having read any book on their teaching and having a library in their classroom with materials on CCI, respectively.

90 per cent of teachers said they deal with CCI in the class. This was the end of the survey for teachers who had responded 'no' to this question. Around 70 per cent stated that they deal with some CCI more than others, and their classification ranged from more to less in this order: peace education, moral and civic education, environmental education, gender education, health education, road safety education, consumer education and sex education

Then I listed many materials and resources and asked them to select those they use for CCI teaching. The most frequently employed in order of more to less used are: the coursebook, the activity book or workbook, songs, role-play stories, games and films. I also asked which learning technologies they use for CCI teaching. Results showed a low take-up of technology for cross-curricular teaching. No more than 10 per cent of teachers said that they use computer programs, cameras, video cameras or the Internet with that purpose and 0 per cent of them said they use data projectors for CCI teaching.

Conclusions

The first hypothesis suggested above is partly right and partly wrong. On the one hand, according to slightly more than half of all pupils, peace education, health education, environmental education, moral and civic education and gender education (though many, 28.5 per cent, said that this issue is never approached) are dealt with in their classes. But, on the other hand, sex education, consumer education and road safety education do not get such positive results. Besides, in relation to teachers' questionnaires, results are more negative, since only peace education and moral and civic education were said to be dealt with by more than half of teachers.

As for the rest of the hypotheses, the second one suggested has to be refuted, since data analysed have suggested that the vast majority of teachers perceive CCI teaching as easy. In contrast, there is enough evidence from the analysis made in the previous section to confirm that teachers rely almost totally on published materials for CCI teaching. Finally, the last hypothesis can now be confirmed: CCI are rarely covered by means of IT.

Email: diegorascon@hotmail.com

4.6 Young learners developing foreign language literacy: voices from the classroom

Irma-Kaarina Ghosn *Lebanese American University, Byblos, Lebanon*

Traditionally, beginning young learner courses are heavily aural/oral focused, with limited reading. Yet learning to read in a foreign language is a complex and time-consuming process, but critical for young learners where the foreign language is also the instructional language.

Learners hold different perceptions about reading. A sound-centred view makes readers focus on the graphic information in the text and a word-centred view on lexical items and syntax. Readers with a meaning-centred view try to interpret the author's meaning. What readers focus on while reading ultimately influences their recall and comprehension. Devine (1988) found that readers who hold a meaning-centred view do best in recall and comprehension tasks. Although she does not speculate where the readers' theories originate, early classroom experiences in reading and the approach to reading instruction undoubtedly play a role. This is suggested by DeFord's (1985) study, which shows that children in traditional skills-based first language reading programmes perceive reading as a letter/sound-related activity. Drawing an analogy with L2, it is likely that focus on practice of vocabulary words and small chunks of language may result in a sound- or word-centred perception about L2 reading rather than a meaning-focused one that would facilitate reading comprehension. In Lebanon, where nearly half of the primary schools teach some academic subjects in English (the other half in French), two types of courses are used to teach English: ELT courses and, curiously, American literature-based basal readers. (Basal readers are 'reading scheme' materials intended for reading instruction of native-English-speaking children.)

I shared results from an investigation of 190 5th grade (9–10 years old) students' reading comprehension skills in seven classrooms. Two classes were in English-medium schools, both using a literature-based basal. Two were in French-medium schools, one using a basal and the other an American ESL course. Three were in Arabic-medium schools, two using an ELT course (one American and one British) one had recently shifted to an American basal with an ESL component. All children were in their 6th year of English language instruction as formal English instruction begins in kindergarten.

Although the study was cross-sectional rather than experimental, the findings revealed something interesting. First, transcripts from classrooms revealed that the discourse around the ELT course tasks focused on practice of chunks of formulaic language, whereas discourse around the basal reader tasks was on the meaning of texts as well as on how language works. Second, results of a standardised reading comprehension test, TORC-3 (consisting of general vocabulary, syntactic similarities and paragraph reading), revealed a wide range of grade level equivalences (GE), the class means ranging from 2nd grade to high 5th, with some children reaching grade levels as high as 7, 8 and 10 (see Table). Children in the basal reader programmes clearly outperformed the others; not surprising, of course, since they had had much more exposure to written English and more experience in reading. The two English-medium classes had also had science and mathematics instruction in English, which considerably added to their exposure to English texts.

The surprising thing was that the French-medium class, which used a basal reader course, significantly outperformed its equivalent counterpart that was using an ELT course. Yet, the two schools were similar as regards socioeconomics, teacher qualifications, the French-medium curriculum, and the hours of English instruction, differing only in their English language coursebook. Examination of the coursebook tasks and the classroom discourse suggests that in the basal reader class, the focus was

School Subtest	English immersion (Basal Reader)	English-medium (Basal Reader)	French-medium (Basal Reader)	French-medium (ESL course)	Arabic-medium (ELT)	Arabic-medium (ESL)	Arabic-medium (Basal w. Phonics)
General vocabulary	3.4	3.8	3.8	2.3	2.3	2.7	2.8
	2.2–10.4	2.4–6.0	2.2–5.4	2.2–3.0	2.3–3.4	<2.2–5.0	2.2–5.0
Syntactic similarities	4.0	5.1	5.7	2.8	3.0	3.4	3.7
	2.2–7.2	2.2–11.7	2.4–12.0	2.2–4.7	<2.2–6.0	<2.2–5.4	2.2–6.0
Paragraph reading	3.4	3.7	5.8	3.7	2.8	2.8	4.0
	2.2–8.4	2.2–5.7	4.0–7.7	2.4–5.7	2.2–4.0	2.2–6.0	2.2–6.4

Figure 4.6.1: Grade level equivalences and ranges in the seven schools in TORC-3 Test of Reading Comprehension (Brown et al. *1995)*

intensely on getting at the meaning of the text, as opposed to reading chunks of language to repeat and drill.

Similar positive indications were found in a 2nd grade classroom in an English immersion school. At the beginning of the year, children's reading levels ranged from mid 1st to low 4th. Catering to such a wide range was a real challenge, but was made possible by implementing a book-based guided reading programme. Children made rapid progress, with the lowest readers reading at high 2nd grade level after eight months of instruction, some reading at 3rd grade level, and the highest readers at 4th and 5th grade level. One child, age 7, was reading at 6th grade level at the end of the 2nd grade.

Further controlled investigations with random-grouping and pretest-posttest designs should be conducted to identify any possible causal links.

Email: ighosn@lau.edu.lb

4.7 Challenge not competition

Andrew Wright *International Languages Institute, Godollo, Hungary*

It is easier to adapt games or to create new games when guided by the notions of 'challenge and invitation' rather than 'competition' as a motivating factor. We can ask students to describe a picture displayed in front of them. As students of English they are challenged to remember the words in English but as whole people they are not challenged. This activity is a language practice activity but not a game.

If we flash the same picture at great speed we are challenging the whole person to try to identify a fleeting image as well as challenging the student of English to remember and to use English. The basic challenge in this case is, 'challenge to identify'.

The student is challenged to identify something (anything) which is difficult to identify.

In thinking of new games or when adapting existing activities to make them more game-like, it is helpful to think of the five senses: seeing, hearing, touching, tasting and feeling. If we combine each of these senses with the idea of presenting information which is difficult to identify we suddenly have access to a lot of games. In the example given above we had 'seeing' and a picture being flashed at great speed. Another example of 'difficult to identify' is based not on speed but on seeing the part and not the whole. Put a picture in an envelope or behind a book and slowly reveal it, asking at each stage, 'What is it?'

In the next example, we change senses to 'hearing' and the information being heard bit by bit. Read a text to the class word by word. Ask the students to give the meaning(s) of the word and then to hypothesise how this word might link with other words and, as more words are added, to hypothesise what the text might be about, who might be writing it and for whom and with what purpose.

Traditionally, we might have held up objects for the students to identify, for example, a book or a key. Why not drop them and ask the students to identify the objects only by hearing the sound of them falling? This simple idea transforms a language practice activity into a challenging game.

What about 'invitation' rather than 'challenge'? Play the students a few seconds of instrumental music, stop and say, 'This is background music for a film. What is happening at this moment?' Play another few seconds of the music, 'Now what is happening?' In this way the students make a story. It is a challenge, in a way, but it is more an invitation to be creative.

Further challenges

Challenge to describe

The student by speaking or by writing must describe something so that other students can do it. For example, they can make, draw or name something. This approach can be used at any proficiency level and for any topic: for example, a doctor studying English for medical purposes might be asked to describe the symptoms of a disease so well that another doctor could identify the disease. Or an engineer might be asked to describe a process. Or a business person might be asked to describe a sales pitch and the other business person might be asked to identify the potential client.

Challenge to match

The student must find a relationship between two bits of information. Remembering the idea of the five senses, the student might be asked to match a piece of music which is played on tape with a picture of a place which it might be associated with.

Better known would be those many matching games when two pieces of card must be matched correctly together: L1 word/L2 word; two halves of a sentence; US English word/British English word, etc.

Challenge to group
The student is challenged or invited to find a relationship between several different bits of information.

Challenge to order
The student is challenged or invited to place bits of information in an order of quality.

Challenge to sequence
The student is challenged or invited to place bits of information into a sequence of development.

Challenge to remember
The student is challenged to remember what he has seen or heard or even tasted, smelt and touched.

These two key words, 'challenge' and 'invitation' can often transform an ordinary language practice activity into a living communicative activity engaging the whole person and offering an experience of language in use.

Reference
Wright, A., D. Betteridge, and M. Buckby. 2006. *Games for Language Learning*. Third edition. Cambridge: Cambridge University Press.

www.teachertraining.hu
Email: andrew@ili.hu

5 English for specific purposes

This chapter comprises reports from the ESP (English for specific purposes) areas of academic, business and medical English. In the first report **Hans Platzer and Désirée Verdonk** look at discrepancies between the stated B2 exit level of the Common European Framework of Reference for Languages (CEFR) for upper-secondary school leavers in Austria and the real English levels of their university business students. They note that the majority of their business student intake will find work on authentic business texts difficult or impossible. **Riitta Purokuru and Hannu Ryynänen** also work with business students in a university of applied sciences. They give an account of Team Academy, a system of teams of students who define their own learning and performance goals and who are responsible for their own and each others' language learning. **Oleksandr Shalenko and Nataliya Todorova** describe the development of the ESP Curriculum for Universities written in 2005 by a group of Ukrainian ELT professionals. It makes use of the CEFR to stipulate entry and exit levels as well as taking into account the Ukrainian Education Qualification Standards. The authors point out that the curriculum is innovative in that it is both learner- and learning-centred.

The next four papers deal with helping EAP (English for academic purposes) learners to make the most of their courses. Such courses should presumably focus on the most frequently required task and discourse types in academic writing or speaking. **Katie Dunworth** emphasizes the necessity for empirical evidence about the most common tasks that tertiary students have to undertake. Her paper summarises a case study that identified assessed task types in the four academic schools of a large Australian university. **Alex Dawson** states that students in British Higher Education (HE) need to be able to work autonomously, but many international students come from teacher-centred cultures and therefore find this difficult. The aim of his project was to turn the students into better processors of information. **Clare Anderson** finds that many EAP materials are dry and alien to the students. She illustrates how communicative activities and longer tasks can be adapted to the EAP class. Clare Anderson maintains that such materials offer the students choices about input and output, allow genuine interaction, collaboration and enjoyment, all while practising academic skills. **Robert Berman and Samira ElAtia** piloted a reduction in contact hours in an EAP class in Canada. The missing hours were compensated for by voluntary, drop-in workshops, which appeared to offer greater benefits than more hours of classroom teaching.

Nadezhda Yakovchuk and **Philip Nathan** consider the problem of plagiarism in British universities. Nadezhda Yakovchuk investigates the reasons for plagiarism, as well as students' attitudes to acknowledging sources in academic writing. Philip Nathan assumes that language problems are often a reason for plagiarism and Nadezhda Yakovchuk's research lends weight to this view. Philip Nathan goes on to explain a system used at Durham University whereby students generate academic texts using a restricted number of academic source texts. Nadezhda Yakovchuk concludes with a number of thought-provoking questions for those involved in EAP to reflect on.

Aysha Viswamohan and Ursula Troche plead for the inclusion of literature and media materials in ESP courses. It is argued that these materials facilitate natural use of language, provide exposure to a variety of Englishes, generate inter-cultural understanding, foster the comprehension of para-linguistic features and non-verbal communication, and are easy to use. **Marjorie Rosenberg**'s summary presents her approach to making business English fun and communicative. She demonstrated the methods she uses to involve learners and in her summary takes us through some sample activities. **Vincent Smidowicz** is also in favour of business English being fun. He shows how language development games popular in general English can be adapted for teaching business English and clarifies their relevance to the new City & Guilds Spoken English Test for Business.

The focus of the two final articles in this chapter is medical English. **Marie McCullagh and Ros Wright** introduce their framework for developing business and ESP materials through the example of a course designed to raise the communicative competence of doctors. **John Tremarco** also emphasizes the need for training medical staff in social communicative English. His research suggests that cross-cultural training and training in successful social interaction should have a high profile in nursing textbooks and language courses.

5.1 English competence and reading comprehension among first-year business students

Hans Platzer and Désirée Verdonk   *Fachhochschule Wiener Neustadt fuer Wirtschaft und Technik, Wiener Neustadt, Austria*

Introduction

With the publication of the Common European Framework of Reference for Languages (CEFR), the Council of Europe (2001) has provided a consistent model of describing language competence on a six-level scale of A1–C2. The Austrian Ministry of Education duly incorporated this scale into school syllabuses and set a standard of

B2 in English as the minimum exit level for upper-secondary schools (i.e. 18/19-year-olds). (A similar standard was set by the German Ministry for their *Abitur*, the equivalent of A-levels in Britain). This exit level of B2 for upper-secondary education consequently represents the entrance level for tertiary education at universities and *Fachhochschulen* (Universities of Applied Sciences).

Competence levels

In the past three academic years, the *Fachhochschule Wiener Neustadt* has subjected all its first-year business students to a placement test to establish whether their English competence meets the expected standard of B2. However, the results (see Figure 5.1.1) show that only about half the intake reaches this level (47.1 per cent B2–C2), while the other half falls below it (52.8 per cent A1–B1). The situation is best characterised by the fact that B1 makes up the largest group (41.4 per cent), even though it falls short of the expected standard.

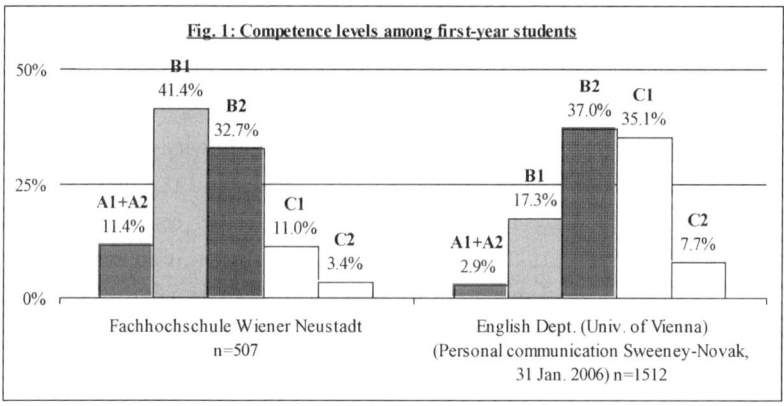

Figure 5.1.1: Competence levels among first-year students

Comparable findings come from the University of Vienna's English Department. Sweeney-Novak (personal communication 31 January 2006) reports that over the past four academic years 20.2 per cent (see Figure 5.1.1: A1–B1) of first-year students of English have not reached the expected level of B2, either. But at least in this sample, the B2 and C1 levels make up the two largest competence groups, both of them falling within the expected range. Clearly, these results are better than those of our business students. However Sweeney's sample consists of students of English, whose main focus is the English language as such, whereas for business students English is only an ancillary subject. While higher results among students of English are therefore to be expected, one fifth nevertheless do not come up to the required standard.

Our first conclusion therefore is that the standards set by the Austrian Ministry of Education cannot be taken at face value as they are not being achieved in practice. Tertiary institutions are consequently well-advised not to base their course design on these theoretical standards, otherwise a substantial proportion of students will be left behind.

Reading comprehension

The second issue we are interested in concerns how these general competence levels affect one specific skill, viz. reading unsimplified business texts. The descriptors of the CEF suggest that work with unsimplified material becomes possible at the B2 level. On this basis 52.8 per cent of our intake will face problems reading the business pages of journals and newspapers. However, to get a clearer understanding of this issue, first-year students at the *Fachhochschule Wiener Neustadt* were subjected to three Vocabulary Levels Tests (VLTs) covering the 2,000 and 3,000 Wordlists (WLs), and the Academic Wordlist (AWL). (See Nation 2001). Even though the CEFR does not associate definite vocabulary sizes with the six competence levels, B2 can be equated with a knowledge of between 2,000 and 3,000 words (Platzer forthcoming). We have therefore correlated B2 with knowledge of the 2,000 WL plus the AWL. Our results show that while 81 per cent of our intake has sufficient knowledge of the 2,000 WL, only 40 per cent are sufficiently familiar with the AWL (and the figure drops to 23 per cent for the 3,000 WL). This implies that about 60 per cent of the intake will find work on business texts difficult to impossible. And this in turn means that reading at the tertiary level will have to involve simplified material at least in the initial stages of study.

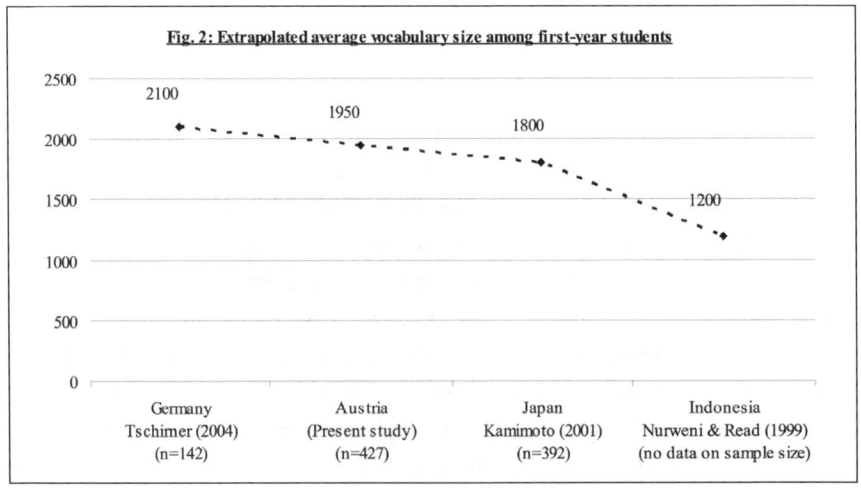

Figure 5.1.2: Exrapolated average vocabulary size among first-year students

Finally, how do these results compare internationally? On the basis of the VLTs, the average vocabulary size of our business students comes to about 1950 words. (See Figure 5.1.2.) Tschirner (2004) reports higher figures for German first-year students, viz. on average 2100 words. However, those are students of English, who focus primarily on the study of language, so higher results are to be expected. Somewhat lower figures are reported for Japanese first-year students (1800 words) and Indonesian freshmen (1200 words).

Conclusion

We can therefore say that the average university entrant does not have a vocabulary exceeding the 2,000 word-level to any significant degree. And as far as their more global language competence is concerned, first-year students do not consistently achieve a level of B2. This also means that unsimplified business articles will prove too difficult for a substantial number.

Email: hans.platzer@fhwn.ac.at
verdonk@fhwn.ac.at

References

Nation, I. S. P. 2001. *Learning Vocabulary in Another Language.* Cambridge: Cambridge University Press.

Platzer, H. Forthcoming. 'Englischkompetenz unter erstsemestrigen Wirtschaftsstudenti-Innen: Eine empirische Untersuchung.' *Arbeiten aus Anglistik und Amerikanistik.*

Tschirner, E. 2004. 'Breadth of vocabulary and advanced English study: An empirical investigation.' *Electronic Journal of Foreign Language Teaching* 1/1: 27–39. http://e-flt.nus.edu.sg/v1n12004/tschirner.pdf (16 November 2005).

5.2 We don't teach, we coach: Team Academy in Finland— a new learning environment

Riitta Purokuru and Hannu Ryynänen *The Language Centre of the Jyvaskyla University of Applied Sciences, Jyvaskyla, Finland*

Team Academy is an inspiring and innovative learning environment for business students within the Jyvaskyla University of Applied Sciences. The basic learning principle of the Academy is that of 'learning by doing', and three years ago they wanted to incorporate language learning as part of their programme.

Learning in Team Academy

In Team Academy a team is a group of students who study together: they define their learning and performance goals and are responsible for their own and each others' learning. All students belong not only to their home teams but also to temporary project teams that can be formed for a specific purpose. The teams have business projects of their own mainly with local and—to an increasing degree—also with international clients. Some of the projects started by the students have become successful businesses that still exist today.

Freedom and responsibility are the basic principles of Team Academy. Instead of lectures, traditional teachers and exams, the Academy uses dialogue sessions run by coaches (not teachers!) as the central tool of learning. Twice a week each team meets with their coach for a learning dialogue. All participants explain what they have learned and how they have learned it. They exchange ideas in the presence of their coach and also tell the group what they have learned from the books they have read.

As mentioned above the students also learn by reading. Each student must earn 120 book points by reading books from the book list—a bibliography compiled over the years, as well as updated annually—where there are more than 1,000 books rated by degree of difficulty covering a wide array of topics. The students give presentations and write essays on the books not by summarising the content but by stating what they have learned and how this has contributed to their projects.

Background to becoming a language coach of Team Academy

Earlier the Team Academy students took part in the 'traditional' language courses of the Jyvaskyla University of Applied Sciences but gradually there was a need for Team Academy to have its own language learning programme based on their learning philosophy. Three teachers from the Language Centre of the Jyvaskyla University of Applied Sciences started working at the Academy and created the following four learning paths:

- guided learning,
- dialogue learning,
- project learning, and
- learning through experience.

Guided learning

According to the principle of learning by doing the students who choose the guided learning path are given learning tasks that also include teaching the outcomes to the others. Here the teacher's role is to focus on elaborating on the content and supporting the students.

Learning through dialogue

This is the most valuable tool in Team Academy's learning system and it also works in language coaching. The students read books and reflect on their learning by giving presentations and writing essays just as in their regular business learning. Only this time they do everything in English. This learning path has become the best functioning tool of the language programme.

Project learning

In this path the students work on real-life projects that take place in English. This applies especially to teams with foreign business contacts. This is in line with the Academy's learning principles because here the students themselves have a clear vision on what they need to learn.

Learning through experience

In this path partnerships with learning communities around the world are set up and the students go for three- to six-month exchange periods abroad where language learning can be one of the objectives. If the students choose to do their language studies in this way, they sign a language learning agreement. This normally includes writing reflective essays on their language (and other) learning experiences, keeping learning diaries and writing reports on the business contacts they have made.

What has Team Academy given us?

We have certainly gained new insights into learning by coaching at Team Academy because their methods present a challenge to the traditional ideas of education. Their 13-year history proves that 'learning by doing' works with academic and business learning. Hopefully the future will see us developing ways and methods of language learning that are even more consistent with the novel approach that Team Academy so strongly believes in.

Email: hannu.ryynanen@jypoly.fi
riitta.purokuru@jypoly.fi

5.3 A national ESP curriculum for universities: generating success

Oleksandr Shalenko *British Council, Kyiv, Ukraine* **and**
Nataliya Todorova *Donetsk National Technical University, Donetsk, Ukraine*

We presented the National ESP Curriculum for Universities developed in 2005 by a group of Ukrainian ELT professionals in response to the growing need for change in Ukrainian higher education. The ESP Project was initiated by the British Council, Ukraine and the Ministry of Education and Science of Ukraine to enhance education reform in the country and thus contribute to Ukraine's integration into the European higher education area. The project was supported by the expertise of British (the College of St Mark and St John) and Ukrainian (Kyiv National Linguistic University) consultants.

The ESP Curriculum for universities is informed by the Bologna Process, the Common European Framework of Reference for Languages (CEFR) and Ukrainian

Education Qualification Standards. It is innovative in that it is both learner- and learning-centred. It also makes use of modern principles of tertiary language learning and teaching by:
- developing language intercultural and language learning awareness, and
- emphasising comprehension, socio-cultural content, the textual nature of communication and methods of teaching and learning that activate the learner's interest.

The document implements the principles of the CEFR from which it stems; it is transparent, flexible and non-prescriptive, specifying levels of language proficiency for university students which are readable within Ukraine and across Europe. The Curriculum recognises the diversity of learners' needs and a full range of the learner's language and intercultural competences and experience. It integrates language learning and content by promoting the notion of language as an integrated system of skills and knowledge and by relating acquired language skills to the learner's area of specialism.

Based on the internationally recognised levels of proficiency (according to the CEFR) and national qualification levels of achievement, the ESP Core Curriculum clearly and flexibly formulates expected learning outcomes for an ESP course, giving due consideration to students' backgrounds and their study and target needs. With B1 stipulated as a school-leaving language proficiency level, B2 is set as a target level to qualify for a Bachelor's degree. The Curriculum envisages that communicative language skills can be further developed at Master's level to C1 and above.

The ESP Curriculum is modular in its organisation. (See Figure 5.3.1.) Meaningful descriptors of expected learning outcomes for each module and an ESP course as a whole serve as reliable criteria for assessment and a resource for developing a Language Portfolio for Professional Communication. Generic job-related situations and areas determine language functions and functional exponents to be learned.

Learners as direct beneficiaries of this project receive the opportunity to acquire professionally relevant communicative competence in English by integrating language skills and knowledge within generic job-related areas and situations. Students become involved in course management and get recommendations for self-assessment. Expected higher levels of language proficiency will contribute to students' academic mobility and increase their opportunities for better jobs.

ESP teachers in Ukraine will benefit from the new Curriculum as it offers a broader outlook on learning outcomes in ESP and is expected to encourage their further professional development. We argue that the Curriculum will contribute to a better quality of teachers' work which, in its turn, will enhance their professional status and acknowledgement within the educational community of Ukraine as well as

A national ESP curriculum for universities: generating success

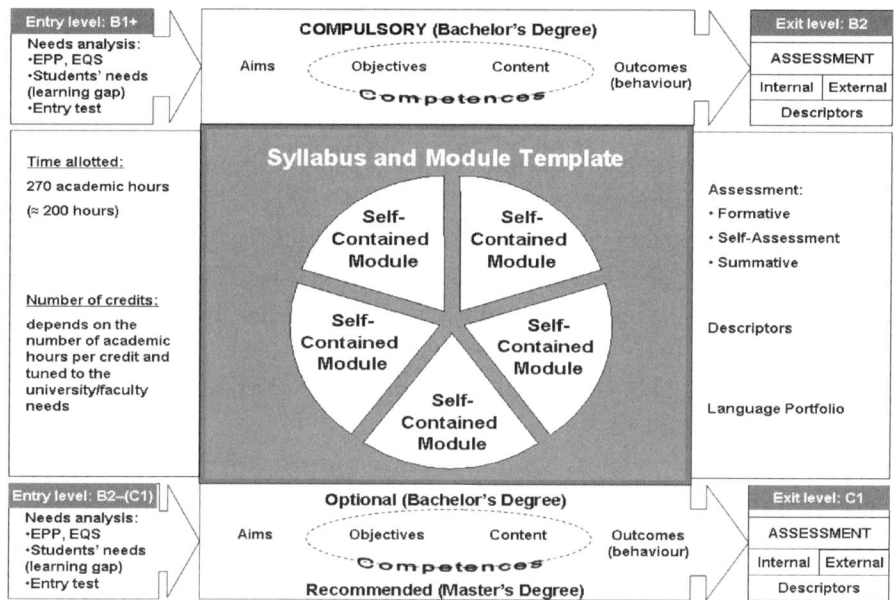

Figure 5.3.1: Modular organisation of the ESP Curriculum

bring increased job security. The Curriculum can also be used as a resource for syllabus designers, materials writers and assessors.

Educational administrators as beneficiaries of the ESP Curriculum receive national guidelines for language education consistent with international standards, as well as meaningful descriptors to measure the effectiveness of the system. The Curriculum has been developed following good practice in quality assurance in the European higher education area.

Potential employers will certainly appreciate that young professionals are multi-skilled, creative, self-sufficient and ready to engage in lifelong learning. The Curriculum gives businesses a reliable yardstick against which they can specify language proficiency of job applicants and meaningfully formulate language requirements for their sector of the national labour market.

The National ESP Curriculum has been piloted nationwide and welcomed by the professional community. To help ESP teachers to implement the Curriculum, a large-scale training scheme has been launched in Ukraine. The scheme enables the authors to collect feedback from their colleagues and use it for a revised edition of the document.

The Curriculum is available from http//www.britishcouncil.org/ukraine.

Email: nutodorova@hotmail.com
Oleksandr.Shalenko@britishcouncil.org.ua

5.4 Linking EAP courses and undergraduate assessment: a task-based approach

Katie Dunworth *Curtin University of Technology, Perth, Australia*

One major aim of EAP courses is to familiarise students with the language required for academic study by providing them with models that they can emulate, particularly those models which reflect tasks on which students will later be summatively assessed. For EAP programmes of limited duration, it is logical that course content should focus primarily on the most widely applicable tasks and discourse types; it is therefore important to have empirical evidence of the most common tasks that tertiary students undertake. This paper summarises a case study which seeks to contribute to our knowledge in this area.

The study identified compulsorily assessed tasks undertaken early in students' tertiary careers before they have had the opportunity to gain experiential induction into the linguistic, academic and social norms of their university. The data were obtained through the analysis of 'unit outlines'—detailed documents provided to students at the start of semester, and through follow-up interviews with unit coordinators.

The site for the case study was a large Australian university with approximately 35,000 students. To identify disciplinary differences, the results were stratified according to the four academic divisions of the university: Business, Engineering and Science, Health Sciences and Humanities. Of 139 compulsory units undertaken at first year, first semester level, 80 per cent, or 112 unit outlines, were obtained from across 32 discipline areas.

For coherence of presentation, a taxonomy of tasks was required. Categories were created according to certain criteria, which were themselves adapted from those utilised in the limited number of prior studies in this area (for example, Moore and Morton 1999). The criteria were: the nomenclature of the task, the quantity of output in words, the time allocated to task completion, the cognitive demands of the task, the predominant macro-skill required for completion and the source of information for task fulfilment.

Using these criteria, nineteen different tasks were identified. They were: participation, formal presentations, timed essays, short essays, extended essays, reports on experiments or field experience, case study reports, journals or diaries, literature reviews or critiques, annotated bibliographies, summaries, computer tasks, non-laboratory based practicals, a library task, short answers, multiple choice questions, designs or drawings, and 'other'. The results were then measured in terms of the percentage of units in which a given task appeared (frequency), and the mean percentage score awarded to that task (value).

The results showed that short answer tasks and multiple choice questions are overwhelmingly prioritised in three divisions in terms of both frequency and value; the exception is Humanities, where folios and drawings predominated, probably because of the presence of the Departments of Art and Design. Tasks involving some kind of oral output were not allocated a high status in any division, but did appear across the board. In all cases participation was much more highly valued than presentations.

In written work, timed essays were most highly valued in Business, although essays in general received more marks in Humanities. Written tasks based on experience were more common and attracted higher marks than essays in both Health Sciences and Engineering and Science. On the other hand, tasks requiring evidence of reading, such as critiques and summaries, were rare in all divisions.

It is conceivable to conclude from the results that EAP courses should, for example, spend less time on essay-writing and more on précis, or less time on presentations and more on impromptu interactive oral communication. Of course, we do need to be cautious, as the case study may not be generalisable, and in any case we may not wish simply to replicate university assignments in EAP courses intended to help students engage with the total range of activities that constitute the university experience.

On the other hand, there are advantages of taking the findings into consideration. Firstly, EAP professionals are often graduates from humanities and may need to develop a wider appreciation of the range of disciplinary distinctions that exist. Secondly, knowledge of this type permits teachers to explore with students those potential linguistic and socio-cultural misunderstandings that might later occur. Thirdly, showing students which tasks are prioritised illustrates the kind of intellectual work which is valued at their university.

In conclusion, while it may not be appropriate in EAP courses to focus narrowly on reproducing those tasks which appear in first year assessments, this information can be used as one of a range of tools we use when we develop content for EAP programmes.

Email: k.dunworth@curtin.edu.au

5.5 Implementing strategy training with low-level EAP learners

Alex Dawson *Cardiff University, Cardiff, UK*

Background to the study

General context

British Higher Education (HE) requires autonomy, but many international students come from teacher-centred cultures, where Western concepts of autonomy are neither recognised nor envied. In particular, many students have no experience of reflecting on their own learning and experimenting with different learning strategies to discover suitable ones. Research has shown that the introduction of self-assessment has fostered a better awareness of self-directed learning amongst students in general at university level (Thomson 1996). There is, however, a lack of research regarding low-level learners in this environment.

Specific context

This project aim was 'not to provide a specified corpus of linguistic knowledge but to make the learners into better processors of information' (Hutchinson and Waters 1987: 70). The seven learners involved were on a ten-week pre-sessional EAP course in the UK. They were in their late teens and early twenties, of mixed sex and nationality. They were pre-intermediate and low intermediate students.

The structure of the study

Two categories of strategies were dealt with:

1. Cognitive strategies

Cognitive strategies are those with which the students interact directly with the material being studied, experiment with the material and apply new techniques to language learning tasks (O'Malley and Chamot 1990: 138). The two sub-categories focused on were:

- practising: working with writing systems, using formulas and patterns, using different techniques, and
- analysing: assessing quality of work and locating errors after completion.

2. Metacognitive strategies

Metacognitive strategies are indirect and involve the students thinking about their learning, planning and monitoring their work and assessing their achievements. They include:

- goal setting and action plans,
- time management, and
- self-evaluation questionnaires and learner journals.

Data collection was via questionnaires and journals, and one-to-one tutorials allowed the students to individualise their self-analysis in the latter stages of the course. Awareness of strategies was raised in classes initially, then the students experimented with them in order to discover personally successful ones. As their teacher, I gradually released control and monitored their progress.

Findings
1. Cognitive strategies
1. Students lacked pre-writing strategies: they were unable to approach a writing task with creative, independent ideas.
2. Students were ineffective at locating errors after essay completion.
3. There was only limited progress in error self-correction: after the ten-week project, there was little improvement in their abilities to locate their written errors.
4. Despite this, however, the employment of both categories of strategies resulted in writing fluency improvements.

2. Metacognitive strategies
1. Little importance was initially placed on metacognitive strategies: students resisted what they perceived as 'irrelevant' learning.
2. The lower the level, the greater the difficulty in exercising independence: the more proficient students adapted to self-assessment more easily.
3. Initial inefficient time management: although aware that weekend mornings were optimum work times, the students reported that they spent that time relaxing. However, by the end of the project, they had learned the value of efficient time management, incorporated it into self-study time, and could successfully reflect on the benefits in their journals.
4. Inexperienced goal setters: they had never been required to set personal learning targets or plan their study time before.
5. Disorganised folders: the students failed to organise their folders for any of their modules. The result was that when asked to locate a particular handout, a chaotic search ensued, often in vain.
6. With support, students began to self-assess, recognise weaknesses and set goals. Students recognised improvement, and confidence rose.

Implications for EAP syllabus designers
1. *Strategy use should be incorporated into low-level EAP syllabi* Course designers need to acknowledge the need for a widespread fostering of autonomy and self-reflection in the UK HE context.
2. *Explicit instruction is needed* Without explanation and support, learners are unlikely to be successful in implementing strategies. Reluctance to engage, and unrealistic goal-setting was common amongst the students and they would probably not have acquired the skills without extensive supported practice.
3. *Improved organisation of student resources is vital* In order to make students effective teachers must help students organise their folders and operate tidy filing systems. This area is often neglected due to limited time and frequent emphasis on linguistic points.

4. *Improved time management* Students must be aware of how best to organise their time before entering an academic culture which requires autonomous organisation of time and multiple assignment deadlines. This can be an area of tangible progress for students, and therefore a confidence booster.
5. *Pre-writing and creative thinking strategies* These are vital if students are to be able to apply creative solutions to academic problems, as they would need to do in a British HE setting.

Email: dawsona@cf.ac.uk

References

Hutchinson, T. and A. Waters. 1987. *English for Specific Purposes*. Cambridge: Cambridge University Press.

O'Malley, J. and A. Chamot. 1990. *Learning Strategies in Second Language Acquisition*. Cambridge: Cambridge University Press.

Thomson, C. 1996. 'Self-assessment in self-directed learning: issues of learner diversity' in R. Pemberton, E. Li, W. Or and H. Pierson (eds.). *Taking Control: Autonomy in Language Learning*. Hong Kong: Hong Kong University Press.

5.6 Interactivity in EAP groups and students' views of effective learning

Clare Anderson *EF Executive Languages Institute, Cambridge, UK and University of Essex, Colchester, UK.*

Why should the business English side of ESP have the best tunes, in other words exciting, motivating, enriching and interactive tasks promoting student participation? Where does that leave EAP? All too often, I contend, with teaching and learning materials that are dry, beyond students' understanding and even culturally alien to them. Such EAP materials focus on the necessary academic skills and language—for example, listening and note-taking, or describing processes—but often reduce opportunities for active student participation. Interactive approaches are well established in many teaching and learning situations, and in BE (business English) there is a wealth of authentic material available; exploiting this and adapting general English tasks for BE are well-accepted and established practices. Why is the latter not often the case in EAP?

My presentation attempted to address this question by suggesting that communicative activities and longer tasks can be adapted to the EAP class, and can overcome many of the problems such as multi-level classes, large groups and lack of commitment and attendance. The presentation described activities which allow students some choices about input and therefore output, allow genuine interaction, collaboration and enjoyment, and practise academic skills. I referred to research I had carried out to discover which activities EAP students rated most effective for EAP vocabulary-learning.

Because many of the tasks required student input, issues of content relevance and development of critical thinking could also be addressed. My research into students' views of how best to learn vocabulary (in a wider and task-based context, and interactively) led to some experiments with multi-skill tasks offering maximum interactivity in other EAP modules. The presentation focus was on the activities I have produced and used. Firstly, the term 'interactive' as used here was defined; secondly, the approach itself was described; thirdly, the implications of the approach were investigated; and fourthly, some activities were described.

The term interactive as used here refers to interactivity between class members and teacher, and interactivity between learner and material. It is desirable because it produces a desire for communication in the student through engaging material and activities, so encouraging an active learning style and experience. In other words, students do more. In addition, if EAP skills and content can be taught through enjoyable activities and tasks, individual needs can be dealt with more easily and an independent learning ability can be encouraged. The tasks described included 'University Student Advice Centre' (describing experiences including study, listening to others' problems, offering advice and report-writing) and 'Editing your essay', which practises second and third draft editing as an information gap pairwork task. The task usually reveals considerable gaps in students' understanding of the extent of this process. Discussing their written work in English is another benefit.

The responses to this talk appear to suggest that although interactive tasks are not new, using them in EAP certainly is. It seems that there is much interest in this area but that specific suggestions are needed for making the transition from more traditional teaching methodologies, and for adapting the tasks to the very diverse EAP teaching contexts around the world, especially to those contexts with large classes and a lack of resources. There also appeared to be a need to show how the changes in student and teacher interaction which can result from using this type of task can operate to bring about student autonomy and empowerment.

Interaction is desirable for the development of transactional, transferable, and communication skills, and also for the development of academic skills such as discussion, debate and justification, group work and responsibility for its completion. It seems that use of interactive materials results in greater student engagement, requiring from them input and decision-making, and in the promotion of critical thinking. Learners also become better able to judge when effective learning has taken place.

Email: anderson_clare@hotmail.com

5.7 An investigation into the effectiveness of time on the teaching of EAP

Robert Berman *Iceland University of Education, Reykjavik, Iceland* **and**
Samira ElAtia *University of Alberta, Edmonton, Alberta, Canada*

There is no consensus among administrators of EAP programmes in Canada on exactly how many hours of instruction are necessary for international undergraduate students to achieve the level of English language proficiency required at universities such as the University of Alberta. For example, in regular EAP courses at that university, undergraduate students attend classes for over eight hours per week for a year, while at other Canadian universities this time commitment may be much less. Clearly, a mandatory, lengthy EAP course limits students' opportunity to attend other courses on campus, which could be detrimental to their progress in those courses while perhaps not significantly benefiting their English language proficiency. This paper reports on an investigation of the feasibility of offering reduced class time, and instead having students control some of their individual contact time by attending voluntary workshops.

At the University of Alberta, undergraduate applicants whose English proficiency is not quite up to the level deemed necessary for successful study (for example, receiving a paper-based TOEFL score of between 530 and 580), but who are otherwise deemed admissible to undergraduate studies, are granted conditional admission, with full admission being contingent upon their passing two, 3-credit, semester-long, EAP courses. These in-session students may take up to two other credit courses at the same time as they take each of their EAP courses.

In the fall of 2005, a pilot section of an EAP course was offered to thirteen in-session volunteers, in which the regular contact hours of over eight per week were reduced to six. Course requirements were identical to those of the 91 in-session EAP students in the regular classes, with the essential difference being that much less language *practice,* either written or oral, was undertaken in the pilot section. However, an MA student supervised voluntary workshops for these students at which they could drop in, up to twice a week, theoretically for up to four hours per week, although most students participated two hours per week or less. A great deal of individualised teaching was provided in the workshops on topics students felt were not adequately covered in class, and where students could practise their writing and ready themselves for homework and assignments.

For this study's pre-test, we used the results of our regular standardised diagnostic test, a sample CAEL assessment, produced by Carleton University. Students in both the pilot and regular classes performed similarly on this pre-test. As a post-test, we used an official version of the CAEL, which we assumed would be parallel to the pre-test. Paired *t*-test analyses of the differences of the means between the pre- and post-test revealed great gains were made by *both* groups in listening and writing from the start of term, but the pilot class made significantly higher gains in writing and listening than the students in the regular classes. (See Table 5.7.1.) Unfortunately, the reading section of the pre-test, in retrospect, turned out to be far too easy, which made students in all sections appear to regress in their reading, although we are confident this was not the case.

	Pilot class (N = 13)			Regular classes (N = 91)		
	Pre-test	Post-test	Difference	Pre-test	Post-test	Difference
Listening	38.46	56.92	18.46	38.46	50.99	12.52
Reading	59.23	55.38	–3.85	56.48	52.64	–3.85
Writing	38.08	48.85	10.77	38.19	46.81	8.62

Table 5.7.1: Comparison of the mean Listening, Reading and Writing scores

At the end of the semester an independent interviewer conducted interviews with the students in the pilot class. All students favoured having fewer in-class hours, compensated for by voluntary, drop-in workshops where students felt that they had benefited from the extensive communication and one-on-one attention.

In order to study the effect of the workshops, we correlated workshop attendance with students' post-test writing score, and found a moderate but significant correlation of .56 (p = .046), showing that students who attended the workshop more often received higher final grades, at least in writing.

Aside from the inevitable methodological problem posed by the self-selection of students who took the pilot course, sample size was a major factor in our study, which may have skewed the results. However, with no student in the pilot group failing the final exam, compared to an overall failure rate in the other classes of over 20 per cent, we are confident that the pilot students did benefit from the optional, one-to-one sessions in place of regular classroom teaching.

Email: robertb@khi.is
samira.elatia@ualberta.ca

5.8 Why students plagiarise: developing plagiarism prevention strategies among international students

Nadezhda Yakovchuk *University of Warwick, Coventry, UK*

Plagiarism has become an important concern within British higher education in recent years. Discovering international students' reasons for plagiarising can provide vital clues for developing effective preventive measures.

The paper reports on a 2004 study aimed at investigating reasons for plagiarism, as well as beliefs about and attitudes to acknowledging sources in academic writing, among international students attending the pre-sessional course in academic English run by the Centre for English Language Teacher Education, University of Warwick. This paper focuses on the findings regarding the students' reasons for plagiarising and discusses their implications for EAP.

The research method used in this study was a questionnaire survey. The question regarding the reasons for plagiarism was phrased as follows: 'When writing assignments, students sometimes copy other people's words and/or ideas and present them as their own. Why do you think this happens?' The ten categories generated from students' responses to this question and the number of response units classified under each category are presented in Table 5.8.1 below:

Cat. no.	Category name	No. of responses
1	Content problems	52
2	'Laziness'	45
3	Language problems	43
4	Desire for a better product	26
5	Lack of awareness	25
6	Work management	17
7	Lack of confidence	7
8	Deliberate choice	3
9	De-motivating task	2
10	Lack of resources	1

Table 5.8.1: Questionnaire response analysis

The category 'Content problems' encompasses all problems relating to students' difficulties in producing the content of their writing, mainly lack of ideas or opinions on the subject, having no background knowledge of the subject, not understanding the topic or having no working experience to stimulate their ideas or opinions. The category 'Laziness' reflects students' lack of desire to work hard and make an effort in their studies. It includes both responses explicitly mentioning laziness, and also ones relating to students' not being serious about studying and thinking that copying saves effort, and is easier and more convenient. The category 'Language problems' encompasses issues relating to various language production difficulties, such as a lack of or insufficient writing skills, difficulties in expressing and formulating ideas, problems with summarising and/or paraphrasing or using appropriate vocabulary (particularly academic). The comments relating to students' desire to get better results and/or produce a better piece of work fall under the category 'Desire for a better product'. The category 'Lack of awareness' includes two major areas: a lack of awareness of referencing conventions and a lack of awareness of the fact that students might be involved in unacknowledged copying. As for 'Work management', the responses in this category relate to problems with time management, inadequate study skills, problems with resource management and work discipline. The category 'Lack of confidence' reflects students' not being sure of their own abilities, ideas, and skills. The category 'Deliberate choice' includes the responses reflecting the students' deliberate decision to plagiarise hoping that they 'won't be found out'. The responses in the category 'De-motivating task' relate to a lack of interest in the assignment topic. Finally, the category 'Lack of resources' reflects the lack of sufficient resources to produce an assignment.

These findings suggest that the three most common causes of plagiarism among international students might relate to content and language production difficulties, as well as to some students' reluctance to make an effort in their studies. Some other relatively common reasons for plagiarising appear to be the desire for better results, unawareness of referencing conventions and insufficient study skills. Interestingly enough, very few students mentioned deliberate malicious intent to deceive a teacher without being found out.

These findings seem to invite those involved in EAP to ponder the following questions:

- To what extent is plagiarism deliberate?
- Why do so many students have content problems? Are they getting enough input? Do they need more guidance or more ideas and stimulating activities?
- What prevents students from working hard? Why do they lack motivation?
- Are we teaching them enough language and skills of paraphrasing and summarising?
- Are we giving them enough academic vocabulary?
- Why do they think that copying others would lead to better results?

- Are we giving them enough explanation and input on referencing conventions and
- the importance of acknowledging sources properly? Are we giving them enough examples?
- Do they always have adequate study skills? How well can they manage time?
- Are we giving them enough reassurance?
- Are our tasks always motivating and reasonably challenging?

Email: n.yakovchuk@warwick.ac.uk

5.9 Teaching against plagiarism in the EAP classroom

Philip Nathan   *Durham University Language Centre, UK*

Plagiarism, the unacknowledged or inappropriate use of source material in academic writing, is an area of major concern on university programmes, with all UK universities having regulations which warn students of penalties or even expulsion in the worst cases, for commission of this academic 'crime'.

Avoiding plagiarism presents a particular challenge for non-native-speaker students faced with the need to produce high-level thinking and writing in what is not simply a second language but what is also a second culture. In the face of these difficulties, Pecorari's research (2003) indicating that there may be significant levels of plagiarism in the work of non-native students on academic programmes, can come as little surprise. All of the non-native-speaker student assignments analysed in Pecoraris' research were found to contain text elements which were either highly similar to, or identical with, passages in source texts or which lacked acceptable attribution. However, many cases of plagiarism may be unreported since the gravity and complexity of plagiarism cases can cause significant difficulties for academics (Sutherland-Smith 2005).

The assumption of the paper presented here is that plagiarism can be largely attributed to the fact that non-native-speaker students (and indeed native-speaker students) are not adequately prepared for the linguistic tasks that they face on their academic programmes. Not only do many such students lack the basic linguistic resources necessary, but they also do not fully understand the role that citations and sources play within the structure of academic argument, and lack the linguistic mechanics to successfully integrate sources within their academic writing.

While the issue of plagiarism is certainly dealt with on most courses in English for Academic Purposes, many of the strategies used for teaching against plagiarism (while valuable to some degree) may not be as effective as would be desirable. Citation and referencing sessions tend to focus on low-level features of conventional form. Teaching paraphrasing at the sentence level can help students avoid using the precise wording of text elements; it may, however, also encourage students to follow a source text too closely. Summary writing approaches may in fact serve to enhance plagiarism, particularly if students are required to underline key elements of the text and join these elements together to form the summary. Warnings and threats do not enhance students' capacity to avoid plagiarism which is in fact where the problems lie. Library-based research projects are invaluable EAP learning tools; however, identifying plagiarism in multiple full-length texts is an almost impossible task in the short time available on many pre-sessional programmes, and even with the use of computerised anti-plagiarism software such as *Turnitin* or *Copycatch*, the news that a text is likely to be plagiarised will arrive too late to have a positive effect on the learning process.

The proposal put forward in this paper, and indeed a major strategy employed on the English and Academic Study programme at Durham University, is to use techniques built around the idea of 'writing from constrained sources'. (See Figure 5.9.1.) In simple terms, students are required to generate academic texts in response to authentic or semi-authentic tasks which centre around limited numbers of academic source texts. This approach has a number of benefits. It requires the fitting of source text information within the framework of an academic argument, requiring the student to engage in thought processes which parallel those required on academic programmes. It requires students to employ language resources required for use of texts in such a manner, and therefore requires teachers to teach core academic

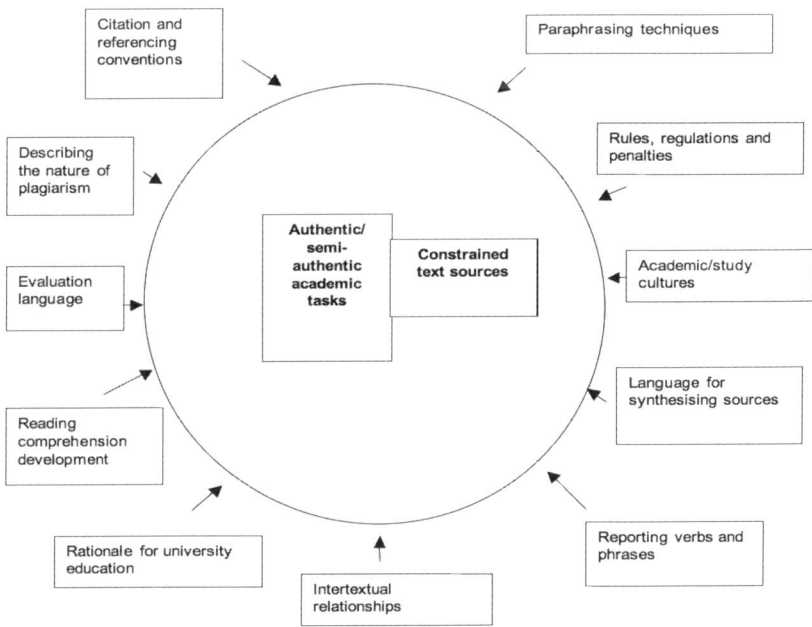

Figure 5.9.1: Teaching to avoid plagiarism with 'writing from constrained sources' coombined with other approaches

language. Teacher feedback is focused around aiding the student to achieve the requirement of effective use of sources. Finally, using constrained sources means that observing whether or not plagiarism has taken place is feasible, and students can be properly advised on how to overcome their difficulties with respect to paraphrasing, evaluation, citation and referencing, and other problem areas. The cycle of teaching and learning can be repeated so that the intellectual process and techniques required for avoiding plagiarism and using sources effectively can be ingrained. Teaching using this approach is combined with a range of other approaches to developing students' ability to avoid plagiarism. Writing from constrained sources tasks are also used for assessment, and as a result students have an additional motivation to grasp the principles of effective and appropriate use of their academic sources.

Email: p.b.nathan@durham.ac.uk

References

Pecorari D. 2003. 'Good and original: plagiarism and patchwriting in academic second language writing.' *Journal of Second Language Writing* 12: 317–45.

Sutherland-Smith, W. 2005. 'Pandora's Box: academic perceptions of student plagiarism in writing.' *Journal of English for Academic Purposes* 4 : 83–95.

5.10 Literature and media in an ESP classroom

Aysha Viswamohan *Indian Institute of Technology, Madras, India* **and Ursula Troche** *Culture-Net-Work, London, UK*

The workshop demonstrated how, in the matrix of ESP, one requires a content-area objective, and subsequently, how the possibilities of innovation/experimentation in an ESP situation can be enhanced. Although literature and media are frequently used in ELT classrooms, they are under-represented in ESP pedagogy and practice. The workshop discussed the necessity for bringing Specific Literature and Media (SLM) materials for the students of technology/management.

ESP is a challenging branch for teachers of English, especially in India, where it has only recently started to develop. Many teachers still have a vague idea of what it is, and since most of them have literature backgrounds, the problem of developing/teaching a tertiary needs-based course is intensified. A typical ESP course addresses the needs of the learners, which includes specific reading and writing, but largely privileges listening and speaking since all content lectures are delivered in English. However, much of the language that learners need may not exist in a pre-designed package because in the real world, few suitable ESP textbooks exist. This necessitates ESP teachers being ready to prepare their own materials. SLM materials—that have a greater rate of success in countries with strong tradition of oracy skills, literature, and cinema—can be used in a variety of ways to enliven an EAP class as well as develop the communicative abilities of learners.

The workshop started with discussing the nature of the language that SLM materials can facilitate. It was pointed out that these materials generate familiarity with the *aesthetics* of the language, including blends, idioms, combinatory possibilities of a word, and recognise *subtechnical* vocabulary. Moreover, being competent in communication involves the understanding of the socio-linguistic aspects of language, which includes the cultural aspects of the target language. Media—in its all-inclusive connotation, embracing films, teleserials, advertisements, journalistic prose, etc.—facilitate natural use of language, provide exposure to a variety of Englishes, generate inter-cultural understanding, foster the comprehension of paralinguistic features and non-verbal communication, and are easy to use.

The workshop highlighted how excerpts from films/TV series, such as *The Insider, What Women Want, The Office,* etc. can be effectively used to develop business vocabulary, make simulations work, and demonstrate how to (or how not to) make presentations. The celebrated 'Greed is good' soliloquy from *Wall Street* was taken as an exemplar for promoting discussion, argument and critical reflections on business ethics. SLM thus engenders a process rather than a product approach to language learning/teaching, resulting in a power-shift from teacher to student. Likewise, clips from *Matrix, Gattaca, Apollo 13, Contact, MI-2,* and *The Astronaut's Wife* illustrated how complex scientific concepts can be articulated and presented in simplified terms.

Literature fostering business English can be accessed in *England, England, Glengarry Glen Ross* and *Disclosure.* For science-related themes *Time Machine, Gravity's Rainbow, A Clockwork Orange, Slaughterhouse Five* and *The Handmaid's Tale* are useful resources. Literary texts can be used for skimming, recognising text cohesion and passive voice constructions. Since literary texts invite more than one meaning, they also promote problem-solving skills besides examining language in operation.

During the ensuing discussion, it was remarked that ESP teachers have reservations because of *self-perception* of being unequipped to handle the materials. They feel that the use of 'unconventional tools' dilutes the purpose of the course. However, we must acknowledge that ESP is an *approach* and not a subject to be taught, and curricular materials invariably get richer by introducing diverse/unorthodox elements. Since the language of science/business is universal, the instructor can access the materials without reservations. SLM materials certainly motivate the participants, help sensitise ESP teachers, and provide an extensive as well as an intensive ESP setting.

Email: ayshachip@sify.com
essaare@yahoo.com

5.11 The fun side of business English

Marjorie Rosenberg *Berufspädagogische Akademie, Graz, Austria*

'Is there a fun side of business English?' was the first question posed to participants in this workshop, followed by 'Is teaching business English fun?' 'Do you and your learners enjoy it?' To my delight, most participants answered with a resounding 'Yes!' indicating to me that even in the 'serious' world of business professionals, we language teachers have found a way to put our special stamp on teaching language for business and make it fun and communicative.

Presenting at IATEFL comes with its own special challenges as well. What do you do when you have the 3 p.m. slot after the lunch break but before the afternoon tea? How do you ensure that the participants will find the energy to actively take part in your session? Do we have the same problems when teaching business people and how do we deal with them?

As this challenge is present as well in a number of courses for professional people, demonstrating methods used to involve learners should help participants take these ideas away with them. We began by handing around cards with instructions to find somebody who could define particular terms used in business. The audience immediately got up and began mingling till they were asked to stop. The next step was a domino game with the same words and their definitions. As there was a group of about 50, we formed two groups of 25 giving each person a domino with a business term and a definition and they were instructed to form a large circle by matching the terms with their explanations. It was encouraging to hear people calling out 'I need the cash cow,' or 'Who has something about USPs?' The exercise was then followed-up with a short discussion about the usefulness of such activities. The general consensus was that they are great ice-breakers but can also be used as valuable assessment tools giving a trainer a good idea of how much knowledge of a subject a group has. However, individual work afterwards is also necessary. After the active parts of the activity, the participants got a worksheet with the definitions and had to remember the terms and write them in the gaps. This method helps to reinforce new vocabulary and gives learners something to take away when the course is finished.

We then moved on to the four Ps. In order to appeal to visual, auditory and kinaesthetic learners, each person was given a card with specific marketing information on it and they had to decide if it belonged to product, price, promotion or place. In the classroom, learners would receive a grid and do this in small groups. In a group this size, it was easier to put the grid on the OHP and have the participants call out their term and say where they thought it belonged. A discussion ensued as several felt that the cards could be put into more than one place and we agreed that this is a necessary element to encourage learners to express their opinions and put forward coherent arguments.

The next activity dealt with sorting out advertisement phrases into physical, emotional and intellectual statements. Discussion again became quite heated as individuals interpreted some of the statements differently from others. We again concluded that it is perfectly fine for learners to disagree as long as they can back up their points of view with sound reasoning, an excellent step towards becoming better communicators in the world of business.

The last part of the workshop involved buying and selling. Here the participants had first to decide if phrases they were given were 'soft' sell (more customer-oriented), or 'hard' sell (more product-oriented). The language of the two types of sales pitches was analysed and then the group was divided into buyers and sellers. The sellers were given product cards as well as role cards indicating whether they needed to try the 'hard' or 'soft' sell approach and instructed to try and sell as many products as possible. In the debriefing after the activity, the buyers were asked to give their opinions about whether or not they felt that they had worked with the more product-oriented or customer-oriented sales people and why they thought so.

In wrapping up the workshop several participants said that they found themselves energised and ready to go on. They felt that they had not only had fun, but had learned new ideas, vocabulary and even some business skills which they could then put to use in their own classrooms.

Email: mrosenberg@aon.at

5.12 City & Guilds Spoken English Test for Business. The BEST teaching ideas

Vincent Smidowicz *Freelance (on behalf of City & Guilds), Sidmouth, Devon, UK*

My presentation gave the background to the development of the City & Guilds Spoken English Test (SET) for Business and suggested practical ways in which teachers can help candidates prepare for the test. For those not yet familiar with this relatively new test, SET for Business is a stand-alone test in the communicative use of spoken English for production and interaction in a general business context. Assessment criteria are based on the 'can do' descriptors of the Common European Framework and SET for Business tests proficiency at all levels from A1 to C2.

The rather vain title 'The BEST teaching ideas' was intended to be tongue in cheek but, as the audience appreciated, was relevant to the theme of the presentation. In the initial stages of development, the working title for the SET for Business was

BEST (Business English Speaking Test). On reflection at City & Guilds, we decided that this put the focus too much on the candidate's knowledge of the topic and too little on communicative competence. The audience revisited the familiar 'Business English' versus 'English for Business' debate and the clear consensus was that the emphasis should be put on the English language element, which was very encouraging.

Encouraging, because in SET for Business it is the candidate's English we are assessing. Business is merely a setting, albeit a very important one, and SET for Business is open to people preparing to enter the world of business as well as those with experience. This also means that effective teachers of SET for Business candidates need not have an extensive background in business itself provided they are competent language teachers with a good awareness of the requirements of English for business purposes. To a large number of teachers this is still a novel idea. My experience in academic management and teacher training has taught me that all too many potentially very effective teachers of English for business assess themselves in terms of 'can't do' statements: 'I *can't teach* a bank manager English because I have never managed a bank.'

Preparing for the presentation I pestered many colleagues with the question, 'What, in your opinion, are the main differences between teaching general English and English for business'. The modality of responses, shared with the audience, was interesting: a high frequency of 'you can't' and 'you have to' occurred. Many teachers seem to feel restricted and see language learning games and fun generally as inappropriate to the context. We agreed that it is good to make ESP courses special and distinctive as this is what the learners expect. At the same time, it is a pity to abandon the techniques and tasks which made us successful in the first place.

The SET for Business assessment criteria are Communication, Accuracy, Range, Pronunciation and Fluency. We looked at how language development games popular in general English can be adapted for teaching English for business and offer ideal practice in the speaking skills used in the four parts of SET for Business. One simple example is the adapted version of the popular radio game *Just a Minute* which the audience played out with ruthless competitiveness. The same basic rules: a speaker must speak on a given topic for one minute without repetition, hesitation or deviation. Adapted to make a pair activity (the group divides into pairs, one pair begins the interaction, the others challenge if one of the rules is broken; if the challenge is accepted by the referee/teacher the challengers continue for the time remaining). Make the topic a familiar situation in a business context and you have a classic fluency and range development activity to help candidates prepare for SET for Business Part 2 situations. Examples offered included 'Partner A—a colleague offered to finish some work for you but the results are not satisfactory: explain what is wrong ... Partner B— put your side of the story to A.'

Similar activities were presented and practised for Part 1: giving personal business-related information; Part 3: exchanging information and negotiating; Part 4: presenting, and responding to follow up questions. Space is too limited here, as time inevitably was at the conference, to go into much detail. The essential message communicated was that the best teaching ideas are sometimes so obvious and familiar that we overlook them. We should encourage ourselves and colleagues to look again at ideas which have worked in one context and adapt them for transfer to another.

Email: vincentfromsidmouth@hotmail.com

5.13 Life and death situation—responding to the *real* needs of ESP learners

Marie McCullagh *School of Languages, University of Portsmouth, Portsmouth, UK* **and Ros Wright** *Freelance editor and materials writer, Paris, France*

An increasing number of qualified non-native English speaking medical professionals are choosing to work in the UK; statistics show that in 2004 some 33 per cent of Senior House Officers and two thirds of junior doctors in district general hospitals had been trained overseas. Here was one target audience with very special needs in terms of communication skills that we felt were not being adequately provided for in terms of published materials, a sentiment also shared by ESP trainers of other disciplines. Currently in the process of developing a course for medical practitioners, we aimed in our presentation to offer a framework to help business and ESP trainers develop materials that really prepare their learners to function adequately in a given profession.

We began by giving a description of our learners. While content knowledge is obviously high for this particular learner profile and language levels at mid-intermediate and above (doctors must achieve an overall score of 7 in IELTS), the level of communicative competence tends to be dramatically lower with only 20 per cent of our target audience likely to have received training in communication skills.

We went on to highlight key communicative competencies for doctors based on guidelines set out by the General Medical Council. These include

- the need for active listening skills: being able to elicit the patient diagnosis and read patient cues,
- awareness of cultural issues: those of the patient as well as the doctors' own culture,
- pragmatics: knowing just *how* to use and interpret spoken language—what is conveyed through intonation and tone of voice, and finally
- verbal and non-verbal communication: the idea that what is said is not necessarily what is being mirrored physically—again being able to 'read' and therefore better understand the patient.

Next, using an evaluative framework developed by Tomlinson (1998), but adapted to the needs of medical English students, we analysed the two main course books currently available. A review of such materials revealed that neither the language covered nor the types of activities provided fully prepared doctors for the range of communication skills—verbal and non-verbal, cultural and pragmatic—required of them to perform their duties, especially in light of increased recognition of their therapeutic importance. It was also apparent that the lack of provision for the trainer, as with any ESP course, could in reality be highly detrimental to the course, not to say the health of future NHS patients.

We then presented a framework devised by Maley (2003), again adapted to the development of competencies specific to communication in the patient–doctor context in order to highlight ways in which our materials are able to address deficiencies in existing resources. Maley suggested writers should be extending the range of *inputs*, *processes* and *outcomes* so as to meet the real needs of the learner. By inputs he refers to the 'raw materials'—written or spoken text in its various forms and genres—which can be used for teaching purposes. Processes refer to what is actually done with the inputs, i.e. activities and tasks. The term 'outcome' represents the results of the learning process, the psycho-social and educational as well as the pedagogical. Educational outcomes such as developing critical thinking, increasing social awareness and psychosocial outcomes such as attitudinal change and increased self-esteem are particularly pertinent to doctors.

To give an idea of how our project was progressing, we ended our talk by demonstrating (with audience participation, of course) a few of the tasks currently being piloted. These were tasks developed using authentic spoken data as well as examples of real-world activities adapted to the classroom situation.

Email: marie.mccullagh.ports.ac.uk
ros_wright@hotmail.com

5.14 Meeting the linguistic and cultural needs of foreign nursing students

John Tremarco *Kagoshima University, Kagoshima City, Japan*

Teachers of English for specific purposes (ESP) often face difficult choices when deciding on syllabuses and classroom activities that best suit their students' needs. One major concern is getting the right balance between the amount of 'technical' and 'social' English we expose our students to. The inspiration for the study came from the critical remarks made by a number of postgraduate nursing students regarding the appropriateness of their English course textbook. They felt that it did not meet their professional or personal needs. To reduce the risk of poor choices, we decided to carry out a needs analysis of Japanese students and professional nurses. From this analysis we produced guidance for the educators of nursing students in Japan in terms of syllabus and classroom activity design. The first part of the presentation focused on the conclusions and implications of this study. The conclusions included recommendations that students need textbooks and activities that promote confidence in social communicative English throughout a course focusing on speaking and listening. It was also clear that 'technical English' should be introduced incrementally and should be limited (at the beginning at least) to basic technical words and functions. Furthermore, 'technical English' should not dominate to the point where social communicative skills are abandoned. It also highlighted a need for a cultural awareness component to be included in language courses.

Following on from these conclusions, I decided to look into the cultural and linguistic needs of nurses wishing to work in an English-speaking country. The purpose of the second study was to look at the culture-related problems faced by nurses trained outside the UK but who are working in UK medical institutions.

At the 2005 Nurse Education Tomorrow (NET) Conference at Durham University, UK, I examined a number of the presentations and papers of the delegates. In addition, I interviewed some of the educators, nurse supervisors, nurses, and other delegates. The conclusions from these consultations along with a literature review formed the basis of the second half of the presentation. There were two major findings: (1) among educators of nursing students in the UK, there is a general consensus that if nurses from one culture hope to interact successfully with a culture different from their own, they must develop a keen awareness of and a strong competence in the culture of the country where they wish to work; (2) nurses without cultural competence often experience difficulties adapting to their new environment and they face professional consequences ranging from the trivial to the serious. To reduce the risk of healthcare incompetence associated with cultural misunderstanding, the language programmes for nurses should include components to strengthen the students' cross-cultural awareness and competence. The culture-training component needs to range from simple class-cultural awareness activities to culturally orientated, task-based projects, preferably within an English-speaking medical environment.

Perhaps the most satisfactory part of the presentation was the enthusiastic response of those present and their strong agreement that communicative skills and cultural awareness are sadly lacking in many nursing textbooks and language courses.

Email: jtrem@ms.kagoshima-u.ac.jp

6 According to teachers

This chapter gathers together a number of contributions that in various ways tell us how teachers think and feel. Firstly, **Jeremy Harmer** outlines the viewpoints presented in a debate on teacher self-esteem. In spite of the frequent lack of resources, good pay and a proper career structure, teachers seem to enjoy their jobs, finding their reward and their self-esteem in their contact with students and colleagues.

Esin Çağlayan describes some self-study research. Her performance as the academic co-ordinator of a teaching unit in an English-medium university in Turkey was evaluated by staff. Four performance areas were considered: administration, interpersonal traits, individual qualities and leadership. She draws the conclusion that upward assessments can help managers to be consistent in their words and actions and can reveal how they might improve their performance. **Valerie Hobbs, Chizuyo Kojima** and **Simon Phipps** discuss teacher beliefs, considering whether they are open to change and the degree of influence they exert on teachers' classroom practices. Valerie Hobbs documented her own experiences as a course participant as well as those of other course participants on a four-week CertTESOL course. She found that most trainees on that particular course reverted to behaviour consistent with their pre-existing beliefs once the Certificate course had ended. On the other hand, Chizuyo Kojima's study of Japanese teachers on an in-service course in the UK suggests that teachers' beliefs may be rapidly affected by certain training courses. Simon Phipps acknowledges, however, that many teacher training courses do not encourage trainees to make explicit or interact with their beliefs about teaching and learning. His research project leads him to recommend that trainees be encouraged to reflect on, question and explore their own beliefs.

Christine Savvidou explores how teachers' stories may become a legitimate tool for professional development. She reflects on the processes of teachers' telling the stories orally, turning them into written text and responding to the stories of colleagues in order to make meaning from their experiences. **Derin Atay** and **Tim Graham and Alice Oxholm** advocate encouraging teachers to become classroom researchers. All three writers aimed to find out how doing research would affect teachers' professional development. They conclude that, with support, teachers benefit from the experience. **Peter Watkins** questions how well initial training programmes prepare teachers for teaching after their course and what things are most likely to affect teacher development during the first year of teaching. Support for new teachers appears to be very limited, he notes, but new teachers value talking to each other as they feel more comfortable talking to peers than to senior colleagues.

6.1 What price self-esteem? Image and self-image in TEFL

Jeremy Harmer *Freelance, Cambridge, UK*
Rod Bolitho *The College of St Mark & St John, Plymouth, UK*
Sagrario Salaberri *University of Almería, Almería, Spain*
Luke Meddings *Freelance, London, UK*

For this event three 'witnesses' were 'examined', and this was followed by interventions from some of the teachers in the audience. The aim was to tease out how we feel about the job of teaching, and to try and say why people keep on doing it, often in not enormously appealing situations. Above all we hoped to be able to celebrate the teaching profession.

Three witnesses

For the first half-hour of the session, Jeremy Harmer asked three 'witnesses' about their own careers and their thoughts on teaching.

Luke Meddings described how much he enjoyed teaching—the contact with the students, the life of the staffroom, etc. Later in his career, however, he decided to branch out and enter the world of ELT journalism; as a result he met and talked to a large number of teachers and writers who fired his enthusiasm for the profession, and how to think about it. But he missed the classroom and so he decided to return to it. Pleased to be back in the classroom he tried (with moderate success) to run a school on a number of egalitarian principles, and now mixes journalism with teaching, market research and other writing.

Luke reminded everyone of some of the less attractive features of the profession, namely the lack of career structure and the frankly unsatisfactory rates of pay that many British people laboured for and under. 'It feels more like a trade than a profession', he said. He would have some trouble recommending teaching as a career to a 22-year-old from that point of view, but was keen to stress that there are many opportunities for teachers who were prepared to branch out into other areas of the profession.

Rod Bolitho comes from a family of teachers and swore he'd never be one. But a spell as a language assistant in Germany got him started and like many born educators (my words, not his!) he discovered a world he felt entirely comfortable with in the classroom. Rod paid tribute to the legendary Geoffrey Broughton, his original mentor at London University Institute of Education. After a spell of teaching both EFL and German, he opted for a full-time career in ELT and has no regrets about this decision

Rod talked with enthusiasm and commitment about the interchange of methodological culture in projects where a UK-based consultant such as himself interacted with teachers from (for example) Central Europe and Russia, and how the development of his postgraduate students and project partners in those situations was the most deeply satisfying and motivating part of his work right up to the present day.

When asked why he stayed in a profession he claimed to have been simply too lazy to change jobs. No one in the audience believed him! When asked what he would say to a 22-year-old who was thinking of becoming a teacher of ESOL, Rod Bolitho's considered suggestion was 'suck it and see'; in other words, like so many things in life, give it a try and see if you are suited to such a demanding job and whether the job is suitable for you.

Sagrario Salaberri described her work as a teacher, a trainer and an inspector in Andalucia in southern Spain. She pointed out that Spanish teachers study for a considerable length of time in order to become qualified. She worried that much of this lengthy and concentrated study was not entirely relevant to the teachers' future especially given the lack of methodology training. She agreed that the length of time that Spanish teachers studied made an ironic contrast with the only-four-week courses that are run for native-speaker teachers and that experience was the biggest single factor in teacher success after initial training. It is experience above all (and training) that separates the pedagogic professional from the 'backpacker'.

She talked, as the other witnesses did, of her love for her job, and of how she enjoyed working with teachers and training them. However, a particular problem for her colleagues in Spain was the continual shift in education ministry policy, leading to a number of education reforms in a very short space of time. This put teachers under a lot of pressure as they had to face new teaching situations, such as the implementation of new curricula and bilingual schools, without the necessary support. Asked why she herself had not stopped teaching and training, she professed the same kind of love and commitment that was already evident from the previous witnesses.

Before we asked for comments from the audience we introduced one of the IATEFL scholarship winners, Valentina Dodge (Learning Technologies SIG travel grant). Valentina works in Italy teaching in a wide variety of situations. She emphasised that the freelance nature of the EFL profession, with its late hours, was not particularly family-friendly. Her own passion for information technology has directed her into new fields and she is now involved in on-line training and development. She mentioned that ICT is also becoming a requirement for those in this already quite complex profession.

At this point it seemed that we had exposed some of the problems that English language teachers face in terms of career structure and life pressures. But our witnesses and our scholarship winner had also demonstrated their love for (and commitment to) what they do. What would the other participants in the room think? Speakers talked eloquently of the inspiration they get from both students and colleagues, factors which make poor pay and conditions (sometimes) bearable. Here are some of the points made:

- A teacher from Korea pointed out that British teachers (for example) had little to complain about since they often earned more than local colleagues and they could travel extensively whereas he would only ever be able to teach English in Korea.
- A teacher from Libya found satisfaction in the gratitude and respect she received from her students.
- A teacher from Kazakstan quoted a Chinese proverb about the lasting influence of good teachers.
- A colleague from Pakistan talked of his admiration for the commitment of many teachers in Pakistan some of whom had little or no resources.
- There was a discussion about the value of training in linguistics and phonetics at tertiary level (in the light of Sagrario Salaberri's comments). Everyone agreed that this should not be at the expense of methodology (and that *how* such subjects were taught was crucial).
- A trainer from Mexico described in heartwarming detail a colleague she had observed in an extremely poor rural school who nevertheless had enormous success with her primary children and how she was still trying to persuade this teacher to share her obvious skill and dedication with others. This echoed an earlier point made by Rod Bolitho. When asked about his 'best moments' he cited watching current and former students of his giving their first presentations at the Harrogate conference, and the pride this gave him.

What price teacher self-esteem? Well the obvious lack (in many situations) of resources, good pay and proper career structure cannot diminish the passion and commitment that devoted teachers feel. And more than this: teachers find their reward and their self-esteem in their contact with students and their interaction with colleagues. And, now that publishers offer such extraordinary support material online and elsewhere, teachers are not alone. Perhaps then, despite all its problems, teaching is a pretty good way to run a life.

Email: jeremy.harmer@btinternet.com

6.2 If you can't measure it, you can't manage it: implications of upward assessment

Esin Çağlayan *Izmir University of Economics, Izmir, Turkey*

My interactive presentation described research I conducted on my performance as an academic coordinator at the School of Foreign Languages at an English-medium university in Turkey. The objective of the research was to apply an upward assessment in order to learn whether the coordinator could meet the demands of the staff (thirty-five instructors whose demographics vary), as well as that of the institution, and carry out the duties listed in the coordinator's job description efficiently.

Methodology

In this research *grading* was preferred as a method of performance appraisal and a questionnaire including seventeen criteria (listed under four categories; *Administration*, *Interpersonal* qualities, *Individual* qualities and *Leadership*) was designed to evaluate the coordinator's performance. Each criterion was evaluated out of 5 points, 5 being *Excellent* and 1 being *Unsatisfactory*. Below is the list of criteria:

Administration
- Planning
- Organisation of work
- Compliance
- Problem solving and decision making
- Evaluation and control

Interpersonal
- Oral communication
- Written communication
- Coordination/collaboration

Individual
- Effort and initiative
- Professional competence
- Objectivity
- Credibility
- Flexibility

Leadership
- Coaching
- Modelling
- Team building
- Self-development

Findings

The research findings strongly indicate that the coordinator achieved desirable results with regard to her responsibilities and the qualities expected of her (average 4.67 out of 5.00).

The first graph of the research results is displayed below, in Figure 6.2.1.

Implications

- Performance appraisals are an important part of managing employee performance. They can be used to establish expectations for employees and to provide feedback on an employee's progress toward meeting those expectations. Upward appraisals and peer appraisals can bring out things which are normally never spoken, reducing tension, improving communications, and most likely raising the employees' or the manager's performance considerably. Therefore, not only do teachers benefit from performance appraisal to improve their skills and knowledge but also coordinators or managers may gain substantial feedback about their job performance. Upward assessments can help managers to keep their words and actions

Examining the effectiveness of the four-week training course

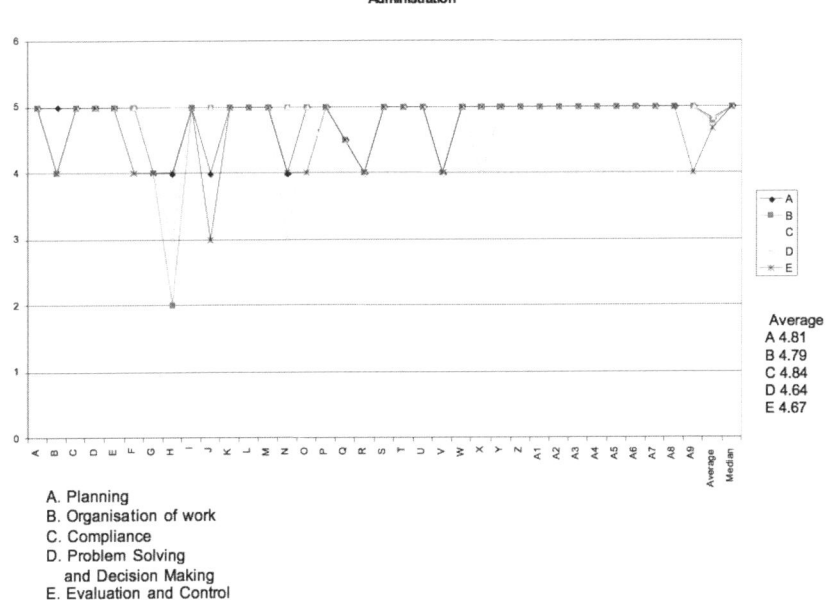

A. Planning
B. Organisation of work
C. Compliance
D. Problem Solving
   and Decision Making
E. Evaluation and Control

Figure 6.2.1: Research results

consistent, while showing areas where managers can improve their performance. This can greatly increase their credibility.

- In a learning organization, which is described as 'a group of people continually enhancing their capacity to create what they want to create', people at all levels should increase their capacity both individually and collectively in order to obtain the desired outcome. Today, learning is the essence of improvement in most industries. Therefore, most institutions should adopt the concept of 'learning organisation' and encourage both upward and downward appraisal as well as a performance management system.

Email: esincaglayan@gmail.com

6.3 Examining the effectiveness of the four-week ELT training course

Valerie Hobbs *University of Sheffield, Sheffield, UK*

Short-term ELT teacher education, such as the four-week CELTA and Trinity London Certificate, well-established in the UK, is quickly becoming popular around the world, warranting a closer look at its effectiveness. Current criticism of these courses includes over-reliance on the PPP methodology, privileging of native-speaker teachers, and the lack of professionalism that such a short course lends to the field. However, a more critical and fundamental issue remains that is less easily solved, even by the most well-intentioned of centres. Current research has shown that pre-service teachers, having already fixed their beliefs about teaching after thousands of hours of classroom learning, often emerge from short-term courses with these beliefs unchanged and unchallenged, calling into question the very idea of such short courses. Is it time for a change?

This presentation detailed recent, overt ethnographic research at a four-week Trinity CertTESOL course in the north of England in July, 2005, where the researcher documented her own experiences as a course participant as well as those of the eleven other course participants. Using a variety of data sources, such as course documents, audio-recorded interviews, conversations and lectures, field notes, teaching practice journals, and follow-up interviews and emails with the other course participants, this presentation offered insight into how the design and implementation of short-term teacher education can limit any impact on the belief systems of ELT teacher trainees.

Several key issues addressed in this presentation were:

1. how hidden course objectives such as the focus on 'survival techniques' and 'instilling teacher confidence' discouraged trainees from engaging in genuine exploration of their own pre-existing beliefs or ideas;
2. the way in which proliferation of handouts made absorption of course content overwhelming and difficult (inhibiting positive change and contributing to the course participants' tendency to wholly disregard lecture content);
3. the seeming 'guaranteed pass' evidenced by the lax attendance policy and comments by tutors that indicated that lessons could only be failed if one didn't show up or didn't turn in a lesson plan;
4. the prevalent disingenuousness of course participants in both their course assignments (particularly the teaching practice journal) and their teaching practice, wherein they often engaged in 'display lessons' and wrote journal entries inconsistent with their genuine beliefs;
5. how the course participants' background, motivations for enrolling on the course, and attitude towards the course contributed significantly to the change or lack thereof in beliefs about teaching while on the course and in the year following the course.

Keeping all of these key issues in mind, data collected from this research points to only very limited change on the part of the CertTESOL course participants at this particular centre. The course participants had very strong opinions about what constituted good teaching and were able to state their convictions quite well in most cases, but most demonstrated little to no understanding of why they held these opinions nor whether or not they were appropriate in a language classroom. There were some visible changes in the observable behaviours of course participants, primarily in areas like time management, instruction-giving, the setting up of activities, and lesson planning. However, observation of and follow-up conversations with the majority of the course participants reveal that most reverted to behaviour consistent with their pre-existing beliefs once the Certificate course ended, perhaps either because of the structure and nature of such a short course or because a great deal of time passed between completion of the course and acquisition of a teaching job. However, recorded conversations between course participants reveal that in many cases, they engaged only in performance while on the course and had no real intention of changing or examining their teaching beliefs.

Attendees at this presentation offered some interesting comments during the question and discussion time, including the comment that certain characteristics of this particular Trinity course provider, such as the lax attendance policy during input sessions, were not characteristic of all CertTESOL providers. Others commented on the fact that change in beliefs is unlikely on such a short course but rather takes a great deal of time and experience. Additional discussion via email continued after the presentation, contributing to the conclusion that the purpose of this presentation, to raise questions regarding the effectiveness of one-month teacher education, was accomplished. As this research project is ongoing, additional feedback and discussion is welcome as it will contribute to a greater understanding of the issues surrounding short-term ELT teacher education.

Email: vhowardhobbs@hotmail.com

6.4 The impact of overseas in-service training on teachers' beliefs

Chizuyo Kojima   *University of Exeter, UK*

Introduction

Teachers have their own beliefs about learning, teaching, learners and themselves, which are gradually built up from a number of different sources such as their own experience as language learners, or experience of what works best. Teachers' beliefs are considered to have a greater influence than their knowledge on their decision-making, and their general classroom practice. An exploration of teachers' beliefs would be useful for understanding any context of English teaching.

As part of the Japanese government's plans for 'improving the teaching ability of English teachers and upgrading the teaching system', a group of Japanese teachers of English were sent to the UK to improve their English and English teaching. They were based at a university in the UK for three and half months. This study reports on the extent to which the beliefs of the Japanese teachers were influenced by their in-service programme.

Methodology

The research questions for this study were:

1. What are the beliefs of the Japanese teachers studying in the UK about learning and teaching English?
2. Did the teachers' beliefs change after their study-abroad programme?

In order to answer these questions, the following research was conducted within an interpretive paradigm, where the main purpose is to explore and understand. The participants were seven Japanese teachers of English. They were involved with this research at the end of their study-abroad programme. Two methods to collect the data were used: an open-ended questionnaire and a semi-structured interview. Twelve questions were asked in total: three questions concerned beliefs about learning, five questions were concerned with beliefs about teaching, and four questions were about changes in the views of the teachers after the study-abroad programme. The data were content analysed in categories according to each question.

Summary of the findings

Beliefs about learning

Many participants considered 'vocabulary' to be a difficult aspect, saying that 'difficulty in speaking and listening stems from a small vocabulary'. One participant stated, 'I can't guess the meaning from the context if there are too many unknown words'. With regard to the best ways to learn English, most participants wrote, 'using English', 'living in English-speaking countries', and 'using authentic materials'. As for the question of 'What kinds of exposure to language best facilitate language learning?', many participants mentioned 'a lot of input' such as TV, radio, films, newspapers, songs and extensive reading.

Beliefs about teaching

The participants thought a teacher should be 'a role model as a learner (or a user) of English' and should 'help students learn English'. Regarding the question of 'metaphors for teachers', participants offered a variety of ideas, such as; 'An actor can perform differently using the same script'. Similarly 'a teacher can teach students by adjusting to the level of each student while using the same textbook'.

Changes in beliefs after the study-abroad programme

All participants wrote that their views had changed to some extent. Three of them noticed that their beliefs and attitudes had changed drastically, particularly with regard to the use of English as a means of instruction, authentic materials, and motivating students. The majority considered the main cause of the change to be the course they took in the UK. Educative experience thus seems to have had a great influence on their beliefs. The participants also said their attitudes towards their students would change because they could understand their students' feelings better as a result of their own experiences as students in the UK. They considered that a teacher's ability and attitudes could affect the process of learning.

Conclusion

This study reveals that participants' beliefs appear to have changed, contrary to the literature which claims that beliefs cannot be easily or quickly modified. It seems that the participants learned a great deal and were influenced by the programme in the UK. The main changes in their beliefs relate to psychological aspects, such as incentive, motivation, empathy, and stress reduction.

One further issue which should be noted is that this in-service training was not a 'deficit model' of teaching (Brown and McIntyre 1992), aimed at overcoming teachers' perceived weaknesses. An emphasis on teachers' weak points is not likely to encourage their existing strengths. In the present study, however, the fact that the teachers' belief changes were positive and ambitious suggests that the in-service training undertaken was both productive and encouraging.

Email: chizuyok@hotmail.com

6.5 Teacher beliefs: an essential element of effective language teacher education

Simon Phipps *Bilkent University, Ankara, Turkey*

Introduction

Teacher trainers are all faced with the dilemma that training input is not always taken up by trainees, and that ideas presented in the training classroom are not always put into practice in the language classroom. Having grappled with this issue for many years, I have gradually come to the realisation that there is a missing element in many teacher training courses: namely that they often fail to acknowledge or interact with trainees' existing beliefs about language learning and teaching.

The importance of beliefs and reflection

The growing influence of constructivism in teacher education and the increase in the amount of research into teacher cognition have pushed the notion of reflection into a central role, such that it is now fast becoming the dominant paradigm in EFL. One of the central tenets of a reflective approach is that teachers should be encouraged to reflect critically on their own practice. This implies that teachers should be aware of their belief systems and reflect on the extent to which their actions are in keeping with their beliefs.

Research into teacher cognition has shown that trainees' existing beliefs about language, learning and teaching greatly influence their pedagogical decisions during lesson planning and in the classroom. Yet these beliefs also tend to act as a filter, often preventing training 'input' from becoming 'intake'. It is, therefore, essential that teacher educators understand the importance of beliefs and that teacher education programmes are designed in such a way as to encourage teachers to make their beliefs explicit and to explore the relationship between their beliefs and their classroom practice.

This paper presented a model of teacher education (see Figure 6.5.1 below) which extends Wallace's (1991) 'reflective model', to include an explicit focus on beliefs, encouraging teachers to critically reflect on their own beliefs and to help raise them to a level of consciousness, so that they can then explore links between their own beliefs, training input and their own teaching.

Study: a reflection task

A small-scale research project was carried out with a group of 12 practising teachers doing a part-time MA, in order to explore the development of their beliefs about teaching and learning.

Students completed an initial Likert-scale 'Define' questionnaire containing statements about language learning and teaching. They then worked on a reflection task, in which they explored their beliefs further by choosing three statements from the questionnaire, attempted to make explicit their current position vis-à-vis each of the three statements, tried to understand the origins of their beliefs, reflected on how their beliefs might be currently manifested in their teaching, looked for evidence for and against their belief (from the course, reading or own reflections on their teaching)

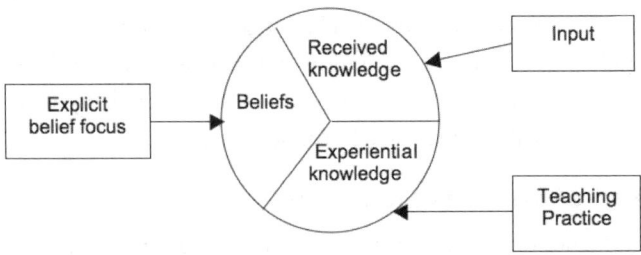

Figure 6.5.1: A model of teacher education

over a two-month period, redefined their beliefs at the end of the two months in the light of their deliberations, and finally outlined how this might then impact on their own teaching in the future. Students then completed the questionnaire again after six months.

The questionnaire results and reflection tasks of the 12 MA students were analysed in order to look for common patterns, and the following conclusions were drawn.

Results

Analysis of the tasks and questionnaires showed clearly that some beliefs change. It was also evident that some beliefs do not change, but are strengthened. This is clearly a desirable outcome, so trainers should not always expect trainees' beliefs to change. It would also seem that awareness is a pre-requisite for belief change, so one of the most important challenges for trainers is to try to increase trainees' self-awareness.

The guided reflection tasks do seem, however, to have helped cause some initial dissatisfaction with trainees' existing beliefs and fostered a desire to explore them further. An explicit belief focus seems, then, to have encouraged both greater belief awareness and initial belief questioning.

Implications

All teacher training courses, both pre-service and in-service, should include a systematic beliefs/reflection strand which acknowledges teachers' existing beliefs. They should include specific tasks that help trainees make their own beliefs explicit, and to then reflect on, question and explore their own beliefs.

A second implication is that belief change requires certain preconditions. Firstly, there needs to be a catalyst for dissatisfaction which helps trainees to initially begin to question their beliefs. Secondly, they need to see evidence of an alternative belief and/or practice. Thirdly, trainees require sufficient confidence and self-esteem to be able to try out new ideas. Finally, their teaching context needs to be conducive to their trying out new ideas.

Email: simon@BILKENT.edu.tr

6.6 Constructing communities of learning and practice: a narrative approach

Christine Savvidou *Intercollege, Cyprus*

The stories that teachers tell each other in the staffroom are more than 'experience swapping' (Lortie 1975). According to Wenger (1998), stories are part of a 'shared repertoire' by which members of a community are mutually engaged in the exchange of tacit knowledge. Specifically, the stories people tell and listen to in the workplace are powerful tools in the development of a community; they allow for the construction of professional identities, the formation of social relationships, the management of conflict and the socialisation of new members.

The aim of this project was to explore how teachers' stories could become more than informal and incidental exchanges that take place in staffrooms and develop as a legitimate tool for professional development. The specific aims of the project included:

- recognising narrative discourse as a legitimate and pervasive feature of teacher learning;
- supporting the development of EFL teachers as research-practitioners;
- supporting the development of a more cohesive research community;
- supporting teacher development rooted in research and technology.

This storytelling project started in October 2005 at a tertiary education college in Cyprus. A total of 13 EFL teachers from the languages department agreed to participate. Eight teachers were videoed talking about a recent or significant learning experience. A few days later, these teachers were asked to review their video story and highlight any aspects of their story that were important to them using Microsoft PowerPoint. Next, using Microsoft Producer 2003, teachers were shown how to integrate the video and PowerPoint to create their own digital presentation. The remaining five teachers then viewed the stories, which acted as triggers for their own stories of learning. They then went through the same process of constructing their own digital presentations.

A total of 13 stories, each between three and ten minutes in length, were made reflecting the multiple perspectives of learning within this TEFL community, for example, learning to manage a classroom; doing research; applying research knowledge to teaching; participating in a teacher-exchange project; juggling personal and professional aspects of teaching and learning, etc. To protect the privacy of the storytellers, stories were stored on a password secure website for a temporary period of time with access restricted to other members of the department.

Having reached this stage of the project, the critical question is how such a storytelling project can help teachers develop. The answer varies depending on whether the teacher or the researcher is asked. As far as teachers are concerned stories can only be meaningful if, as Bruner (1991) points out, meaning is ascribed by the narrator and not by any externally imposed criteria from the researcher. Therefore, it is the teachers who select their own story to tell and then author their own digital presentation.

From a research perspective, my interest is in analysing the process of storytelling rather than the story itself and gaining insight into the journey that teachers take in coming to an understanding of their professional experiences. For this reason, the design of the tool means that the telling of these stories enables teachers' voices to be heard in three different spheres:

- *reflection*: teachers tell their story orally;
- *meta-reflection*: teachers retell their story through shaping it into written text;
- *dialogue*: teachers respond to stories and become engaged in a process of meaning-making with their colleagues. It is though the resonance of the story that teachers are able to co-construct meaning and new understandings of their learning.

To conclude, this is an ongoing project and I am still considering the potential of storytelling for the development of a community as well as for individual teachers within that community. This project has highlighted the idea that stories are not told in a vacuum but are shaped by the context in which they are told. From this perspective, it is also worth considering:

- the ways stories *cohere to* or *deviate from* community stories;
- which stories are told and which ones are withheld;
- who tells their stories and who remains silent.

Since there is no such thing as a typical story, this storytelling project is about helping teachers come to their own understanding of their experiences; it is not about the researcher classifying those experiences and applying a typology of stories to other contexts. This is a narrative approach designed to help teachers in a community create connections between learning and practice through reflection with *self* and dialogue with *others*.

Email: christine.savvidou@cytanet.com.cy

References

Bruner, J. S. 1991. 'The narrative construction of reality'. *Critical Inquiry* Autumn, 1–21.
Lortie, D. 1975. *Schoolteacher*. Chicago: University of Chicago Press.
Wenger, E. 1998. *Communities of Practice. Learning, Meaning and Identity*. Cambridge, Cambridge University Press.

6.7 Can primary school teachers be researchers?

Derin Atay *Marmara University, Istanbul, Turkey*

The eight-year compulsory education system starting in 1997 brought significant changes to foreign language education in Turkey. Under this law it became obligatory for public primary school students to start studying a foreign language from the 4th grade upwards. Although the 4-year degree programmes underwent certain modifications, the majority of in-service teachers in public schools have not received sufficient in-service training for teaching a foreign language at the primary level.

Chapter 6: According to teachers

Despite an emerging consensus in the teacher education literature about the need to change dominant practices in teacher development (Little 1993; Lieberman and Miller 2001), a 'training model' generally unconnected to teachers' daily work continues to persist as the most common form of professional development for teachers in Turkey. The limitations of 'training-models' have in recent years led educational researarchers and practitioners to reassess what constitutes professional development (Darling-Hammond 2003; Lieberman and Miller 2001). Consequently, there have been many attempts to alter the methods of teacher professional development so that teachers can assume control of classroom decisions and actively participate in their own instructional improvement on an ongoing basis (Knight and Boudah 1998). From this perspective, rather than relying solely on generalisations or input provided by outside researchers, teachers are encouraged through in-service training to carry out research to resolve problems or to increase their understandings of their individual classes or situations.

The study I described in my presentation aimed to find out the effects of a research-oriented in-service programme on the professional development of participating teachers. Thirty-nine teachers, 27 female and 12 male, from different schools participated in this study. Data were collected by means of field notes and journals. The in-service programme which lasted for six weeks consisted of two phases: in the first three weeks the teachers were provided with the relevant theoretical knowledge on research and on issues related to instructional practices. From the fourth week on they started doing their own research in their own contexts. During the second phase of the programme the focus was on their research, i.e. their questions on narrowing down their research topics, data collection, analysis and discussion were dealt with one by one by the researcher.

At the end of the programme all teachers submitted their journals. The analysis of the journals revealed four major themes, i.e. research process, collaboration, personal outcomes and challenges. In-depth analyses of these categories showed that, although the prospect of launching into the realm of researcher on top of the many things that they already did probably seemed very intimidating at the beginning, teachers benefited from participating in the programme in general. Many indicated that research enabled them to question many things in their own contexts and understand the relationship between their beliefs and classroom practices. Their experiences in becoming a researcher had changed their ways of teaching and approaching the students. Others discussed the value of a collaborative research process where they could all share ideas, listen to each other and contribute suggestions and ideas with one indicating that 'it helps to hear other views from teachers who value their job'.

I believe the programme was successful because of the following characteristics: firstly, teachers were volunteers and they felt the need for personal and professional growth. Secondly, the programme content was tailored according to their needs. I was highly flexible with the content and the teachers realised this. I believe that if the teachers had been given some time off, the process would have been even more effective. Finally, although they had an active role in their research, I directed them through the process. Direction in this programme was not like the one in the traditional transfer models, in which the facilitator transfers theory via instruction and the teacher is expected to apply the theory. My guidance was process-oriented and teachers were aware that I was not trying to impose things on them.

The hope, goal, and potential of teacher research is to enable teachers to shift from teaching as 'telling' to teaching as 'listening' and 'learning'. I believe that most of the participating teachers have begun the journey. They came to view teacher research as a process of changing or becoming transformed themselves as a means to facilitate effective practices for their students.

Email: dyatay@yahoo.com

6.8 Two hats or the same one? Exploring the changing attitudes of TESOL teachers to classroom-based research

Tim Graham and Alice Oxholm   *Sheffield Hallam University, UK*

Introduction

Teachers are often the driving force behind classroom innovation. Potentially they have a huge amount to tell the profession but often see themselves as isolated voices without an obvious means of communicating their experiences widely. Pure researchers, meanwhile, can find that their studies strike the non-researcher as too esoteric or unactionable as to be readily consumed, drawing into question their utilitarian value.

We have experienced some success supporting students' production of Masters level research projects. The classroom-based research project (CBRP) that teachers undertake is designed to enable them to focus on existing classroom activities. Its key function, for those unfamiliar with research as part of normal teaching duties, is to encourage them to begin to critically examine their environment from a question-oriented perspective (Graham and Oxholm 2005).

Teachers' context and background

The research group involved 13 pre-research teachers and 18 post-research teachers. All 31 teachers taught full- or part-time and studied individually via elearning and communication and were internationally based. None of the teachers involved had previously carried out systematic research. Questionnaires were sent to all 31 teachers. 10 were completed and returned from each group.

Selected results
Pre-researchers

Nine people reported feeling positive about undertaking research, whilst one saw it as negative. Six saw the process as enabling, though two also saw it as potentially time-consuming.

On practicalities, included were concerns over availability of subjects (4) and, perhaps related to this, the willingness of participants to cooperate (5). Six people cited concerns about fitting their research work into their timetables.

Challenges elicited a range of factors. Amongst these were time (5); deciding on a research focus (3); placing their own research in the context of past research and estimating its value (3); and deciding on the methodology for data collection (3).

Post-researchers

On the question of value, initially none were positive, one was negative and the remaining nine all declared themselves neutral. However, following the completion of the task, there was a sizeable shift with nine now seeing research as having value, one reporting neutrality and none seeing it as negative. In response to how they had felt on the whole about doing research ten were positive and none negative.

Whether or not engaging in research had helped in furthering understanding, all ten respondents declared that it had. Of these two said that it had added to their capacity for reflection and seven stated that it helped in finding practical solutions to things in their classroom duties.

Discussion and conclusion

The size of the sample in this study is low and its generalisability is at best questionable. However, the internal consistency of the results obtained from respondents is compelling with regard to the specific experience of undertaking research on their course at SHU. Our main findings are that:

- doing research in teacher education is seen as challenging but rewarding, and
- research itself appears individualised and non-collaborative.

The most significant finding is the shift in perception of the value of research in the before and after estimations of post-researchers. It is encouraging to note that virtually everyone saw doing research as part of their studies as positive despite inherent practical difficulties and challenges. This might suggest that the practitioner/researcher divide may not be so broad as is sometimes suggested (Ellis 1997). Interestingly, although electronic input of various kinds by tutors was valued, the electronic mode of study and the peer contact it afforded was seen as largely insignificant, suggesting that specificity of research focus militates against collaboration. We earlier suggested that teachers' voices were muted on many of the issues discussed here, so it is apt to quote from one of the respondents to this survey:

> Although I still am not particularly good at the recording of research info, I found that research is very much practical and should feed teaching practice and was hugely beneficial to my teaching as I created a whole new programme of materials which has been very useful. Also it made me think about how theory relates to practice.

Email: T.Graham@shu.ac.uk
A.M.Oxholm@shu.ac.uk

References

Ellis, R. 1997. *SLA Research and Language Teaching*. Oxford: Oxford University Press.

Graham, T. and A. Oxholm. 2005. 'Research as conversation: developing a positive approach to action research' in B. Beaven (ed.). *IATEFL 2005. Cardiff Conference Selections*. Canterbury: IATEFL.

6.9 Pre-service training and the first year of teaching

Peter Watkins   *University of Portsmouth, Portsmouth, UK*

This presentation reported a small-scale piece of research which followed eight new teachers through their first year in the profession. All eight had previously followed a Cambridge CELTA course. There were two main aims. The first was to look at how well initial training programmes, such as the CELTA course, prepare teachers for taking up work and the second was to look at what things are most likely to affect teacher development during the first year of teaching. The teachers were interviewed at intervals throughout their first twelve months of teaching.

The first finding related to the things that shape teacher development. After 12 months of teaching only two of the teachers had observed others teaching (those observed being classroom assistants in an ESOL context). Only four had been observed (two of those by classroom assistants) and only one had received substantial feedback on the lesson. Books were used for reference and as source of material but very rarely to find out more about teaching. Only one teacher had attended a workshop of any description. Most of the teachers had talked about teaching to others. There was evidence (based on frequency and duration of conversations) that new teachers felt more comfortable talking to other newly qualified teachers and rarely sought guidance from those that they considered 'senior' to themselves. All the teachers reported that they thought about lessons after teaching them and felt that the CELTA course prepared them well for a cycle of planning, teaching, reflecting, and then planning again, and so on.

When asked about the criteria used for assessing the success of lessons, all the respondents seemed to use interpersonal criteria (based on perceived rapport and enjoyment) and also the amount of speaking in English that took place. When asked what they had changed about their teaching in the light of their reflections, the dominant themes concerned choices of material (of which they tended to be quite critical) and also catering better for the needs of individuals in the class.

The second set of findings concerned areas that teachers felt they needed to develop in order to cope with their first year of teaching. Some needs were highly context specific, such as 'more on teaching young learners', but all but one reported that they found it difficult to find the 'right' material. It seemed that in searching for material much was rejected and all respondents followed similar criteria to assess material. The first criterion was 'is it fun?' (this is related to how they judged the success of lessons—see above), the second was 'is it too similar to something I've recently done?', and the third was 'does it fit in with the theme of the lesson?'. Failure to meet the first or second criteria led to rejection of the material but failure to meet the third did not always lead to rejection.

The third set of findings related to how their teaching had changed since the course. All felt that the general methodology they used remained the same. There was little evidence of experimentation with new techniques, but this is hardly surprising as it could be assumed that new teachers would find security in the familiar and would want to establish teaching 'routines' before experimenting. All respondents commented on planning. During their courses they tended to worry about such things as the precise wordings of aims, extremely detailed timings, and in some cases including things that they felt would please the observer. In the 'real world' respondents felt they could be more flexible in their approach. They planned in less detail and were less rigid in following their plans—often happy to allow activities to continue if they felt they were 'going well'. Aims were nearly always described in a 'procedural' form, such as 'do a discussion', with little attention paid to linguistic aims.

What implications does this have? Amongst other things, support for new teachers is often limited and support networks of peers are very important—new teachers like talking to new teachers. New teachers often appear to value interpersonal aspects of lessons over linguistic input. Finding material considered appropriate is a constant problem and so more on potential sources and then fully exploiting material may be useful during initial training. Teachers make a lot of 'in-flight' decisions during lessons, diverting from plans. Training courses could encourage experimentation with this in the protected environment of the training course.

Email: peter.watkins@port.ac.uk

7 Teacher development

The range of topics considered relevant to teacher development has grown considerably in the last few years. Chapter 7 demonstrates that range, taking a broad view of the term 'development' by including both development through training and development that teachers may initiate and carry out without trainers. **Bena Gül Peker**'s account of her plenary talk emphasises the importance of teachers building rapport in the classroom in order to interact effectively with different kinds of learners. She advocates teachers tuning into the mood of learners and suggests ways of doing this, including PALE (pacing and leading). She did not merely describe these techniques from neurolinguistic programming (NLP), but also showed how she believes they work in practice, including audience participation in her session. **Zeynep Onat-Stelma and Juup Stelma** review training they have undertaken based on adjectives that teachers use when talking about their classroom practices. The adjectives become 'reflective vehicles' for teachers to reflect on their work. Studying their own use of adjectives can reveal to the teachers discrepancies, a lack of coherence, or an emphasis on classroom management at the expense of considerations of language improvement.

The next two papers indicate how needs differ in our very varied IATEFL contexts. **Kristen di Gennaro and Bede McCormack** from New York appeal for teachers to become more knowledgeable about ELT theory, particularly SLA (Second Language Acquisition) theory. This public theory, they feel, provides a necessary underpinning to the personal, practical knowledge that teachers develop with experience. **Andrew Sheehan**, on the other hand, suggests that in his context in Chile, a move towards teacher education firmly rooted in classroom practice is required. He takes us through two in-service training courses that he devised, which had as an additional aim a knock-on effect on initial teacher training.

Peter Beech focuses on guidelines for the observation of peers on a training course, guidelines for peer observation for experienced teachers and the potential of developmental peer observation as an element in the wider context of classroom research. **Rachel Appleby** defines behavioural competencies, including those for teachers, looks at examples in practice and discusses the rationale for using them.

Naďa Vojtková and Světlana Hanušová and **Briony Beaven** present teacher training and trainer training activities. Naďa Vojtková and Světlana Hanušová summarise two innovative pre-service teacher training courses containing task-based activities, together with the results. Briony Beaven reports on a workshop that demonstrated some practical ideas for those preparing classroom teachers to become teacher educators, and specifically, preparing the new trainers to lead workshops and training sessions.

The chapter ends with a report on a presentation, convened by **Rod Bolitho**, which was given by a team of Hornby Scholarship holders from all over the world. The report summarises opinions and data on five issues of common concern: the culture of reading; large classes in countries in transition; curriculum issues; the balance between language and teaching skills in teacher training programmes; and teacher development/ in-service training for English teachers in transitional countries.

7.1 Plenary: The spirit of the dance—taking one step further

Bena Gül Peker *ELT Department, Faculty of Education, Gazi University, Ankara, Turkey*

Introduction

An act of communication, like a dance, undoubtedly calls for knowledge, skills, and expertise. Star performers, however, go one step further and create exquisite performance by 'being' and 'feeling' in this act of communication, whether they are in the classroom or on stage. It is such competence that we can be aiming at as English language teachers, that is to say the 'spirit of the dance.' This dramatic presentation focused on, discussed and demonstrated the use of an exhilarating communication strategy; building rapport, in the classroom. It focused on how building rapport can help us become adept communicators able to interact effectively with different kinds of learners, dancing the dance of rapport and adapting to whatever the situation calls for, hence taking one step further.

With the aim of conveying such a state of being and feeling, the session was delivered in a dramatic style drawing on the metaphor of dance. By way of introduction, first, I discussed briefly non-verbal communication and rapport. Second, I defined rapport and then moved on to how we can establish rapport through the technique of pacing and leading, building on the dance metaphor. Next, I questioned whether we can learn this dance, a discussion that unfolded an awareness of different emotional states followed by a discussion of challenges involved in learning the dance of rapport. I then provided theoretical underpinnings touching on issues that relate to the mind, body and emotions. The session then turned to the choreography of the dance of rapport based on four major moves in order to demonstrate how we can build rapport very much like a dance and maintain that rapport and start to influence people. Finally, I made suggestions as to tips that can help us in our efforts to establish rapport.

About non-verbal communication and rapport

There is a myriad of ways to build rapport in communication. In fact, rapport can be built and maintained through non-verbal and verbal strategies. (Alder 2000; Gün 2003; Robbins 1986). In this session, I am talking about non-verbal communication; however, it would not be my conscious intention to give the impression that rapport can only be established through non-verbal means. There are also many ways of establishing rapport through verbal means.

There is a broad academic spectrum in which non-verbal communication is researched: psychology, sociology, anthropology, communications, and linguistics. Psychiatrists, for example, investigate connections between body language and conversation, while social scientists focus on the relationship between non-verbal communication and cultural differences analysing how body language affects conversation across cultures. For the interested reader, articles on body language and non-verbal communication may be found in the following journals: *Business Communication Quarterly*, *Journal of Communication*, *Communication Studies*, *Communication Quarterly*, and *Journal of Psychology*.

Non-verbal communication strategies are extremely important as the classic study by Albert Mehrabian (1972, cited in Revell 1997) shows. As can be seen in Figure 1, 7 per cent of the meaning of communication comes from verbal elements, while vocal elements like tone, pitch account for 38 per cent of the meaning, that is to say the language we use. It is interesting to note that body language—the movements or attitudes of the body—is responsible for 55 per cent of the meaning in communication. For this reason, it is likely that facial expressions, for example, influence the attitudes and judgements of the receiver as much as, or more than, our

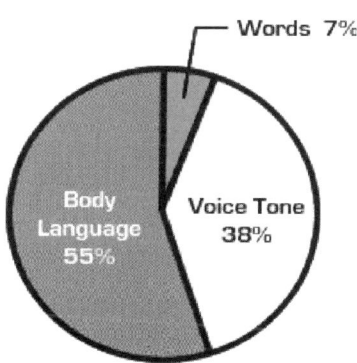

Figure 7.1.1: Elements of communication

verbal message, convincing us that communication is more non-verbal than verbal, hence the importance of body language.

In effect, body language has been the first means of communication and the first language of human beings, enabling many people to share their thoughts, emotions, wishes, and needs with others (Ekman 1994). And yet, body language is perhaps one of the areas of communication that has been unjustly neglected with the result that most of the time we fail to realise how important non-verbal communication is. Whether you are a mentor, a teacher, a lawyer a doctor, or a psychologist, your success in your work career is closely related to your ability to communicate through your body language; even before you have said any words in any act of communication, you have made a non-vebal statement and have communicated a message. To give an example, if you are leaning forward while listening, you could be giving the message that you are willing to listen and are open to conversation. The opposite case may also be true: if you are leaning backward, it could be stating that you want to decline the conversation. We should be warned however, against judging all body language within fixed parameters: non-verbal communication may be ambiguous, hence change from culture to culture and sometimes from person to person. As a result, it may not be possible to read exactly what a particular gesture means. If a learner is crossing her or his arms it does not necessarily mean that she or he is closed to conversation. It could be that the person just wants to support their back or rest their arms in that position. For this reason, the better course of action would be to get to know the person first before passing any judgement on their body language.

The art of rapport: becoming adept communicators

> The most important thing in communication is hearing what isn't said.
> (Peter F. Drucker)

Rapport can be defined as matching 'other people's behaviour, thinking or levels of energy' (James 2001: 63). When you match another person at such levels, an environment of trust, confidence and participation is created naturally. In fact, you must have noticed this kind of an atmosphere at cafés, restaurants and in classes. You can immediately notice that people who get on well, whether they are a couple or friends or mother and daughter, or teacher and learner, are matching each other's body language because they are in agreement. These people seem very comfortable and relaxed in each other's company. What this shows is that by creating rapport, an environment of bonding, affinity, empathy and a certain kind of harmony has been created (Alder 2002; James 2001; Robbins 1986).

The fact that such an environment has been established allows you to join the other person in their model or map of the world (Revell 1997). It shows that you are acknowledging the thoughts and feelings of the person that you are communicating with. If you are good at rapport skills, this can enable you to get on easily with most people in most contexts. It will also make it easier for others to communicate with you.

What is perhaps the most powerful aspect of rapport is the fact that when people match each other, rapport happens without conscious awareness, that is to say it is spontaneous. A common example can be given from the context of a conference or a concert where audiences are usually expected to applaud after the performance. In order to applaud the speaker or the performer on stage, the audience would usually applaud in perfect unison without a signal or a leader. That is to say, the synchrony would be spontaneous. One would also assume that it feels comfortable, relaxing and pleasant to be a part of this audience; perhaps very much like the feeling of togetherness one would experience among people supporting the same football team.

A final aspect of rapport is that it is closely related to the expression of emotions. In other words, a person will reveal what is being felt at the particular moment in the communication through facial expressions and other indicators of body language like body postures or positions of the arms and legs. It is important to remember that you cannot avoid communicating non-verbally. Imagine for a moment that your manager or director of studies became somewhat emotional and started to raise his voice: would you not give an emotional reaction of anger that will reflect in your facial expressions as frowning? Or perhaps you could not help falling asleep when you were listening to a boring lecture? A case in point is when the movie producer Sam Goldwyn fell asleep when he was listening to a proposal for a film. This made the person speaking to Goldwyn angry and he demanded an explanation about why Goldwyn fell asleep. Goldwyn made it clear to him that sleeping was also a statement! On a more personal note, as a speaker at a conference, I would not choose to talk from behind the lectern as that would be making a non-verbal statement of a style more closely associated with objectivity and a non-emotional state.

'Pacing and leading' (PALE): the dance of rapport

Would it not be possible to create in the classroom the same feeling of oneness which would naturally occur when we are with the ones that we love and that we get on well? This feeling and state of being makes up the essence, the foundation for establishing rapport. It is said that Milton Erickson could enter the worldview or the map of his patients by establishing excellent rapport as a result of which he was able to intervene and make extremely beneficial suggestions to his clients in order to help them resolve their problems.

An effective strategy in establishing rapport is that of 'Pacing and leading' (PALE) which comes from the field of neurolinguistic programming (NLP). NLP is considered to be a methodology and a technology of the study of human excellence used widely in many fields such as business, therapy, and education. The PALE strategy was born out of the investigations of the founders of NLP, Richard Bandler and John Grinder, who were modelling three of the world's most successful therapists, Virginia Satir, Fritz Perls and Milton Erickson (Alder 2002; Revell 1997; Robbins 1986).

Pacing, also known as mirroring or matching, means the emulation of the behaviour of one person by another in communication. Pacing may be done by matching some of the following aspects of non-verbal communication:

- *posture*: position of body/legs; feet/weight distribution; position of arms/hands/fingers; how shoulders are held, inclination of head;
- *facial expressions*: eye contact, look, gaze; happiness, sadness, anger, fear, surprise, disgust;
- *voice*: pace, volume, pitch, tone, intonation;
- *breathing*: rate, position;
- *movement*: rhythm; fast, steady, slow, still.

I would like to argue that establishing rapport can be compared to dance when viewed from many perspectives. First of all, a dance is a form of communication between follower and leader; as one moves the other follows. Another similarity is related to the moves. In order to dance, you must learn the moves. In time, you assemble the moves in a spontaneous way. As this process continues, eventually steps are blended. You can no longer tell who is leading and who is following. At the beginning, the leader may be leading 100 per cent. As the follower learns the moves, gradually the leader leads less. This leads to complete rapport which has a certain flow, is powerful and is pleasurable. At the same time, it is very elegant, and graceful. In PALE, once you have established rapport, you can start to lead or influence the other person. This is the same kind of spirit, the spirit of the dance and what star performers do as mentioned earlier—the state of 'being' and 'feeling'.

Whether you are doing the Argentinian tango, or an African dance, what you are doing is creating is a conversation in body language between two people. As would happen in speech, it ebbs and flows, sometimes with humour, and sometimes with passion and joy. That is to say, rapport in dance is driven by extremely powerful emotions like happiness, and joy. These emotions are also driven by the music which adds to the power of that relationship and the moment. I would like to argue that the same is true for the dance of rapport which we may call the PALE.

A valid question at this point in the argument would be to ask whether as teachers, we can learn how to dance the PALE? We can indeed say that it is a learnable skill. And yet there are challenges in learning the PALE. Before we turn to a discussion of these challenges, however, let us embark on an awareness raising activity to see if we can consciously become aware of different dance styles which are expressions of different emotional states.

Let us imagine that there are four different characters on stage. The first character is a rather aggressive person, perhaps somewhat like a macho man with body language confirming it. Watch the way he approaches people, the position of shoulders and the way he moves. The second character is rather snobbbish, with snobbery coming naturally to her. She walks in her peculiar cool manner with her head high and feeling over-confident. The third character is very active, and energetic and somewhat flirtatious, moving her body to the sides and swaying her hips, looking very happy. The fourth character takes each step very cautiously and is very conscious of everyone around him. His facial expressions and hesitant body movements indicate a rather shy character. What would happen if we asked them to dance, the macho man with the cool lady and the flirtatous with the shy? Imagine for a moment that they are on stage and trying to dance the tango. Would you say that there is any rapport between the two couples? I would doubt it.

This lack of rapport may help us to question our body language when we are dealing with our colleagues or learners. I am sure we can recognise some aspects of non-verbal behaviour and the emotions revealed through the body movements of these characters. We may be engaging in such non-verbal behaviours in particular moments of our personal and professional lives. When dealing with a difficult student, for example, do you raise your head a little higher than you ordinarily would? Or do you tend to lower your shoulders when listening to a serious piece of advice from your manager or director of studies? What about how you may be reacting to your spouse when he does not give the impression that he is listening to you since his head is tilted to one side and avoids eye-contact?

Challenges of learning the PALE

I have argued that the PALE is a learnable skill and pointed out that there are a number of challenges we face in learning it. The first challenge is overcoming the limitations that have been imposed on us by traditional conceptions of thinking and acting, hence issues of the mind. As established wisdom goes, mind and body are two different and separate systems. This is a rather 'limited understanding' of the brain (Pert 1997: 26). Today, as a result of recent research and interdisciplinary insights, it has become apparent that the brain is a marvellously complex and intricate organ of the body and neurologists inform us of the many different ways of the brain's capacity to think and to feel. Thus, we no longer talk about the mind-body system as two separate systems; on the contrary, we talk about one system: the mind in the body or the 'bodyminds' (Pert 1997: 141). Such unity has been enabled following the discovery of 'neuropeptides' which are the 'information molecules' (Pert 1997: 26), carrying information from the brain to the body and vice versa. Emotion, which has been kept out of the scientific picture, is no longer thought of as inaccessible, with the conclusion that 'Emotions are not just in the brain; they're in the body' (Pert, cited in Jensen 1995: 36). According to the theory of somatic markers, (Damasio 1994, 2003), when emotions are felt, they are marked somatically.

To sum up, the assumptions that come out from recent groundbreaking research are two-fold:

- body, thought and emotion are intimately bound together and function as a whole,
- emotions provide the essential criteria on which we base our rational decision-making
  (Damasio 1994, 2003; Pert 1997).

Learning the PALE: finding your own model of internal representation

I will now address the issue of how we can learn to dance the PALE given the challenges mentioned in the previous section. If it is true that emotions are critical to our rational decision-making, then in learning the dance of the PALE, the very first step needs to be tuning into the mood of the person that we are communicating with. This, however, may be easier said than done. If we are in a happy mood and the other person is sad, it may not be possible to suddenly access a sad state simply by telling our conscious mind to do so.

I will argue that there is one possible avenue for accessing intended mental states: keeping an internal representation of particular emotional states. Remembering the four characters that we have observed, you may want to remember the shy character for example, and use that image to match or mirror the non-verbal behaviour of a shy learner in communication. This internal representation is in effect a cue that will trigger the desired mental state. Such a representation may be a visual or auditory or kinaesthetic cue, meaning that it can be:

- an image,
- a melody,
- a feeling, or
- all of these.

Using any of the above cues will be effective as we now know that there is no need to live the actual experience: creating images in the mind will also create the experience. Having said that, I would like to emphasise that music can act as a powerful trigger of emotions. As Kotulak (1997) notes, 'Music is nature's version of a free lunch because it exercises the same neural networks we use for learning and memory'.

PALE: The dance moves

We can argue that the dance of PALE consists of four major moves as follows:

- warm-ups,
- scatting,
- pacing: matching/mirroring, and
- leading.

As discussed previously, you may need to do the dance steps in the order suggested here. In time, however, when you become more professional at pacing and leading you may wish to create your own moves spontaneously and perhaps in your own sequence. Each move is intended to enable the dancer to proceed toward the full experience of pacing and leading. In so doing we will complete the whole procedure to achieve the spirit of the dance. It is important to keep in mind that the aim is not to rate or judge ourselves or others but to learn how to establish rapport by matching and mirroring others, with the ultimate aim of rejoicing in and exploring what and who we are.

We will start with warming the body and we will explore our own movement of particular body postures. We will enter into the rhythm defined by the music but experienced in our own way of living a particular rhythm. We will be learning each move. You may be confused just as you would be when you are first learning the steps of any dance. There is no need to worry as with practice you will achieve spontaneous choreography. And remember the sequence is no longer important, you will improvise and do as star performers do.

Move 1: Warm-ups
The aim to help you get into the spirit of the dance. For this reason, you may wish to move any part of your body that will get you to do that. You may try rotating shoulders or swinging your hips. You may even try some belly-dancing movements which are excellent for warming up.

Move 2: Scatting
Scatting is a technique that I have borrowed from the world of jazz. I believe that it is an invaluable tool for enabling trainees to understand the importance of voice tonality and experiment with their voices. By substituting nonsense syllables for the words of a song, story or anecdote and trying to sound like a musical instrument, you can increase awareness of your voice tonality or use it in a training session.

Now take a moment and work with a partner. You can tell your partner a personal experience or story that is sad, only using nonsense syllables like 'dabba doo', or 'dubba duup' or any other nonsense syllables that you may think of. You can then try a happy story or anecdote. You partner can show that she is listening by using fillers or conversational gambits such as 'Oh!', 'Uh-uh', or 'Hmm …' (An aside: thanks Tessa, Jane and Ken for the wonderful demonstrations of 'micro-scatting'!)

You can practise this second step, scatting, by using different kinds of music. I find that the song *Candle in the Wind* by Elton John is particularly effective in creating a sad emotional state.

Move 3: Pacing: matching/mirroring
We have done warm-ups and scatting; it is now appropriate to move on to actual pacing steps. This is the stage when you get into rapport, that is to say, pace, by matching some aspect of your partner's body language. You may match or mirror the learner's posture, for example. More specifically, if the student is slumping, you could get into a slumping position, too. Or, if the student is sitting with shoulders down then you can lower your shoulders, too. Remember that you are at the pacing stage and you need to match or mirror whatever you feel is appropriate. Recalling the various body postures, facial expressions and breathing rhythms, you can try to get into rapport/pace by matching any and as many as possible.

Why not try matching facial expressions this time? Let us assume that your partner is looking angry. Try to mimic an angry facial expression. If you feel that you cannot get into an angry state of mind, again think back to an image, a sound or kinaesthetic cue. How about remembering a picture of a very angry person? Would that be helpful? What would you do to mirror a happy facial expression? Would thinking of your class help or would you rather imagine a chocolate cake? This then completes the third dance move.

Move 4: Leading
This is the fourth stage when you try to change the other person's behaviour by getting them to follow your lead, which could be leading them from slumping into a more upright posture, or leading them from sulking to smiling cheerfully. This is one way to test whether you have established rapport. What you are doing is that after checking that you have established rapport, you are beginning to lead or influence by changing your body language. If it is the case that you partner does not follow your lead, it means that you have not paced her as much as needed, which tells you that you need to re-pace.

Final tips in establishing rapport

To sum up, the following tips can be helpful in establishing rapport and getting into the spirit of the dance.
- Experiment so that you can decide what works for you.
- Avoid trying to match every aspect of body language. (Try one aspect at a time.)

- Practise with different kinds of music. (Different emotions are triggered by different pieces of music.)
- Feel free to design your own practice!
- Observe people. (This will give you many ideas about what particular gestures there are and how they can be matched.)
- Always keep the principle of flexibility in mind. (If one style of matching does not work with a particular person, change it and see what results that can produce.)

If you get carried away in the spirit of the dance, much as star performers do, then it can become your passion, living complete joy and happiness with the dance becoming a dance of passion. Happy dancing!

References

Emotion theory

Elster, J. 1999. *Alchemies of the Mind*. Cambridge: Cambridge University Press.

Fridja, N. 1986. *The Emotions*. Cambridge: Cambridge University Press.

Goleman, D. 1999. *Emotional Intelligence*. New York: Bantam Books.

Hargreaves, A. 2000, 'Mixed emotions: teachers' perceptions of their interactions with their students'. *Teaching and Teacher Education*, 16: 811–26.

Lane, R. D. and L. Nadel (eds.). 2000. *Cognitive Neuroscience of Emotion*. New York: Oxford University Press.

Lazarus, R. D. 1994. 'Appraisal: the long and short of it' in P. Ekman, and R. J. Davidson (eds.). 1994. *The Nature of Emotion: Fundamental Questions*. New York: Oxford University Press.

Lazarus, R. D. and B. N. Lazarus. 1994. *Passion and Reason: Making Sense of Our Emotions*. New York: Oxford University Press.

Oatley, K. and J. M. Jenkins. 2001. *Understanding Emotions*. Oxford: Blackwell Publishers.

Parrott, W. G. 2004. 'The nature of emotion' in M. B Brewer and M. Hewstone (eds.). *Emotion and Motivation*. Malden, Mass.: Blackwell Publishing.

Parrott, W. G. and R. Harré. 2000. 'Some complexities in the study of emotions' in R. Harré and W. G. Parrott (eds.). *The Emotions: Social, Cultural and Biological Dimensions*. London: Sage Publications.

Rosen, S. 1982. *My Voice will Go with You: The Teaching Tales of Milton Erickson*. New York: W. W. Norton and Company.

Sylwester, R. 1997. 'How emotions affect learning.' *Educational Leadership:* 60–5.

Sutton, R. E and K. F. Wheatley. 2003. 'Teachers' emotions and teaching: a review of the literature and directions for future research.' *Educational Psychology Review*, 15/4, 327–58.

Neuroscience, the brain and NLP

Alder, H. 2000. *Neuro Linguistic Programming*. Ankara: Sistem Yayıncılık.

Alder, H. 2002. *Handbook of NLP: A Manual for Professional Communicators*. Aldershot, Hants., UK: Gower Publishing Limited.

Arnold, J. (ed.). 1999. *Affect in Language Learning*. Cambridge: Cambridge University Press.

Damasio, A. R. 2003. *Looking for Spinoza: Joy, Sorrow and the Feeling Brain*. New York: Harcourt.

Damasio, A. R. 1999. *The Feeling of What Happens: Body and Emotion in the Making of Consciousness*. New York: Harcourt.

Damasio, A. R. 1994. *Descartes' Error*. New York: Grosset/Putnam.

James, T. and D. Shephard. 2001. *Presenting Magically*. Bancyfelin, Wales: Crownhouse Publishing.

Jensen, E. 1995. *The Learning Brain*. San Diego: Calif.: The Brain Store.

Gün, N. 2003. *Neuro Linguistic Programming: NLP*. İstanbul : Kuraldışı Yayıncılık.

Hannaford, C. 1999. *Smart Moves: Why All Learning is Not in Your Head*. Arlington, Va.: Great Ocean Publishers.

Knight, S. 2005. *NLP at Work: Neuro Linguistic Programming*. London: Nicholas Brealey Publishing.

Kotulak, R. 1997. *Inside the Brain: Revolutionary Discoveries of How the Mind Works*. Kansas City: Andrews McMeel Publishing.

O'Connor and Seymour. 1993. *Introducing NLP: Neuro-linguisticProgramming*. London: Thornsons.

Pert, C. 1997. *Molecules of Emotion: The Science behind Mind-body Medicine*. New York: Scribner.

Revell, J. and S. Norman. 1997. *NLP in Your Hands*. London: Saffire Press.

Revell, J. and S. Norman. 1999. *Handing Over: NLP-based Activities for Language Learni*ng. London: Saffire Press.

Robbins, A. 1986. *Unlimited Power*. New York: Fawcett Columbine.

7.2 Understanding dynamics supportive of learning in the young learner classroom

Zeynep Onat-Stelma *School of Education, University of Leeds, UK* **and**
Juup Stelma *School of Education, University of Manchester, UK*

In this paper we present 'reflective vehicles' as a way of understanding dynamics supportive of learning in the young learner classroom. We define reflective vehicles as any adjective that describes classroom practice at some level, such as, for example, the level of class activity or the level of class environment. The paper showed how an explicit focus on such adjectives could aid reflection on classroom practice, and provide a bridge between theory and practice.

Our presentation was motivated by recent case-study research with secondary-trained English teachers in Turkey during their first year of teaching English to primary age learners. English was introduced into the Turkish primary school curriculum in 1997, and it was common for primary schools to recruit secondary-trained teachers to cope with this new demand. However, while experienced English teachers, these secondary teachers often did not have training in the particularities of teaching English to young learners.

Data from semi-structured interviews with four teachers revealed a great deal of concern for class management, in a general sense, and very little concern for the actual activity of teaching English to the young learners. Also, the teacher's talk about class management was seldom 'linked' to the teaching of English. Interviews and observation over the teachers' first year of teaching English to primary age learners indicated that this failure to link class management issues with the actual teaching of English resulted in missed opportunities for English language learning.

As researchers we needed a way to communicate this finding, and as teacher trainers we wanted to develop a way to help these and other teachers to develop a more integrated or dynamic understanding of their classroom practice. To achieve this, we identified adjectives that we felt described the class environment and class activities that the teachers aspired towards. Where possible, we used adjectives the teachers themselves used in talking about their practice. Where this was not possible, we selected adjectives that we felt captured the meaning of what the teachers expressed in their talk. We also paired each adjective with the level of practice that they seemed to describe. The adjectives we identified from the data included:

- an 'organised' class environment;
- a 'quiet' class environment;
- an 'incentive-filled' class environment;
- a 'caring' class environment;
- 'fun-filled' class activities.

This list of adjectives reflects the teachers' great concern for class management. It also shows how they focused more on the class environment as a whole, and very little on class activity or activities. In addition, we noticed a lack of coherence between the adjectives. For example, the wish for a 'quiet' classroom seemed in potential conflict with 'fun-filled' class activities. Finally, there was no articulated focus on English or the teaching of English.

Next, thinking as teacher trainers, we began seeing the adjectives we had used to describe the teachers' practice as vehicles for reflecting on their practice. The 'fun-filled' vehicle illustrates a possible next step. We felt that 'fun-filled' might usefully be replaced by a different adjective not in conflict with 'quiet', such as, for example, 'familiar' class activities. Alternatively, the potential conflict between a 'quiet' classroom and 'fun-filled' activities could be replaced by a more sophisticated notion of activities, and how activities affect the class environment as a whole. For example, Halliwell's notion of activities which 'stir' and activities which 'settle' might be helpful here.

We also presented the reflective vehicles as a way to bridge the gap between practice and theory. For example, we felt that the adjective 'incentive-filled' (teacher's variously talked about praise, rewards, etc.) revealed a theoretical underpinning best described by behaviourism (as in 'positive' reinforcement). Hence, looking carefully at the adjectives we identified could reveal coherence or a lack of it in an everyday sense ('fun-filled' seemed to conflict with 'quiet') as well as coherence in a theoretical sense. (In fact, much of what the teachers articulated was coherent with a behaviourist view.)

Finally, using the literature, we suggested our own set of adjectives, or reflective vehicles, describing a 'generic' best practice on the levels of class environment and class activities. We felt that these sets of reflective vehicles illustrated both an everyday and theoretical sense of coherence, as described above. However, as our final advice we suggest that teachers generate their own adjectives, describing their own practice, and then use these as reflective vehicles to further develop both everyday and theoretical forms of coherence, thereby promoting dynamics supportive of learning in their own teaching practice. We also suggest that this might be a useful addition to for example, in-service teacher training programmes, and we intend to follow up this suggestion in our own work with teachers of young learners.

Email: zeynep@onat.org.uk
Juup.Stelma@manchester.ac.uk

7.3 Promoting knowledge of theory in teacher practice

Kristen di Gennaro *Pace University, New York, USA* **and**
Bede McCormack *Hunter College, CUNY, New York, USA*

Professional EFL instructors work in a variety of situations, allowing them to become knowledgeable as to which methods and techniques are most effective considering their students' ages, proficiency levels, purposes for learning English, and educational settings. That is, EFL teachers are very informed in their specific areas of practice. Such practice, in fact, helps teachers develop personal theories of what works and what doesn't, depending on the teaching situation. How many EFL teachers, however, are knowledgeable of relevant established theory in the field of ELT? What might teachers gain from greater awareness of and access to formal theory?

First, all teachers make pedagogical decisions on a regular basis, such as deciding how much time to spend on a task, how to order tasks during lessons, and what type of corrective feedback to provide students with and when, just to name a few. Many teachers also make curricular choices whenever they select books and design materials to address their students' needs, levels, skills, and desired goals. In some cases, teachers are responsible for assessment. Without experience in formal theories about language learning, teachers must rely on their experience and intuition to define constructs, realistic expectations of learners, and what constitutes evidence of learning.

While drawing on personal theories of teaching and learning gained through experience can be effective, based on our observations and comments made by practising teachers who lacked a background in ELT theory, we believe it is necessary for teachers to have access to both types of theory. Specifically, professional EFL teachers should be knowledgeable about seminal research questions and findings in ELT in order to promote learning in their classes and improve the status of the field. In particular, teachers should have a sense of the history of ELT, both to see themselves as part of an established and active research field, and to understand what has been done in the past so as to avoid less-than-effective teaching methods, while drawing on what has worked. Such knowledge can also give teachers a sense that a theory is just that—a theory—and that it can be challenged and even dismissed. Things change.

Understanding the role of input in second language acquisition is vital to creating comprehensible, salient material, written or aural, that makes noticeable those structures (phonology, syntax, or discourse) that the teacher intends to target. Having a basic knowledge of the role of Universal Grammar in both first and second language acquisition gives teachers a sense of the creativity of language and, more importantly, that not everything can be taught. The notion of learner language, or interlanguage, as systematic, rule-governed, and prone to fossilisation is perhaps one of the key theories to understand. Recognising not only what learners can't do, but also what they can do, and why, goes a long way towards informing teachers' curricular decisions. And an understanding of the linguistic and non-linguistic influences causing variability in second language learning allows teachers to see how their learners' age, first language, motivation, aptitude, etc. affect their learning.

Teachability issues implied by empirically based studies, such as the order of acquisition of relative clauses or the tense-aspect system, can help teachers decide what to attempt and what to postpone. In a similar sense, findings on error correction, both written and spoken, can give teachers a sense of what, when, and how to correct, as well as what to leave alone. Finally, understanding the value of classroom-based, or 'action' research allows teachers to recognise that a 'study' need only be as complex as is useful for the teacher/researcher.

Accompanying the need for increased awareness of theory amongst EFL teachers is the need for programme administrators and teacher trainers to encourage and promote greater access to theory for developing teachers. For example, teachers can be encouraged to join professional organisations and subscribe to affiliated journals, perhaps subsidised by their employers. Programmes can create coffee circles and reading groups, where teachers congregate socially to discuss theoretical issues and share ideas.

Although several audience members commented that expecting teachers to be knowledgeable of theory is a luxury not all can afford, we argue that in addition to the above-mentioned benefits, emphasising the role of formal theory in ELT can increase the professionalism fostered by the presence of more knowledgeable teachers who contribute to the field through their own observations and involvement in theoretical debates.

Email: kdigennaro@pace.edu
bede.mccormack@hunter.cuny.edu

7.4 Killing twenty-five birds with two stones: strategies for implementing innovation

Andrew Sheehan *Ministry of Education, Santiago, Chile*

As Senior ELT consultant for the Ministry of Education, I realised that my responsibility for the in-service development of teachers of English was akin to the toil of Sisyphus, because the teacher-training universities were continuing to generate inadequately-prepared graduates. Having tried, overtly and unsuccessfully, to remedy the situation, it became obvious that more 'devious' strategies were required. I therefore placed two 'Trojan Horses' in the universities: two ostensibly *in-service* programmes, but with the covert intention of achieving *pre-service* reform.

The first 'Trojan Horse' was an innovative 200-hour English and ELT pedagogy + methodology course that I designed specifically to address the needs of state-school teachers of English, delivered by teacher-training universities whose bids to offer the course were accepted by the Ministry, which heavily subsidised the course. The second was a mentor trainer training programme I initiated, involving university professors who each then went on to implement a mentor training programme for school-based teachers of English working in schools in their vicinity.

The English and ELT pedagogy + methodology course has a mandatory, three-phase structure: Phase 1 is 120 hours of English, in which lessons are video-taped and the participants (the university professor 'teachers' and their school-teacher 'students') all keep diaries; Phase 2 is a 50-hour ELT pedagogy + methodology component, in which the video sequences and diary entries from Phase 1 are used to initiate observation, analysis and reflection on key ELT pedagogical and methodological issues; Phase 3 is a micro-teaching component in which the teacher-students implement what they have learned in the preceding phases.

The course was innovatory in its interlinked phase structure and, more significantly, its extensive use of videos and diaries, both virtually absent from existing pre-service programmes in Chile. These factors proved a major—and revelatory—

challenge for the universities (which some took two years to meet, and others failed to adequately meet). Some universities, for example, wanted Phase 2 to be a 'potted history' of ELT methods and approaches (something they devote a whole semester to at pre-service level, but completely unacceptable for practising teachers on this course). For the majority of the university professors, however, the power of video sequences as a tool for observation, analysis and reflection quickly became apparent, and their use was implemented at pre-service level.

The fact that university professors were working with school teachers rather than undergraduate students—often for the first time—also had profound consequences. The school teachers were quick to react if their university 'teachers' were talking about a theoretical reality remote from that of their own classroom situation (which typically happens in pre-service courses), or suggested a technique which was unrealistic.

These consequences were, of course, exactly what I had hoped for. One professor, who had been invited to visit some 'teacher-students' in their schools, and saw first-hand the classroom conditions, admitted to me, 'I think we are preparing students sometimes for a reality they will never have—so I think students who are now in our programme should start attending schools earlier on'. Another, who has now begun using videos at pre-service level, wrote excitedly about the teachers, 'And when they saw themselves you could have heard a fly, they became so involved'.

The second 'Trojan Horse', the mentor training programme, had an even more profound effect, partly because I 'hand-picked' the university professor participants for their dedication and openness to change. My sessions began by 'unpacking' their own attitudes and beliefs about ELT, which had such a powerful influence on them that they all incorporated similar activities in their own mentor training programmes and in their pre-service classes. The participants and I developed a strong network of friendship and professional collaboration, despite the considerable distances which separate us (Chile is 4000 kms. long). Sharing experiences was a mainstay of the course, and they communicated frequently about their sessions with their groups of teachers. One wrote:

> I realised we had achieved the breakthrough. Each of them, in their own terms, acknowledged that for the first time they were aware of where they stand as teachers, they have come to understand why they do certain things, why they behave in a certain way, and most importantly, they are questioning their own teaching.

At the IATEFL TDTR Conference in Chile in 2005, all the university-based mentor trainers did joint presentations with their school-based mentors, the first time these two normally disparate groups have ever collaborated in Chile. That in itself was an indication that my 'Trojan Horse' strategy was beginning to have an impact.

Email: andrewjspider@hotmail.com

7.5 Peer observation in teacher development

Peter Beech *Anglo-Hellenic Teacher Training, Corinth, Greece*

This presentation began with a consideration of the elements that teaching practice on an initial teacher training course is designed to promote (Gower 1983, 1995), including:

- sensitivity to problems of language use for learners;
- sensitivity to how learners learn, the skills they need, the strategies they employ and the problems they have;
- classroom management skills;
- teaching techniques.

I then proposed a series of guidelines for the observation of peers on a training course. Guidelines are provided for each day's teaching practice, with a focus each day on a different area of teaching skills, such as grading language, staging instructions and checking meaning. This gives the peers observing their teaching partners an additional opportunity to focus on the practical implementation of some of the key teaching techniques taught on the course, which enriches both their contributions to the feedback discussion and their own teaching practice. In the final week of the course, instead of specifying guidelines, we ask the observed teachers to tell their peers what they want them to focus on.

We studied in detail two examples of peer observation notes from Scrivener (1994), noting that comments should be objective, supportive and non-judgmental, but in fact often include interpretative comment on the intentions or attitudes which the observer thinks might underlie the observed behaviours.

In the context of the training course, formal observation is often based on the trainer's expectations, and linked to assessment, focusing on the aims and objectives of the course, not those of the trainee teacher. Feedback is therefore likely to be corrective, and teacher change resulting from such feedback is likely to be convergent, with the teacher required to move closer to some agreed norm (Kurtoglu-Hooton 2004). This narrow view may stem from preconceptions about the processes of teaching and learning that can usefully be challenged (Gabrielatos 2004), and the identification of such preconceptions allows us to make feedback to trainee teachers more constructive and so more likely to facilitate teacher change. Some of the preconceptions discussed include:

- learning has specific and uniform goals;
- there are specific ingredients that a good lesson absolutely must have; and
- there are specific models for good lessons.

Having explored the distinction between initial training and further development, I posited a parallel distinction in the objectives of teaching practice in these two contexts. In the training context, the objectives of teaching practice may be summarised as:

- to provide an arena for assessment;
- to have your teaching evaluated and criticised.

In the context of ongoing development, objectives of peer observation might be:

- to encourage self-awareness;
- to enable you to make decisions about how you teach.

Based on the various reasons for observation, guidelines for peer observation were suggested. These were designed to promote the development of self-awareness for experienced as well as novice teachers. They focus on the use of observation as a tool to provide constructive and formative feedback.

Finally, we considered the value of peer observation as an element sustaining development in the wider context of classroom research. As White (2003) notes, 'Where two experienced teachers are involved they should take the opportunity to reflect on the underlying rationale of their teaching, rather than more superficial issues of procedure or technique'. Being observed and reflecting on feedback is the most immediate way for teachers to increase their awareness of how they teach, while 'Peer observation can provide opportunities for teachers to view each other's teaching in order to expose them to different teaching styles and to provide opportunities for critical reflection on their own teaching' (Richards 1995). This kind of reflection on practice, stimulated and supported by a colleague's observation is an important factor in the cycle of ongoing development. As Norrish (1996) states, 'Once the virtuous circle of establishing a climate of non-judgmental professional interest is established, then teachers will begin to regard themselves as researchers with a professional stake in their own theory generation'.

During the discussion, colleagues commented that it was very useful to provide detailed guidelines for the peer observation during the pre-service training course, and we explored the possibility of linking these more closely to the areas covered in the input sessions on each day of the course. It was also noted that our guidelines focus very much on teacher behaviours, and colleagues suggested that a focus on the learners and learning outcomes should also be included.

Email: mail@peterbeech.com

7.6 Giving your staff the best chance possible

Rachel Appleby *British Council, Budapest, Hungary*

Behavioural competencies are used by many companies in performance management. They are a tool whereby companies can motivate staff, discuss and set individuals' and departmental targets, as well as evaluate performance. This session aimed to define behavioural competencies, look at examples in practice and discuss the rationale for using them.

A behavioural competency is an observable skill, characteristic or application of knowledge displayed by a person and required for effective performance. Highly developed behavioural competencies differentiate outstanding performance from more typical performance in a given job, role, organisation or culture.

Behaviours tend to be more difficult to see than skills and knowledge (which include certificates and qualifications), and they are therefore more difficult to identify and measure. However, behavioural competencies have been found extremely effective in the area of recruitment, specifically on the basis that a person's past behaviour is likely be similar to the behaviour they will demonstrate in the future.

The British Council has identified 13 behavioural competencies as of particular relevance to the work of its entire staff. Ideally, they are used to improve one's own performance, as well as that of one's working unit. The competencies are as follows:

- achievement,
- analytical thinking,
- customer service orientation,
- entrepreneurship,
- flexibility,
- holding people accountable,
- intercultural competence,
- leading and developing others,
- professional confidence,
- relationship building for influence,
- self-awareness,
- team working, and
- working strategically.

At the British Council, each job description includes a maximum of 6 behavioural competencies, each graded according to a given level (1– 3, or 4). A teacher's job description, for example, will usually include customer service orientation, flexibility, self-awareness and team working. These are usually required at level 1 or 2.

The session looked in detail at self-awareness, defined in the British Council competencies dictionary as:

an understanding of your own emotions and 'triggers', and how they impact on your own behaviour and/or the behaviour of others. It is also about understanding your own strengths and limitations.

In brief, the levels of self-awareness can be summarised as follows:
1. knows and acknowledges strengths and weaknesses,
2. accepts feedback from others without being defensive,
3. understands how feelings and emotions may impact on performance,
4. sets up support structures to manage stress levels.

The session went on to describe how behavioural competencies operate in three areas of school management.

Development and training Examples included developing one's own career aspirations—looking ahead at future positions within the organisation—and defining what behavioural competences might be required at what level. As each competency is divided into 3 or 4 levels, and clarifies a range of actions of the competency concerned, it is easy to see what is required to progress to the next level.

Measuring performance Specifically within performance management, when each post has clear criteria as to what is required, then tasks carried out over the performance period can be evaluated in terms of behavioural competencies. For example, a teacher who has been involved in setting up a peer-observation programme by getting teachers together and deciding what aspects of teaching to focus on, could be seen as developing 'team-working'.

Motivation Behavioural competencies enable tasks to be defined and measured. They do not replace qualifications, but help staff recognise tasks achieved. This is important for the manager as well as the person being managed.

Besides looking at current global British Council practice, the session also touched on three related areas:

1. A survey carried out by Paul Kimm (British Council, Seoul), aimed to find out which competencies and levels are being used for teachers' job descriptions within the British Council, and the extent to which teachers deemed them appropriate. Besides general support from teaching staff in favour of the competencies used, the survey also identified that almost 75 per cent all these job descriptions are standardised.
2. A supplementary set of criteria is being used by some British Council centres. These aim to give more relevant focus to teaching skills. Initiated by staff at British Council Singapore, the teacher competencies include such areas as course and session planning, classroom management skills, promoting learner autonomy, etc. These complement the thirteen behavioural competencies used globally by the British Council, and are used in some centres in performance management.

3. Following a British Council presentation on behavioural competencies (Munich, April 2004), EAQUALS—the European Association of Quality Language Schools, www.eaquals.org—has recently started working groups to develop behavioural competencies for the purpose of giving greater definition to both teachers' roles, and managerial duties. These are now being piloted by a number of schools Europe-wide.

Email: rachelappleby@mail.datanet.hu

Reference

http://www.britishcouncil.org/teacherrecruitment-competencies-dictionary.doc

7.7 Task-based teacher training activities

Naďa Vojtková and Světlana Hanušová *Faculty of Education, Masaryk University, Brno, Czech Republic*

We presented two pre-service teacher training courses containing task-based activities, reflected on them from the trainers' perspective and showed how we integrate a Virtual Learning Environment (Moodle) into teacher training.

We believe our students (prospective English teachers) need the approach which Michael Wallace calls the 'reflective model' in which received knowledge, previous experiential knowledge, practice and reflection are well-balanced and lead to professional competence (Wallace 1994). Our activities followed the principles of Jane Willis's framework for task-based learning. Although Willis set the framework for language learning we found it equally relevant and useful for teacher training. We propose a definition of a teacher training task as an activity where theoretical materials (methodological principles) are used by the trainee for a learning purpose in order to achieve an outcome (Willis 1996). Our tasks are goal-oriented, having a specific objective that must be achieved in a given time. To achieve the goal students have to employ a number of skills including IT skills.

Using authentic literature in English classes

A course for future lower primary teachers. Initiated as a result of research and the 'Using real books' conference in Munich, Germany in 2004.

Aims and objectives

- to provide solid theoretical background for using authentic literature in the young learners´ classes,
- to equip the participants with hands-on experience in developing and running a series of lessons based on real books for children,

- to teach the participants how to keep a record of a project,
- to link theory with practice,
- to make the participants reflect on their learning and teaching practice,
- to integrate face-to-face sessions with distance learning elements and reflect on their use.

Task: a preparation of a teaching sequence based on a realbook

1. Pre-task phase
   Trainees look for the rationale of using real books in lessons, identify criteria of their choice and get ready to use the books.
   Techniques used: drama, for and against brainstorm, reading and written assignments in VLE Moodlinka (http://moodlinka.ped.muni.cz/course/view.php?id=638).
2. Task cycle (students work in pairs)
   Choosing the book.
   Planning: plan pre-, while- and post-reading activities, microteach.
   Teaching: teach parts of your plans in real school environment.
   Report: reflect and comment on your teaching in VLE Moodle, keep your records in the project logs.
3. Methodology focus
   Analysis: evaluation in project logs online.
   Further planning and conclusions.

Results

Positive aspects
- trainees motivated by the practical activities on the course,
- practical activities piloted in the seminars (which boosted the trainees' confidence),
- positive support from school teachers (mentors),
- positive feedback from learners.

Negative aspects
- demanding in time and work load for the trainees,
- insufficient IT competence of some trainees,
- limited opportunities of teaching practice.

Methods and approaches in language teaching

A course for future secondary teachers.

Aims and objectives

- to familiarise prospective teachers with ELT approaches, methods and techniques from both theoretical and practical perspectives,

- to engage prospective teachers in reflective thinking about their attitudes, opinions and beliefs concerning teaching English,
- to identify positive aspects of different methods and approaches and to consider their suitability for learners of different ages, learning styles and learning contexts.

Course requirements

Preparation of a teaching sequence based on the principles of a particular method or approach to language teaching. Microteaching in the seminar and subsequent discussion (innovative form) revealing key issues of underlying theory.

Task cycle

1. Pre-task phase
   Students receive detailed information about the task, are warned against possible shortcomings and receive lists of recommended resources.
2. Task (Students work in pairs).
   Planning: at least one consultation with the trainer required.
   Report: a 20-minute microteaching in the seminar.
3. Methodology focus
   Analysis: the discussion in the seminar and subsequently online in VLE Moodle
   Practice: feedback from the trainer. Trainees introduce innovations into their own teaching and comment on their experience in VLE Moodle.

Results

Positive aspects
- hands-on experience popular among trainees,
- very good performance in the exam.

Problems
- tendency to 'improve' the original and supplement it with some interesting activities,
- eliciting in the discussions seemed to be challenging. Some trainees prefered to present the theories they had studied instead,
- some students do not contribute to discussions online unless it is a course requirement.

Interesting suggestions from the IATEFL conference participants during the discussion following the presentation were to introduce an induction courses for students (an introduction to the VLE Moodle) and to video students perfomance and then post the videos in VLE Moodle.

Email: svetlana.hanusova@gmail.com
vojtkova@telecom.cz

7.8 Practical ideas for trainer training and teacher development

Briony Beaven *Freelance, Munich, Germany*

'Walking the dog: If you don't know how to do it, I'll show you how to walk the dog'. This song introduced the workshop. It served as a means of establishing the presenter's view that, although you can show someone how to 'walk the dog', you cannot just show someone how to be a teacher trainer.

Teachers who move into training require new knowledge and skills (Wallace 1991; Roberts 1998) and therefore some preparation for the job. Teacher trainers need to be self-aware, to be able to self-monitor and to attain sociality. Often they need to provide tools, rather than solutions. The workshop offered practical ideas for those preparing classroom teachers to become teacher educators, and specifically, preparing the new trainers to lead workshops and training sessions.

Firstly, some common problems of new teacher trainers were reviewed. New teacher trainers may have:

- no clear concept of what the job entails;
- simplistic ideas about effective teacher training (show and tell, provision of classroom 'recipes');
- little background in theories of teacher learning (how teachers may differently interpret workshop content, if and how new learning will be transferred to classroom practice);
- difficulty in working with peers (other teachers) and being *primus inter pares*; and
- poor self-evaluation skills.

The activities which were demonstrated and described aim to deal with these problems. They fall into two groups. The first group of activities is designed to raise awareness of issues in teacher training, while the second group provides skills training.

The activities
Group 1: Awareness raising

1. Trainee trainers reflect on their experiences of teacher trainers they perceived as 'good' and decide which trainer behaviours led them to that opinion.
   Aim: to start trainee trainers thinking about what a good teacher trainer does while training.
2. Trainee trainers consider statements about learning, teaching and teacher training. They decide which they agree with and which they consider most important. Statements for the area of teacher training could include:
   - Teacher training is getting trainees to copy experienced teachers;
   - Teacher training is showing or telling teachers about new activities or exercises;

- Teacher training involves getting teachers to reflect on their teaching;
- Teacher training involves linking generally accepted knowledge about teaching to teachers' experiences and beliefs.

Aims: to raise awareness that new teacher trainers' approaches to teacher training will depend on their conceptualisations of learning, teaching and teacher training. To suggest that teacher training is not (only) about passing on methodological tips or techniques.

3. A list of knowledge and skills needed by teachers is presented or elicited. Prospective teacher trainers use the list as a starting point to consider what extra or different knowledge and skills are needed by teacher trainers.

Aim: to focus prospective teacher trainers' attention on the knowledge and skills they need to acquire in order to be effective teacher trainers.

Group 2: Skills training

1. The theme of the relationship between teachers' beliefs and their practice is introduced by means of a picture of a head with items such as 'teacher's use of language' and 'teacher's attitude to the school' to place inside or outside the head according to whether the item is visible or hidden. Trainee trainers then read some teachers' statements about their practice and considered what beliefs might underlie them.

Aim: to provide skills practice in relating statements about practice to possible underlying beliefs or assumptions.

2. Trainee trainers modify blunt teacher trainer utterances into true yet face-saving statements for working with a group of teachers. Blunt utterances could include:

   You're wrong.
   What you should do is …
   Stop talking and let someone else have a chance to make a contribution.
   I always …

   Aim: to provide skills practice in working harmoniously with other teachers and in dealing with unexpected input from participants (for cultures where a collaborative mode of work is expected or acceptable).

3. New trainers together run a micro-training session for teachers, training for twenty minutes each. The new teacher trainers give and get feedback from their peers and the trainer trainer using a form that focuses attention on key skills.

   Aim: to provide practice in skills for teacher training in a secure environment with the opportunity for peer and self evaluation.

After experiencing or listening to descriptions of the different activities attendees discussed which ones might be useful or appropriate in their contexts. I am grateful to those present for suggesting modified, alternative versions of some of the activities that could make them suitable for an even wider range of contexts.

brionybeaven@t-online.de

References

Roberts, J. 1998. *Language Teacher Education.* London and New York: Arnold.

Wallace, M. J. 1991. *Training Foreign Language Teachers.* Cambridge: Cambridge University Press.

7.9 Issues in ELT in transitional countries: a presentation by Hornby scholars

Convenor: Rod Bolitho   *The College of St Mark & St John, Plymouth, UK* with **Ika Lestari Damayanti** *(Indonesia)*; **Abdullah Tambul El Malik** *(Sudan)*; **Hasan Shikoh** *(Pakistan)*; **Atanu Bhattacharya** *(India)*; **Tesfaye Habtemariam Gezahegn** *(Ethiopia)*; **Gabrielli de Fatima Zanini** *(Brazil)*; **Mohammad Rahim Samadi** *(Afghanistan)*; **Kapesha Chrispin Ngulube** *(Zambia)*; **Pablo Silva Rios** *(Chile)*; **Dinh Thanh Lam Nguyen** *(Vietnam)*; **Consuela Vargas** *(Colombia)*; **Gabriel Mohr** *(Argentina)*; **Mahjabeen Hussain** *(Bangladesh)*; **Fredrick Odhiambo** *(Kenya)*; **Gospel Ikpeme** *(Nigeria)*; **Dorothy Atuhura** *(Uganda)*; **Eleanor Occena** *(Mexico)*; **Mariela Navarrete** *(Chile)*; **Virginia Morales** *(Colombia)*; **Naeem Sadiq** *(Pakistan)*; **Rosa Maria Funderburk Razo** *(Mexico)*

Introduction

This paper is based on a presentation given by a team of Hornby Scholarship holders from all over the world who, at the time of the Harrogate Conference, were all studying on courses in the UK leading to masters degrees in some aspect of ELT. The scholarships are awarded annually to appropriately qualified and experienced applicants from countries in transition of one kind or another, many of them in the developing world. The scholars' names and provenance appear in full above. Though I was asked to convene the session, the preparation and research that went into it and the opinions represented are entirely to the credit of the group. At a preparatory meeting in Oxford in December, the scholars, all experienced ELT professionals in their own right, identified five issues of common concern in their home contexts. They then gathered opinions and data on these five issues, and the five sections in this paper summarise their findings as presented in the conference session as well as incorporating some of the points made by a very lively and interested audience.

The culture of reading

There seems to be a general absence of a reading habit in the language learning environment of countries in transition. Many language learners do not seem to read enough these days, and this is likely to have a negative impact on their progress in learning English. A small-scale survey was conducted to find out how the current Hornby scholars and their colleagues view reading habits in L1 and L2 in their respective countries. Most of them agree that students have poor reading habits and hardly read either in L1 or L2, regardless of their access to reading materials. They also point out that most teachers leave it up to their institutions to solve the problem, although some do try to encourage students to read in different ways. At the institutional and curriculum level, there is hardly any stress on silent sustained reading, although there are clearly strong correlations between extensive reading and language proficiency. On the contrary, the main institutional and curricular focus seems to be on examinations, and this tends to foster reading for learning, not for pleasure. The high cost of L2 reading materials, addiction to electronic and new media, etc. also impede extensive reading. Quite interestingly, teachers seldom make any conscious efforts to familiarise students with reading materials as a means of promoting reading for pleasure. In some cases, they consciously or subconsciously resist any institutional effort to promote reading, as was evident in the abortive attempt to institutionalise a sustained reading programme at a school in Liceo Antofagasta, Chile. The project had to be discontinued although it had certain positive effects on the students. A major reason for the discontinuation was actually the indifference of, and even resistance from, the teachers. Clearly, the question is not only of resource constraints but also of systemic resistance—a question that ELT professionals in countries in transition need to seriously ponder on.

Large classes in countries in transition

Class size is one of the prime concerns of teachers in countries in transition. According to the mini-survey involving nine countries—Sudan, Ethiopia, Mozambique, Afghanistan, Mexico, Indonesia, Pakistan, Brazil, and Chile—the definition of a large class varies between 20 and 300 students at different levels of education from primary to tertiary. For example, at tertiary level in Chile a class of forty students is considered large but not necessarily in Sudan, where student numbers could be as high as 300. The survey shows that there are things which teachers think that they cannot do in large classes such as effective classroom management, monitoring individual progress, providing feedback, and giving students sufficient practice. However some teachers also state that large classes can provide positive opportunities for variations in the dynamics of group work and presentations, collaborative learning, and for exploring cultural diversity.

Students' views of large classes on the other hand are both negative and positive. Some say that they are often left out and disturbed by other students while others think that large classes increase their chances of doing some work outside the classroom and make fewer demands on them to participate in the classroom.

The survey shows that teachers adopt the following strategies to deal with large classes: pair and group work, project work, peer to peer feedback and process evaluation. Two main training priorities were mentioned: how to help teachers to be aware of the possible advantages of large classes, and how to cope with their disadvantages.

Curriculum issues

English language teachers in transitional countries are frequently unable to participate in discussions related to curriculum issues. This is because teachers in many contexts do not participate in curriculum planning or are not even aware that a curriculum exists. Findings from a survey conducted with current Hornby scholars and other international students in the universities where they study have revealed that the English curriculum in their respective educational institutions falls into one of the following three main situations:

- The curriculum is a plan developed by a higher authority where implementation has been difficult for the simple reason that teachers were not involved in its development.
- Curricula which are developed *with* teacher participation at institutional level.
- In some cases, teachers do not know that a curriculum exists; a textbook was handed to them to work with when they were hired to teach; in such cases, the textbook *is* the curriculum.

These situations cover most cases in our countries and identifying which one applies in a given context is, as we found when we approached the problem for the purposes of the presentation, a prerequisite for a useful discussion on curriculum issues.

Before research advances further in the field of curriculum, it is worth considering the current situations in different contexts because they vary so much and therefore what is discussed at an abstract academic level might be too idealistic or unrealistic.

The balance between language and teaching skills in teacher training programmes

In this presentation we tried to raise issues related to teaching development and language improvement in three countries—Brazil, Colombia and Ethiopia. We mainly focused on the importance of the balance between language and teaching skills in programmes for teachers of English in our countries.

Chapter 7: Teacher development

We started our discussion on the basis of a typical teacher's plea for help in those countries—the desire to improve language proficiency and teaching skills at the same time. Generally, programmes for English language teachers tend to focus either on language or on methodology development. We decided then to find out whether any action has already been taken in our countries and our investigations revealed that:

a) In Ethiopia, an English Language Improvement Programme—ELIP—has recently been introduced, starting with a focus on language and gradually including some methodological aspects.

b) In Brazil, two English language teaching projects were implemented—one in the state of Paraná, starting in the late nineties and the other one, more recently, in the state of Tocantins. In both projects the main focus was on teaching skills development but elements for language improvement were also added.

c) As for Colombia, the Ministry of Education and some universities came together to work on a project aimed at the development of a local in-service Certificate for English Language Teaching—ICELT—based on internationally recognised guidelines. The course helps English teachers to improve not only their language proficiency but also their teaching methodology.

All those programmes shared the following features:

- they were designed for in-service teachers;
- they had elements for language improvement moving towards teaching skills development or vice-versa;
- they were designed in and for contexts where English is taught as a foreign language; and
- they had British Council involvement and support.

We agreed that programmes which tend to follow a cyclical development process brought more benefits for the participants and had more chances to succeed when implemented in contexts with similar conditions as those in our examples. However, some concerns still remain; for example, how can these programmes be sustained when they come to an end, or what could teachers of English do to improve their level of proficiency in a foreign language environment? We hope that our presentation emphasised the importance of the balance between language and skills improvement in programmes for English Language teacher education in other countries as well as our own.

Teacher development/in-service training for English Language teachers in transitional countries

In many transitional countries, there have been a lot of programmes aimed at improving the professional knowledge, skills, attitudes and performance of in-service

ELT teachers. In Nigeria for instance, while the government—mainly from a lack of funds and resources—has not done a lot in the area of in-service training or development, the British Council in conjunction with the National Teachers' Institute has recently initiated a Continuous Professional Development programme for English language teachers. Zambian teachers, on the other hand, have been participating for a long time in school-based Continuous Professional Development programmes despite the fact that there have been a number of setbacks. In Mexico, there is a policy of continuous development of teachers in most sectors of education. In Pakistan teachers participate very actively in ELT conferences. In Vietnam, on the other hand, in-service training is mainly provided through summer schools.

In spite of all these efforts in a number of transitional countries, teachers still have a lot of problems. In many countries, teachers have been provided with very few opportunities to broaden their experience and to keep abreast of changes and innovations in the field of ELT. It seems that teacher development is either not a priority or that it is constrained by other issues.

In our investigation we found that teacher development is affected by some or all of the following factors:

- Lack of resources—many governments/authorities complain that there are not enough funds or resources to enable them to provide support or in-service training for teachers.
- The absence of motivation and of any incentive for teachers—no substantial reward for teachers who participate in teacher development/in-service training activities.
- Insufficient organisation and co-ordination of teacher training/development programmes. All too often, the programmes do not address teachers' real problems. Sometimes it seems the trainers have a different agenda from that of the teachers.
- Insufficient training sessions: in most cases, teacher development programmes are not continuous or progressive. They are organised as 'one-off' events or only during summer vacations.

8 Focus on the learner

The English language teaching community continues to investigate the factors that affect learning and to look for ways to help individual learners. Firstly in this chapter **Dede Wilson** shares her research into learner perceptions and expectations of a good teacher with us, as she did in her workshop, comparing the attendees' beliefs with those of the respondents in her study. Her respondents thought it important that the teacher be able to motivate them; this mattered to them more than whether the teacher was a native or non-native speaker of English. **Brian Tomlinson** and his team of speakers in the materials development symposium also stress the benefits of affective engagement. Brian Tomlinson addresses the effects of using emotionally memorable texts and tasks. Then **Hitomi Masuhara** notes that affect is often regarded as a peripheral phenomenon but bearing in mind the neural architectures in the brain it should be seen as playing a vital role in the learning process. **Michael Rodden** focuses on the role that affect should be playing in EAP textbooks and on EAP courses. The final symposium speaker was **Alan Maley** who shows how creative writing is both feasible and motivationally powerful with learners of English.

Magdalena Keblowska tackles the problem of language anxiety. She surveyed third-year university students of English and found that many of them experience this type of anxiety and, furthermore, not only in connection with speaking, as might be expected, but also when performing in English in the other skills areas.

The following three reports argue for increasing learners' metacognitive skills so that they can take more responsibility for their learning. **Mojca Belak** explains an experiment she conducted with her university students. In line with learning organization and quality school theory, the students shared power with their teacher and found that the success of their working groups depended on their actions. They took decisions about their courses and created their own grading criteria. **Sanja Wagner** examines the rationale for and use of 'work plans', frameworks for learning activities that allow school pupils to find out ahead of time what they are going to study. The 'work plans' also include suggestions for how to learn, for language improvement and for small projects, thus increasing learner autonomy. **Judy Garton-Sprenger and Philip Prowse** begin by citing research which suggests that the notion of learning cycles, the consistency of visual, auditory and kinaesthetic preferences, and the value of matching teaching and learning styles are all 'highly questionable'. They go on to advocate an approach which involves raising the learners' awareness of different ways of learning through experiments with various learning styles according to the nature of the task in hand. **Samuel Lefever** discusses the findings of an evaluation of English language teaching in Icelandic compulsory schools. Both pupils and teachers have positive attitudes towards learning English but more focus is needed on spoken communication and using English during lessons. Next **Sarah Mercer** explores the self-concept of tertiary level learners of English as a foreign language and offers a framework that may be useful to others who are concerned to foster positive learner self-concepts. Finally **Anne Margaret Smith** highlights an area of ELT that is seldom discussed, namely learners with what are often called 'learning difficulties'. As she points out, ELT professionals will in the future need to be well-prepared to help such learners. She recognises that this is not an easy task, clarifies the kinds of difficulties that ELT teachers may come across and makes a number of useful, practical suggestions.

8.1 Nature and nurture, the best of both worlds

Dede Wilson *Freelance, London, UK*

Does it matter whether teachers are native or non-native speakers, or is it a question of good teaching? This workshop aimed at exploring what learners, rather than teachers, thought and in a context where they were taught by both regularly. It was based on my research into learner beliefs about good teaching and how important they thought the teacher was in motivating them. I also wanted to find out how central their expectations and cultural contexts were to their perception of their native and non-native teachers.

The majority of non-native English language speakers around the world learned the language successfully in classrooms, not by acquiring it through everyday exposure. They learned with non-native teachers who made it possible in a non-English-speaking environment.

Good teaching was central to this successful cognitive learning process. Languages are not only acquired, as a great deal of research would have us believe, they are both learned and acquired in classrooms round the world. The numbers of World English speakers are testimony to this. However, education ministries, influenced by research, have introduced collaborative teaching schemes to facilitate language acquisition from exposure to native speakers in the classroom. To see what advantages were to be gained by the learners from this approach, my research also focused on the students' perceptions of learning and their expectations of the teacher's role.

The research

The research involved thirty 14–16-year-old students in Romania who were taught regularly by both non-native (non-NESTs) and native speakers (NESTs) in a 3 to 1 time ratio. It was an open field study that aimed to consider a broad scope of classroom variables that challenge learners' beliefs about their ability to learn, their aptitude and self worth and their attitudes to their teachers. A teacher's approach can mean the difference between success and failure when there is a mismatch of beliefs and attitudes, or expectations between the two (Howitz, 1987).

According to Dörnyei (2001), key teacher motivational behaviours for success are:

1. teacher enthusiasm,
2. commitment to and expectations of progress and success,
3. teacher encouragement and expectation of individual learner achievement,
4. good relationship—genuine involvement with the students,
5. supportive atmosphere—making it a safe and secure environment, valuing student participation and encouraging autonomy, making the classroom environment theirs,
6. establishing a cohesive learner group through establishing group goals, cooperation and maintaining group dynamics.

Classroom variables

Three key learning situation factors were considered in the workshop: learner perceptions and expectations of a good teacher; the importance of the teacher role in motivation and learning; and feelings about speaking in English.

To examine the first factor, in my workshop there were fourteen wall cards around the room with various attributes of a good teacher. The attendees walked around and read them all and then selected the eight they considered the most important. They numbered them in order of importance and then compared their choices with one another. We then looked at what the students in the study had decided. Knowledge of the language was of key importance but so was the ability to make learning fun but serious, provide variety and realistic opportunities for practice.

Workshop attendees then completed the same task as the students, looking at various teacher behaviours and deciding how important they were to their motivation, marking them V (very important) I (important), N (not important). Students felt the most important attribute was that teachers enjoy teaching, followed by a high expectation of the teacher to motivate them to learn and be interested in their progress. The results reinforced Dörnyei's findings.

Conclusions

To decide on what they would consider the ideal learning situation, the students used the criteria from the previous tasks to help them answer three questions:

a) Did it matter if a teacher was a NEST or a non-NEST, or was it just a question of good teaching?
b) Did the combination help their learning?
c) What did they learn from each and why?

It was overwhelmingly the case that students believe the following:

- teachers are vital to their learning;
- good teachers need the skills that both non-NESTs and NESTs traditionally bring;
- learning and acquiring from both kinds of teachers is rich and memorable;
- realistic practice opportunities are important for students to become fluent, accurate and competent speakers;
- cultural awareness as intercultural speaker is an important advantage;
- good teaching and teacher enthusiasm, with teachers using motivational strategies, are important to their learning.

No single definitive method or approach is 'the best'. What matters is a variety of approaches in dealing with language to meet students' overall needs, different learning styles and maintaining learners' motivation to learn. Together, NESTs and non-NESTs enable students to recognise the importance of the link between culture and language and to value themselves as intercultural speakers.

The following quotation sums up the position of the students:

> It was helpful when learning was fun, but serious. By fun and serious I think I meant enjoyable but useful. That includes the variety of work which I think every English class should contain. Some teachers emphasise too much on a point of English language. For example, some teachers make just grammar exercises on and on. That makes English dull and boring, and usually in these kind of cases, I don't enjoy learning anymore. Furthermore, I had a Native English teacher once who used to sit around doing nothing during the class. Or, he didn't prepare the lessons as he should. That's a pity!

Email: dede@dedewilson.wanadoo.co.uk

8.2 Symposium on materials development: ways of developing materials to achieve affective engagement

Convenor: Brian Tomlinson *Leeds Metropolitan University, UK*

The convenor introduced the Symposium speakers and appealed for interaction from the unexpectedly large audience. He stressed that each of the speakers would focus on a particular aspect of affect but that all four would be leading discussion on ways in which language learning materials can be developed and adapted to maximise opportunities for affective engagement. He stated the team's basic position as being that affective engagement can lead to the deep processing that is essential for long-term learning to take place and that without affective engagement no effective and durable learning is possible. He then concluded his introduction by saying that in the four presentations the focus would be on the following three main aspects of affect:

- self-esteem,
- positive attitudes towards the learning environment, and
- emotional investment.

Brian Tomlinson then focused on 'leaving a gap activities' as ways of stimulating affective engagement. He first of all discussed and demonstrated activities which could be used to raise and maintain self-esteem and stressed that these should leave a challenge gap. He demonstrated how understanding and producing riddles and jokes and predicting endings of stories and poems could achieve this. He insisted that the challenge in such activities must be ultimately achievable and suggested ways in which useful assistance could be provided by other activities, by teachers, by peers and by time. He then demonstrated this point with an activity which involved predicting football results from intonation and described activities he had done with students overseas which involved inventing a device to save water, writing group episodes of a class soap opera and writing individual novels. He also looked at ways in which learners can be helped to develop and sustain positive attitudes to the learning experience by being involved in decisions about the learning environment, placement, the syllabus, texts and tasks and by taking part in activities in which they are encouraged to localise texts and tasks, personalise texts and tasks, make their own personal use of texts and tasks and select from a menu of texts and tasks. Finally he demonstrated how texts and tasks can be used stimulate emotional involvement. He stated that both positive and negative emotions (for example, joy, amusement, disturbance and anger) can be useful for making experiences significant and memorable and provoked a lively discussion by reading potentially disturbing texts.

Hitomi Masuhara (*Leeds Metropolitan University*) started her session by asking the audience to list what they remember having learned during their primary school days and to reflect upon the factors that induced such durable learning. The major factors identified were 'frequent exposure, repetition and reinforcement', 'significance to the learners' lives', and 'involvement of strong affect'. It was very interesting how these factors coincided with some optimal conditions for learning as summarised by Hitomi Masuhara based on her studies in second language acquisition and in neuroscience. She then referred to current understanding in neuroscience and in second language acquisition in that what is taught never equals what is learned. Despite this awareness, she argued that syllabus, methods and materials still are predominantly focused on input, as can be seen, for example, from the current emphasis on automatic word recognition and lexical approaches to language teaching. She then stated that what really matters is to consider ways of maximising intake. Affect is often regarded as a peripheral phenomenon, but Hitomi Masuhara counter-argued by showing the neural architectures in the brain and indicating how affect plays a vital role in the learning process. Finally, she demonstrated an example of how an affectively engaging poem may be further exploited to facilitate intake.

Michael Rodden (*Leeds Metropolitan University*) focused on the role that affect should be playing in EAP textbooks and on EAP courses. He did so by first of all referring to his own experience teaching on EAP courses and by criticising the knowledge transmission mode of delivery which typifies many of these textbooks and courses. In particular he was critical of the approach which seemed to be based on the assumption that because EAP students usually have high instrumental motivation they will inevitably learn what they are taught, provided that it is relevant to their needs. He stressed the importance of catering for human wants as well as academic needs and advocated and demonstrated an approach to EAP teaching which aimed to stimulate affective engagement as well as to provide useful experience, information and advice.

Alan Maley (*freelance*) focused on creative writing and showed how it was both feasible and motivationally powerful with learners of English. He began by demonstrating a few practical classroom activities, including making permutations of a sentence, using word arrays, and writing haiku. He then drew from this some of the key points for discussion, which were presented under three headings: creativity in life and language; creativity in learning; creativity for learners. He stressed that linguistic creativity is everywhere about us in everyday life. It includes the way we tell stories (and the importance stories have for our survival), the way that language is shot through with metaphorical and other figurative tropes, the way we play with language, the way we respond to the aesthetic dimensions of language and not just the utilitarian. In terms of learning, using creative techniques helps redress the balance between the affective and intellectual dimensions, it fosters the expression of personal meanings and allows scope for learning style preferences. The disciplined nature of creative writing (contrary to popular belief) gives a live focus to matters of form, patterning and rules in language. In purely practical terms, student-generated texts can be reused with other learning groups. For learners, successful creative writing gives an enormous boost to self-esteem: hence to motivation. It fosters joyful learning, personal as well as linguistic discovery, and a greater awareness of the language being learned. In short, it helps develop 'whole-person' learning.

There had been many interesting questions raised and important points made by the audience during and at the end of each of the individual presentations but there was still time and energy left for a lively exchange of views after all the presentations had been given. The general consensus seemed to be that most commercial course-books fail to achieve sufficient affective engagement (partly because the publishers are understandably reluctant to risk provocative content) and the focus was on ways in which teachers could add affect themselves. The most popular way seemed to be through a personalisation process in which the teacher contributes her own experiences and views and the students connect and evaluate content and tasks in relation to their own previous experience.

Email: B.Tomlinson@leedsmet.ac.uk

8.3 The factors contributing to proficient English users' language classroom anxiety

Magdalena Keblowska *A.Mickiewicz University, Poznan, Poland*

Until the mid-1980s language anxiety was considered as a transfer of anxiety from another domain, which led to contradictory research results (Chastain 1975). It was Horwitz, Horwitz and Cope, who in 1986 proposed language anxiety as a *unique* form of anxiety *specific* to L2 contexts. The uniqueness of the situation stems from L2 being both the object of study and the means of expressing oneself, which makes it so difficult for learners to show their true selves.

The aim of the presentation was to show that, contrary to what many researchers claim (Djigunovic 2000; MacIntyre and Gardner 1989), proficient users of English also experience language anxiety and that their anxiety is not only associated with speaking, as it is commonly believed, but also with performing the other skills in English.

In order to find support for her claim, the author circulated a questionnaire among 57 third-year undergraduate students at a university school of English in Poland. The questionnaire elicited the respondents' definitions of language classroom anxiety, examples of situations in which they felt anxious, and suggestions for reducing learner anxiety. Below are the most significant findings from the survey:

- Thanks to their ELT methodology course, the students are familiar with the concept of anxiety, so they are able to provide an adequate definition. (For example, they know that anxiety can be facilitating or debilitating.) However, in their descriptions they emphasise its *detrimental*, and not potentially positive, effects: inhibiting the process of learning and making students' performance difficult or impossible.
- The most significant causes of learner anxiety are: the teacher and his/her behaviour, the very fact of using L2 and not L1, speaking in L2, students' low self-esteem, as well as competing or comparing oneself with others.
- All the respondents have experienced anxiety at the university and its symptoms can be physical (stomach ache, shaking hands, blushing) or performance-related (inability to perform, impaired performance, poor concentration).
- Although almost 20 per cent of the respondents don't believe effective strategies of counteracting one's language anxiety exist, most students provide a number of techniques, like positive self-talk, preparing for classes, forcing oneself to participate, using relaxation techniques; those for whom classroom-related stress is unbearable skip classes or refuse to participate.
- The respondents have experienced anxiety when performing different skills, not only speaking, especially at the beginning of their academic career; still, the skill that has caused them greatest stress is speaking (especially speaking in public and because of the testing atmosphere when they speak), followed by writing (because writing in Polish is so different from writing in English or because of an incompetent or unhelpful instructor).
- The respondents suggest two types of teacher strategies for reducing language anxiety: affective (pleasant atmosphere, friendliness, empathy, respect for learners) and cognitive (clear requirements, guidance in learning).
- While almost 20 per cent of the respondents claim that a certain amount of anxiety can be beneficial for systematic work, the effects of limiting anxiety indicate they would prefer their classes to have provoked less anxiety. Reducing language anxiety would result in better learner performance and more effective learning. The students seem to realize that the energy and cognitive potential they waste on their anxieties could be put to better use.

While some researchers claim that 'anxiety decreases with increasing language competence since the more proficient the learner becomes, the more positive are his experiences of learning and using the new language' (Djigunovic 2000:11), the study shows that highly proficient learners of English do experience language anxiety. Thus anxiety is not merely related to low linguistic competence and does not miraculously disappear when a certain level of proficiency has been achieved. The respondents emphasise the role of teachers in creating their anxieties, and in particular: high or unrealistic expectations, an atmosphere of constant testing and evaluation, emphasis on absolute correctness combined with the inherent difficulty of the courses. Teachers should remember that their role in the classroom is twofold: teaching or helping to learn, and taking care of students' well-being, without which the former is unlikely to work.

While the study may show certain tendencies, its generalisability is questionable. More groups of proficient English users should be investigated in different contexts and additional data collection tools (for example, interview, classroom observation) should be used in order to achieve triangulation. Nevertheless, this small-scale survey may serve as a starting point for a more comprehensive study of foreign language anxiety among proficient learners.

Email: KMagdalena@inetia.pl

8.4 Mission possible: English class as a learning organisation

Mojca Belak *University of Ljubljana, Slovenia*

I teach general English and my students are future English teachers. They are motivated and proficient in English but tend to come to classes less-well prepared than I would wish them to be. For many years I had wanted to become part of a learning organisation, which is why I suggested the creation of it in my classes. What I expected from my students was high-quality work and readiness to change and keep changing. In return I treated them as my equals, led and not ruled them and supported experimentation and individuality.

I carried out my experiment in two groups. I chose first-year students because I wanted learners who had not yet been influenced by the way of assessment at our department. My fourth-year students, however, joined the experiment because of the good rapport we had built over the three years I had taught them.

Theoretical background

Instead of using the term *learning organisation* I should perhaps modify it to *the learning school* (Underhill 2004) because I used the concept of learning organisation in a school environment. At the core of the experiment lay my own values: I expect students and me to grow as individuals during the learning process, I am convinced that teaching and learning are enhanced if the class atmosphere is good, and finally, according to Choice Theory (Glasser 1984) students and I have to satisfy the four basic psychological needs—belonging, power, freedom and fun—in order to feel happy and be more productive. I expected all of us to be ready to change. We would develop or consolidate honesty, sensitivity, and friendliness in the group and share power. All that would help students do high-quality work. In order to 'ground' my vision I decided to blend the elements of the learning organisation with elements of Glasser's Quality School (Glasser 1998).

Learning organisation elements

At monthly meetings (pow-wows) we discussed process questions. Any disagreements or problems among group members were discussed on this level. We took decisions by voting; my vote was worth the same as any other member's.

Pow-wows were extremely good for the group as they united the students. Besides, it soon became obvious that the system allowed them to have a say on certain issues concerning my running the course and we sometimes changed the rules or I adapted to the wishes or needs of the group. Sometimes the newly acquired freedom in decision-making resulted in their being too strict and demanding on themselves.

In order to follow their own development better, students wrote individual progress diaries and I carried out individual half-term interviews with them, encouraging them to assess their progress.

Quality school elements

Instead of my grading them, I suggested at the beginning of the course that they should decide on the grade each wanted to have so that they could work towards it throughout the year.

In order to achieve that, they had to first create their own criteria. That proved to be a rather trying and challenging task for them and I noticed that both groups initially focused on negative rather than positive criteria for grading and that they needed a lot of guidance to change in that respect.

Results

First-year students proved to be a mixture of ultra-high achievers and diligent but not very successful learners. They were all rather shy; I had a feeling that they felt insecure, unsafe and that they didn't really trust me, as if they expected me to punish them for their mistakes in the end. It took more than six months for them to feel comfortable enough to start taking an active part in the work we did. Their colleagues in the fourth year, however, were very different: they always had views on absolutely everything, but the problem was that the more daring ones dominated while the quieter ones shied away. One of my goals for this group was to help them learn to respect others and communicate in a civilised way.

Chapter 8: Focus on the learner

Most students in the fourth year achieved their goals and got the grades they had set for themselves at the beginning of the course. The strict criteria they had set made them participate in class work even more, which made this group particularly lively and successful. First-year students, on the other hand, were not so good at reaching their goals, but, surprisingly, they still want to continue the project next year. Despite all its teething problems, the learning organisation project proved to be rather successful and certainly an experience for all who were involved in it. How we changed!

Email: mojca.belak@guest.arnes.si

References

Glasser, W. 1984. *Take Effective Control of Your Life*. New York: Harper & Row.
Glasser, W. 1998. *The Quality School*. New York: HarperPerennial.
Underhill, A. 2004. 'Continuous professional development'. *IATEFL Issues* 149.

8.5 Towards autonomous learning

Sanja Wagner *Erich Kästner-Schule, Darmstadt, Germany*

The aim of this talk was to show how to structure larger units based on a topic for young learners (11–16 years old). The examples illustrating the new design of the lessons were developed and tested at a comprehensive school in Hesse in a highly multicultural suburban community. The scheme is based on three fundamental concepts:

1. task-based learning,
2. self-assessment, and
3. learner autonomy.

Teaching English with the help of a 'work plan' (as the template is called in this context) means encouraging self directed learning and self assessment by implementing the European Language Portfolio.

A 'work plan' is a template which can be used at any level, with any course book and even more so if you provide/create your own learning material without any course book at all. All the material and tasks/activities included should be carefully chosen, meaningful, challenging and authentic (as far as possible). They should meet the manifold needs of young learners in an unstreamed classroom in a German state school.

After the teacher has introduced a new topic, pupils are given a 'work plan', a frame for all the learning activities during the following two to three weeks. In this way the pupils know what they are going to learn and how, which makes the teaching and learning transparent. The plan includes various methods and tasks for learning vocabulary, for reading and listening comprehension, for writing and communication, for activities or small projects as well as a part which focuses on language use and language awareness. Examples can be seen and downloaded from the internet (http://s1.teamlearn.de/b-1-eqt, under 'library' and www.bag-englisch.de).

For students the 'work plan' is a scaffold which supports their engagement in learning and in negotiating while the teacher is able to stimulate reflection on learning progress, achievements, problems as well as likes and dislikes when learning a language. Pupils learn how to learn a new language in general, as well as developing their capacity to plan, monitor and evaluate their own learning and building up a dossier of their best work.

For this purpose there is a self-assessment grid which corresponds to the tasks given in the work plan. A teacher can easily develop formats for self-assessment, choosing certain tasks from the plan and evaluating them with the help of the descriptors taken from the European Language Portfolio or CEFR (Common European Framework of Reference). Once pupils know the criteria, they know how to assess their own performance, what language skills they are good at and what language skills they must improve. They also learn how to set themselves new goals and how to learn and prepare for a test so that the test result is just a kind of a confirmation or a correction of their self-assessment.

Having a structure for lessons in which the learners can work autonomously, either individually or collaboratively in groups, the teacher has much more time to observe the pupils at their work and discover their hidden talents. The teacher's role becomes increasingly one of a coach, organising the learning environment, providing the necessary material and counselling individual or group of students who work on specific tasks. This makes it much easier to adapt the teaching step by step to their needs and learning styles without giving up the attainment targets set up by the state syllabus. The English lessons become really rewarding for both pupils and teachers. Since the plan includes all four skills, the teacher has a sound base for assessing the student's overall performance, not only written assignments and isolated contributions to classroom talk.

Teaching with the help of a 'work plan' also meets the recent demands of scholars who work on second language acquisition, because it offers much more time, space and free experimental areas for pupils to process the new language (Bleyhl 2001; van Patten 2004). Additionally it enables extensive and intensive language input, be it by reading, listening or watching films, as well as intensive and creative output in spoken or written form, using new media as well as traditional ones.

Email: sanja-wagner@web.de

8.6 Learning in style!

Judy Garton-Sprenger and Philip Prowse *Freelance, London and Cambridge, UK*

In this workshop we looked at recent research which raises important questions about learning styles. Participants then tried a learning styles questionnaire and, through experiencing a number of activities, considered to what extent the integration of learning style awareness in language teaching materials is valid and worthwhile.

Two reports on learning style identification have been produced, one by Professor Frank Coffield and the other by a team at the School of Education, Communication and Language Sciences at the University of Newcastle, UK. Both reports, published in 2004 by the Learning and Skills Research Centre, deal with education in general, not language teaching in particular, and both raise important questions about the research basis for the learning styles approach. The first report is a critical review of the literature on learning styles and pedagogy, and the second considers what research has to say on the question 'Should we be using learning styles?'

The reports conclude that none of the most popular learning styles theories have been adequately validated through independent research, and go on to say, for example, that the idea of a learning cycle, the consistency of visual, auditory and kinaesthetic preferences, and the value of matching teaching and learning styles are all 'highly questionable'.

A conclusion is that 'self-development is more likely to result from increasing learners' knowledge of the relative advantages and weaknesses of different models, than from learners being assigned a particular learning style'. (Coffield *et al.* 2004)

A third report deals with Multiple Intelligences, Howard Gardner's theory of learning styles. In 'Howard Gardner: the myth of multiple intelligences', John White of the Institute of Education in London argues that the theory has no scientific basis, and is only better than the old IQ view of intelligence in that it is a pluralistic version of it. Most would agree that intelligence has a lot to do with being flexible in pursuit of goals: 'There are therefore as many types of human intelligence as there are types of human goal' (White 2005).

Where does this leave us? We react against the use of learning style theory to pigeonhole students, but do not reject the whole idea.

We support an approach which involves raising the student's awareness of different ways of learning, rather than saying, 'You're this kind of learner'. This has two benefits. Firstly, by becoming aware of different learning styles, students can be encouraged to experiment, and therefore extend their learning repertoire. Secondly, through talking about learning styles, students gain a 'vocabulary of learning', so that they can discuss the learning process, thus heightening metacognitive awareness.

The workshop then moved from research to concrete examples. Having completed a learning styles questionnaire which we had devised for secondary learners, participants shared reactions. These included: 'I don't fit into one category', (Our response: 'No, the aim is not shoe-horning, but seeing that there are different ways of learning'), 'I'm like all of these people at different times', (Our response: 'Exactly. While we may have a preferred style we need other styles depending on the task. If intelligence means behaving in a suitable way to achieve aims, or complete a task, you could argue that there are as many intelligences as there are aims or tasks').

Our suggestion is that after doing the questionnaire students are regularly offered a choice of activities, which we labelled as Construction, Reflection, Action and Interaction, to take account of different learning styles. Students choose an activity in a familiar style, or experiment with another one. Workshop participants sampled a range of activities, assigning each to a particular learning style.

However, there is a danger of 'ghettoisation' if treatment of learning styles is restricted to a particular slot in the timetable or section of a book. For the remainder of the workshop, participants tried activities which showed how awareness of learning styles can infuse a whole book or course.

Our conclusion was that a non-dogmatic approach to learning styles can enable learners to widen their repertoire, adopting that style which is most appropriate to the language learning task in hand. We also argued for the infusion of different styles throughout a book or course.

Email: judygs@btopenworld.com
philip.prowse@ntlworld.com

8.7 An evaluation of English language teaching in Icelandic compulsory schools

Samuel Lefever *Iceland University of Education, Reykjavík, Iceland*

This presentation discussed the findings of an evaluation of English language teaching in Icelandic compulsory schools. The presentation focused on two main areas: (a) whether there was a discrepancy between teaching practices and learning outcomes and the National Curriculum objectives, and (b) what factors and classroom practices were found that contributed to effective teaching and learning of English.

English language instruction in Iceland typically begins in grade 5 (10 year olds). The amount of English instruction ranges from two 40 minute lessons per week in grade 5–7 to 3–4 lessons in grades 8–10. The National Curriculum guidelines for English instruction focus on communicative language teaching principles. Emphasis is on the four skills of reading, listening, speaking and writing, and the integration of grammar and vocabulary with skills-based instruction. Teaching methods and materials should motivate the learners and encourage active use of the language.

Participants

Eight schools representing a cross-section of school sizes and geographical areas in the country participated in the evaluation. Data was obtained from a number of sources such as school curricula and syllabi, lesson plans, school assessments, teacher and pupil questionnaires, interviews with teachers and classroom observations.

A written questionnaire was given to pupils aged 10–16 years old and their English teachers. The questionnaires surveyed the pupils' and teachers' attitudes towards the teaching and learning methods and materials used in English instruction. Pupils were also asked to comment on their use of English outside of school.

Results

The findings of the evaluation show that both pupils and teachers have very positive attitudes towards learning English and they recognise the value of knowing English. Most pupils stated that English was important to be able to communicate when abroad and to understand English movies, TV programs and music. A majority felt English was important for future study and work. Many boys (75 per cent) stated that English was important for using the Internet and playing computer games, twice as many as girls. Despite positive attitudes towards learning English, only 46 per cent of the pupils said they liked the English teaching materials used in their lessons.

Pupils were given a list of teaching methods and approaches and were asked to rate how much they learned English through their use. The teachers were given a similar list and were asked to rate how much they emphasised the methods in their English teaching. The correlation between pupils' and teachers' responses was generally positive. Teachers tended to emphasise the same methods that pupils ranked as helpful for learning English.

The methods that both pupils and teachers ranked highly were:

- using English listening materials,
- workbook use,
- reading English books and magazines,
- grammar exercises, and
- going over homework in class.

A majority of pupils also gave high ranking to traditional grammar-translation methods. However, teachers said that they did *not* emphasise translation activities in their teaching! Other methods that did *not* correlate well between pupils and teachers were:

- watching English videos in class,
- speaking activities,
- working with English songs and lyrics.

Pupils rated these methods as helpful for learning English but the majority of teachers reported placing only 'some' or 'little' emphasis on using them in lessons.

Several teaching techniques, such as the use of games, role play, theme work and computer use that are effective in activating students in creative and/or authentic or semi-authentic language use received very little emphasis according to the teachers' responses. Likewise, pupils said that these methods were seldom (or not) used in class.

The National Curriculum emphasises that teachers should use English as much as possible during instruction. Pupils reported that less than half of the teachers use English always or often during lessons and they said that pupils use English even less than the teachers during lessons.

On the other hand, pupils stated that they had several opportunities for authentic use of English outside of school. They use English primarily for entertainment through English media, i.e. film, television, music, internet and computer games.

Conclusions

Although teachers were aware of the National Curriculum guidelines and used them to plan their teaching, the evaluation showed that certain discrepancies exist between teaching methods recommended by the National Curriculum and those used in English instruction. More focus is needed on spoken communication, using English during lessons, and using teaching methods that 'activate' the learners and give them more chances to use English for fun and creative use. Teachers need to more effectively capitalise on the positive attitudes and authentic learning opportunities of their pupils in their English teaching.

Email: samuel@khi.is

8.8 Understanding the English language learner self-concept

Sarah Mercer *University of Graz, Austria*

My presentation reported on a study carried out as part of a PhD project. The study aimed at exploring the self-concept of tertiary level learners of English as a foreign language. This report attempts to answer the research question: what are the sub-components of an English language learner self-concept?

Self-concept is the beliefs one has about oneself, one's self-perception, both cognitive and affective. Considerable research within the field of educational psychology has already shown such beliefs to be important for successful learning in terms of, for example, achievement, motivation, strategy use, goal setting, persistence and self-regulated learning. Surprisingly, however, very little work has been done on self-concept within ELT, although related work can be found in a plethora of fields, such as learner beliefs, attitudes, metacognition, individual differences and motivation. Language learner self-concept is a problematic area for research, given the overlapping, interrelated constructs and lack of clarity in terminology use. However, if we accept the possibly unique, social nature of language learning, it is likely that self-concept plays a particularly significant role in the learning of a language.

In an exploratory study, students from a first-year university level English language course (N = 64) were asked to write narrative texts entitled, 'Me as a language learner' to describe themselves as language learners. Following an earlier pilot study it had been decided to provide some open guidelines to help learners with the writing of their texts. Following some of the principles of exploratory practice (Allwright 2003) the texts were intended to have both a research and pedagogical purpose, i.e. they were also intended to raise learners' self-awareness and help them set goals for the term.

The resultant data were analysed for content using Atlas.ti. It has been shown that narratives are particularly suited to research on the self (McAdams 1997) and they were particularly appropriate for gathering the open, complex data required for this study. As the learners had just made the decision to study English at university, it is possible that they were more self-aware than other learners would be. One limitation in the method chosen was the possible influence of the guidelines on the data collected.

Although the framework presented below is representative of the commonalties and similarities across the data, it should be noted that the data also revealed the individuality of the learners in the specific experiences, beliefs and interests that they reported, which were unique to just one learner in some cases. Here the subcomponent parts identified in the data are presented in terms of main headings and the subheadings.

1. Beliefs about one's competence

- Belief in general intelligence
- Belief in ability in languages in general
- Belief in ability in specific language
- Belief in ability in skill area
- Belief in ability in specific task
- Ability to achieve goals

2. Beliefs about the type of learner one is
- Learning style
- Learner type
- Learning preferences
- Learner characteristics

3. Beliefs about characteristics as a person

4. Beliefs about one's likes/dislikes/interests
- Travelling
- Languages in general and cultures
- A specific country (for example, USA, UK, New Zealand, etc.)
- A specific language itself
- Literature/Song lyrics/Films
- Communicating with others

5. Beliefs about future self
- Living abroad
- Doing a specific job
- Being like a 'native-speaker'

Space precludes a discussion of each individual heading and the data supporting these categories. However, a few key features are worth noting. From the data it seems that the language learner self-concept works in domain-specific ways in all aspects. Crucially it appears evident that it is composed of more than just competence beliefs; there are other significant subcomponents and affective beliefs. The learners also display a high degree of specificity in their competence beliefs from more global, holistic beliefs right through a hierarchy of specificity to the individual task level.

This provisional framework will hopefully help researchers, teachers and learners to have a better understanding of the language learner self-concept. If we accept that an accurate but positive self-concept is a desirable pedagogical goal, then it seems possible and helpful to use such a framework to consider what can be done in the teaching-learning environment to encourage such beliefs, to what extent such beliefs may be dynamic, as well as what may affect or be affected by the self-concept. It is hoped that these and other aspects of this PhD research project can be reported on in the near future.

Email: sarah.mercer@uni-graz.at

8.9 'Learning difficulties' or teaching challenges?

Anne Margaret Smith *ELT well, Lancaster, UK*

How best to support learners who experience difficulties is something that all teachers will at some stage in their careers have to consider, and yet neither the identification nor the accommodation of 'learning difficulties' are well covered in the average initial teacher training course. In this talk the question of what constitutes a 'learning difficulty' was considered, and it was argued that, rather than seeing *learners* as having problems, it is more helpful to think of difficulties in the classroom as being a challenge for us as teachers, which stretch our creativity (and patience!), requiring us to maintain the best possible classroom practice.

There are several reasons why ELT professionals should be better prepared to support students who have particular difficulties. Firstly, the global role of the English language is such that learning it is—for many—no longer optional; in our classrooms we will meet not only those who are gifted language learners, but also those who struggle with it. Our duty as teachers is not only to work with the capable students, but to help all the members of our classes to achieve as much as they can. There is also a financial argument to be made: put simply, it makes good business sense to be able to accept students with a wider range of needs. Students with learning difficulties pay fees too, and may be more attracted to schools which market themselves as (for example) 'dyslexia friendly'. Finally, in some countries there is a legal responsibility to provide services that are accessible to all, and to *anticipate* needs, as well as to accommodate them. (In the UK, for example, the Disability Discrimination Act (DDA) now covers all educational establishments.)

Most people experience a 'difficulty in learning' at some point in their education, so it seems odd that some students are labelled as having 'special' needs, thereby locating any problems in the individual. Booth (1996) suggests that a more helpful approach is to see these difficulties as the result of a 'mismatch between learner, syllabus, teacher and environment'. Our challenge is to provide the best possible fit for all our learners, and minimise the difficulties encountered in our classes. However, that is not to deny that there are certain causes of difficulty that teachers need to be better informed about.

The UK DDA covers a wide range of disabilities: *physical disabilities and illnesses* (including diabetes, epilepsy and mental health problems), *sensory impairments* of all degrees and *specific learning differences* (for example, dyslexia, AD/HD, Asperger's syndrome). Many teachers may not feel confident that they would be able to recognise symptoms of all of these 'conditions'. However, putting a name to a difficulty is not always necessary; as teachers it is not usually our job to diagnose, but to respond to the needs of the individuals in our classes. The advice given to teachers of students with specific difficulties usually includes the following:

- give clear, simple instructions, and be consistent;
- break tasks down into small, manageable chunks;
- remember that all learners are individuals: those with the same diagnosis may not have the same problems in learning;
- as far as possible, involve the whole class in supporting each other.

Most ELT professionals would probably agree that this simply constitutes 'best practice' that we strive to implement all the time, and that all students benefit from these elements of our teaching. Some learners may also have particular requirements in terms of seating arrangements or modified materials, or allowances may have to be made for increased fatigue or irregular attendance because of health problems.

Supporting learners who have difficulties is not usually about making radical changes in the classroom, but about ensuring that the materials, environment and teaching methods are adapted, if necessary, to match different needs. Admittedly, this is not always easy, and can frequently be frustrating, but teachers should not feel that they are on their own; when there is a challenging situation in the classroom, the support of colleagues is essential, and specialist advice can be sought from another institution or organisation, if necessary.

Most importantly, I would urge all teachers who find themselves in this situation to have faith in their own abilities, and show their students that they believe in them, too. Learners with particular difficulties may already have some coping strategies that can be adapted for the classroom situation, and knowing that their teachers have high expectations for them should boost their self-esteem, which is a key ingredient of success.

Email: ams@ELTwell.co.uk

Reference

Booth, T. 1996. *Learning for All.* Milton Keynes: The Open University.

9 Information and communication technology (ICT) in ELT

As **Aidan Thorne** says in his report, the first in this chapter, it is surprising that in our digital age the usefulness of technology in educational environments is still for many a subject of debate. He goes on to argue for adapting ELT curricula to include technology at the heart of delivery, teaching materials and approaches to assessment. **Jana Jilkova** also pleads for more use of ICT in both teacher training and teaching. She illustrates the practical uses of ICT through some teaching activities that were developed as products of new training modules for trainer and teacher training in the use of ICT in ELT in the Czech Republic. **Nicky Hockly**, on the other hand, deplores the lack of ICT training in many teacher training programmes and offers a possible outline syllabus.

Next, **Maggie Bouqdib and Beate Vogel** survey the advantages of an electronic language portfolio based on the Common European Framework of Reference. **David Shepherd** describes some research conducted by postgraduate TEFL students at a Brazilian university. They were aware of the lack of enthusiasm for learning English amongst Brazilian teenagers although the teenagers regularly use ICT in English in their personal lives. The researchers focused on the digital genres that formed the learners' main reading interest outside the classroom as a means of improving their motivation. **Valentina Dodge and Sheila Vine** explain some of the problems facing e-moderators and introduce their free exchange mechanism called ChatBox, which comprises ten areas of interest to e-moderators. Lastly **Elżbieta Gajek** takes us through the concept of e-twinning. E-twinning allows teachers and pupils to develop intercultural, technical, linguistic and communication skills through electronic communication with a partner school.

9.1 New technologies and instructional design models: a UAE experience

Aidan Thorne *Abu Dhabi Men's College (HCT), United Arab Emirates*

It is often said that education is the only business still debating the usefulness of technology. Paige, in the USA Government 'Visions 2020 Report', argues convincingly that 'most schools remain unchanged for the most part despite numerous reforms and increased investments in computers and networks'. He also notes that 'the way we organize our schools and provide instruction is essentially the same as it was when our founding fathers went to school'. He clarifies this with the powerful statement that 'we still educate our students according to an agrarian timetable in an agricultural setting, but tell students they live in a digital age'. In the presentation I pressed a case for adapting traditional English Language Teaching (ELT) curricula to include technology at the heart of new methods of delivery, new types of teaching materials and approaches to assessment.

Why? There is general agreement that with ongoing technological change the world is changing from an industrial to a knowledge-based society. Firstly people are expected to be able to process ever increasing amounts of information on a daily basis from both hard- and soft-copy sources. In addition, they are hired to work with the expectation that they are self-starters, able to work in teams, ask the right questions and solve problems as they go. Survival in the workplace currently depends more on one's ability to use what have been termed higher-order skills such as collaboration, being able to ask the right questions and come up with answers, to be able to research and filter information on the fly rather than simply relying on acquiring a bank of knowledge learnt prior to entering the workplace.

Current technological developments have set the scene and made the task easier. Mills (2006) succinctly argues that the internet provides a perfect background for the type of task-based research, problem solving and collaborative learning that enable learners to develop the skills they require for the contemporary world. Furthermore it now supports various technological tools like databases, spreadsheets, graphics, graphing and charting programs that can help, guide and even extend the thinking process of learners. Mills (2006: 3) calls these 'cognitive tools'.

I explored various delivery models we have been experimenting with in the Higher Colleges of Technology (HCTs) in the United Arab Emirates including:

- Treasure Hunts (www.treasurehuntadventures.com),
- Subject Samplers (www.kn.pacbell.com/wired/fil/formats.html),
- Webquests (http://webquest.sdsu.edu).

These were developed in western rather than Arab contexts and frequently did not fit well into the Arab learning context as they do not always match local learning styles or the teaching expectations. I outlined the problems and advantages we have experienced with training teachers to develop, design and introduce them into the UAE tertiary context. I also looked at student feedback on the new initiatives and detailed how we wanted to continue to introduce these new ideas in the future. I then discussed an in-house initiative called E-tasks and Challenges. This was developed by English language teachers in Abu Dhabi Men's College (HCT) to extend students' language skills practice beyond the boundaries of the classroom and hours of the teaching day. The initiative, which is WebCT-based, is linked to course assessment and utilizes various internet technologies such as discussion boards and chat channels as well as more traditional web-based language practice activities. Students are expected to do a variety of activities on a weekly basis and their progress and grades are tracked via WebCT. Feedback on this initiative has been very positive and now it is used by six HCTs. Every semester over 2000 students are registered to take part and do up to 60,000 tasks through the course of an academic year. Currently access to the site is restricted to HCT students but further information and viewing access may be arranged by request to the author.

Email: athorne@hct.ac.ae

References

Mills, S. 2006. *Using the Internet for Active Teaching and Learning.* New Jersey: Pearson Merrill Prentice Hall.

Paige, R. 2004. 'Visions 2020 Report' cited in *National Education Technology Plan*
http://www.ed.gov/about/offices/list/os/technology/plan/2004/site/edlite-background.html.

9.2 Enriching ELT with ICT

Jana Jilkova   *ICV Kutna Hora and VUP Pedagogical Research Institute Prague, Czech Republic*

> Give students a more active role in learning. Someone who is 'playing' doesn't get up to mischief.

Computer and web-based resources give learners opportunities for meaningful language use within a supportive teacher framework, maximising rewards while minimising negative outcomes. My presentation considered practical uses of information and communication technology (ICT) in English language teaching (ELT). Participants took an active part in the tasks. Some of them remained in contact and successfully used some of the activities in their institutions.

The session drew on practical experience with newly created training modules for trainer and teacher training in the use of ICT in ELT in the Czech Republic. These courses were prepared and implemented in 2005 under the auspices of the Ministry of Education, Czech Republic, and the British Council within the framework of the National Strategy for ICT in Education (SIPVZ) programme.

The activities described were developed as products of the courses and have been successfully piloted in English classrooms. The most popular ICT uses by trainers and trainees were:

- 'Hot Potatoes' activities,
- webquests,
- projects.

In their own preparation they especially valued:

- using search engines,
- creating worksheets.

You can try out the following activities yourselves; they are focused on searching for and working with information. You could ask similar questions about other countries and topics. Try to answer the following:

What do you know about the Czechs?
- Do you know any Czech places of interest?
- Do you know any Czech customs or traditions?
- Have you eaten any typical Czech food?
- Have you seen any Czech products in your country?
- Have you heard of any notable Czechs?
- Can you say Ř?

With respect to their individual needs learners can acquire information using the internet, through prepared links (for example, webquests, special web pages, worksheets, etc.), from search engines (http://www.google.com, http://uk.ask.com, http://www.askforkids.com, etc.), and through various other sources (encyclopaedias, library databases, blogs, web pages of institutes and companies, questions to companies, experts, and friends via email) in the foreign/target language or their native language.

Many activities give students opportunities for independent learning using teacher-designed and/or facilitated activities. There are opportunities for cross-curriculum teaching and supporting learner autonomy.

Example activity: two views of one picture

Prepare a picture, preferably something unusual or provocative.

Instructions for pupils
- Look at the picture.
- Write quick notes on how you feel about this picture.
- Write down everything you can associate with this picture.
- Have you ever seen a similar picture? Have you ever experienced anything similar?

- Show the picture to your friends, parents and so on and ask them to think about the same aspects of the picture as above. Note down their responses.
- Compare/contrast your answers or comments with theirs.
- Write a summary of the replies and comments on the picture. Add questions on things which further interest you about the picture and give them to the author of the picture.

This activity was successfully used in the framework of an eTwinning partnership and supported both written and oral communication in a foreign language. The students chose a picture, then photographed it themselves, described it as they thought their partners would describe it and sent it to them. The partners worked with the picture according to the instructions above and returned their descriptions with questions attached. The authors of the pictures compared their original descriptions with the actual descriptions and comments sent by their partners.

When using ICT, remember to consider what technical equipment it will be necessary to provide, what technical skills you and/or your pupils need, and last but not least the reason for doing the activity. Who will benefit and how? Select activities suitable for your students, and provide for feedback.

A web page which besides other things contains structured and continually supplemented links, monitored for individual graduates of instructor training, can be found at http://www.fi.muni.cz/ICT4ELT/websites/ict4eltportals.html

Further details of the history and background of the development of courses in the Czech Republic are available at the official web page of the Czech Education in English at http://www.e-gram.cz/English_version.htm

Email: jilkova.icvkh@tiscali.cz

9.3 Making IT or faking IT?

Nicky Hockly *The Consultants-E, Barcelona, Spain*

After over a decade of so-called 'normalisation' of computers in education, why are we no closer to real integration of technology in the TEFL classroom? This workshop examined reasons why teachers may be loath to use technology with students, and posed an ICT (information and communications technology) skills set of relevance to both practising classroom teachers, and to trainers and Directors of Studies who wish to implement a principled ICT training programme with their trainees/staff.

There are a couple of extremely effective *teacher development groups* dedicated to exploring technology in the EFL/ESL classroom*, but these groups of self-motivated early adopters of technology are far from the norm. Why is this so? A cursory look at most syllabi for teacher training, at both pre- and in-service level, indicate that very little attention is given to training new or experienced teachers in how to apply technology to the classroom. Two respected awarding bodies state the following as the aims for technology/CALL in in-service training courses:

> Uses of resources and technology (including audiovisual aids and CALL) and familiarity with published and, where available, online reference and other professional materials which may foster personal and professional development.

(Trinity Diploma syllabus)

> Using aids and equipment effectively—demonstrate understanding of the role of a wide range of technical aids and media including Information and Learning Technology ... for classroom teaching, materials and classroom research.

(Cambridge DELTA syllabus)

Neither of the above syllabus extracts gives trainers any real idea of what CALL/ICT areas to cover with trainees. As teacher trainers themselves have typically received little or no ICT training, this is an area which is hugely neglected in teacher training, and the result is that teachers join the profession with no knowledge of how to apply ICT to their classrooms, and little inclination to try (unless they find the area interesting on a personal level, and are self-motivated enough to try things out). Typically institutions themselves provide little in the way of extra training or support for ICT adopters in our profession. There are of course exceptions to this; the Polish government has put together an ICT syllabus for both pre-and in-service training of teachers, as have some other countries, and examination boards such as Trinity College, London are now providing a special 'ICT in the Classroom' course for EFL/ESL teachers (see http://www.trinitycollege.co.uk/site/?id=705).

Any teacher training programme, whether externally assessed or moderated by an examinations board, or in-house training, needs to seriously consider including a *coherent and relevant ICT syllabus*. Although exactly what is needed in this syllabus will vary depending on the local context and needs, and the individual needs and current skills level of the trainee teachers, there are some basic ICT areas that teachers these days should be familiar with. After all, many of our students are already conversant with, and using, these technologies in their everyday lives.

Table 9.3.1 provides a rough outline of some elements of an ICT syllabus, which is by no means complete or definitive, but which may serve as a basis for teachers, trainers, or directors of studies to work from. The syllabus consists of two main areas: *computer literacy* (or computer skills) and *methodology* (or the practical application of ICT to the classroom).

Computer literacy	Methodology
• Word-processing skills (making worksheets, adding images, etc.) • Email (opening file attachments, file formats) • Internet search skills and search engines • PowerPoint and presentations • Simple authoring tools (e.g. Hot Potatoes, Survey Monkey) • Security (protection against viruses, firewalls etc.)	• Internet-based activities (e.g. Treasure hunts, WebQuests, exploiting online materials) • Email (e.g. how to set up and implement a key pal exchange; email for homework, etc.) • Chat (using text and/or audio chat with classes) • Blogs, wikis and podcasting • Online dictionaries and corpora/concordancing • Online professional development (teacher development groups, online courses and resources for teachers, etc.)

Table 9.3.1: Outline ICT syllabus

* For teachers interested in developing their own ICT skills, and how to apply these to their classroom practice, we particularly recommend joining either or both of the following groups:

Webheads
http://groups.yahoo.com/group/evonline2002_webheads/
Dedicated to exploring uses of technology in f2f (face-to-face) teaching.

Learning with computers
http://groups.yahoo.com/group/learningwithcomputers/
Set up in March 2006 for those who are less confident with technology in the classroom, but would like to learn more.
Email: nicky.hockly@theconsultants-e.com

9.4 The electronic language portfolio

Maggie Bouqdib *Bremer Volkshochschule, Bremen, Germany* **and**
Beate Vogel *Landesinstitut für Schule, Bremen, Germany*

The idea for this workshop arose during our work on the European Language Portfolio. Supported by the network 'Learning Regions', which is sponsored by the National German Agency for European Affairs, the twelve most important educational and cultural institutions in Bremen founded the 'Bremen Round Table of Languages' as a joint venture early in 2003 with the aim of encouraging multilingualism and life-long learning. Our main goal is to develop different web-based portfolio modules based on the Common European Framework of Reference (CEFR) and which can be adapted for the primary, secondary and tertiary sectors in education. Our project is called 'epos', being both a German acronym ('elektronisches Portfolio für Sprachen') and implying a huge underlying task.

Our main workshop aims were to illustrate and discuss the following:

1. the connection between the paper version and a web-based version,
2. the description and functions of an e-portfolio,
3. the advantages and potential drawbacks of an e-portfolio,
4. practical examples of our web-based portfolio.

The e-portfolio follows the principles and guidelines of the European Council (2000) such as promoting plurilingualism and learner autonomy, European comparability and providing an overview of the full range of the learner's competence whilst remaining the property of the learner. Epos uses the CEFR's six-level system. This important point is a strength of the portfolio as the CEFR is increasingly becoming the standard to which courses, materials and tests are linked all over Europe in school, vocational and higher education.

The functions of the epos portfolio are:

- *The reporting function*: this is most evident in the Passport, which documents fully, informatively, transparently and with comparisons which languages and intercultural experiences the learner has gained, and is the most externally-used element.
- *The pedagogical function*: alongside their reporting role, the Language Biography and Dossier offer learners the opportunity to focus on the challenge of learning languages as an autonomous activity for which they are personally responsible.
- *The educational-political function*: it documents the continuous learning of foreign languages and assists in overcoming the interfaces between different educational institutions both nationally and internationally.

As Helen Barrett (2000) wrote:

> An electronic portfolio allows the user to collect and organize artefacts in a variety of formats, such as texts, graphics, videos and audio materials. It is not a haphazard collection of artefacts (i.e. a digital scrapbook or multimedia presentation) but rather a reflective tool that demonstrates growth over time.

It is thus both standard and performance based.

After discussing the general advantages of epos, such as providing an easily accessible and adaptable common platform for different users in various kinds of educational institutions all over the world, a partner activity to decide on the top three advantages for the individual learner followed. Attendees chose points from the list below:

- the possibility of uniting different educational language institutions in a common web-portal,
- adaptability for different user groups in the form of a shared web-based system,
- greater transparency in bridging the gap between different classes, courses and educational systems,
- more economic use compared to the paper version,
- new, flexible, economic ways with open source software,
- easy upgrading,
- more responsibility in selecting items for publication to fellow-learners, tutors or others,
- simpler and clearer archive systems (no bulky storage),
- greater flexibility in use, layout and documentation of the individual language learning process,
- more accessible, direct access to digital references,
- multiple and flexible media storage,
- permanent, aesthetically appealing layout,
- highly motivating means of exhibiting personal work,
- cross-referencing of student work through hyperlinks,
- easy use of criteria-oriented tasks to evaluate one's own level of proficiency,
- easy access to the descriptors and levels of competence according to the CEFR and their concrete adaptation to the respective educational levels and systems,
- access to learning aids/institution-specific/blended-learning within the specific organisation,
- immediate access to all the necessary documents for job applications.

Its flexibility compared with the traditional print version provides an ideal opportunity for the individual learner to document progress during the life-long acquisition

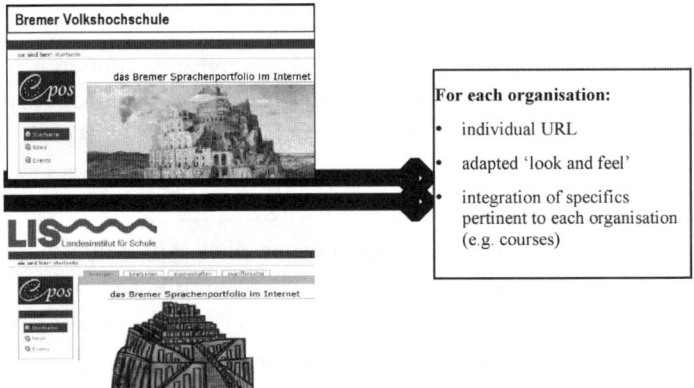

Figure 9.4.1: Sample portal

of foreign languages. It is also an interactive tool for both self- and external evaluation.

A short demonstration of epos was given by our programmer, Dr. Walter Jaisli, starting with one of our individual portals (Figure 9.4.1).

We concluded our session with the following quotation:

> The integration of the different functions of the ELP towards an almost complete didactical learning environment (...) can hardly be catered for by a paper version of the ELP. Only a web-based portfolio would cater for all those needs.

(Gerard Westhof in Babylonia, Nr. 2/04, 56)

Email: Maggie.bouqdib@vhs-bremen.de
bvogel@lis.bremen.de

9.5 Motivating Brazilian female ELT teenage learners using the rhetoric of digital genres

David Shepherd *Universidade Federal Fluminense (UFF), Niterói, Brazil*

This presentation began by describing the background for the research in question. The setting involved Brazilian public sector teachers who were taking postgraduate TEFL diplomas at the Universidade Federal Fluminense (UFF) conducting six-month action research projects. Their exploratory starting point was the definition of teaching/learning puzzles. Between 2002 and 2005 the initial puzzle/question of a sizeable minority was: 'Why is it that my teen groups have little motivation for learning English?' This lack of interest was surprising given the widespread popularity among young Brazilians of films, pop music, computer games, websites, blogging, etc., all in English. In general, the public sector teachers' immediate response was to adopt a 'games, songs 'n' fun' approach. These pedagogical options resulted in what they recognise as long-term learning failures. It was also argued that these options have meant that EFL practitioners lost the respect of pupils, parents and fellow teaching professionals, distancing them from the on-going dialectic on integrated learning objectives within Brazilian public-sector education.

Why have Brazilian EFL teachers consistently adopted this 'circus ringmaster' stance in the light of accepted failures? It was argued that, in order to survive, most practitioners work in several public and private sector schools. Recent UFF research, analysing the language websites of twenty large-scale Brazilian EFL private franchise schools, was then cited. This revealed that the franchise discourse is promotional rather than educational, concerned with the selling of products rather than formative learner development. Examples from the twenty websites demonstrated their exclusive aim of legitimising their products by offering three compensatory gains to their prospective customers: they promised fun teaching; pleasant, easy learning; and classroom use of the latest technological gadgets. The websites' discourse thus failed to interface with applied linguistics and TEFL methodology. For these reasons, it was argued that Brazilian EFL teachers might be seen as belonging to a schizophrenic discourse community. Evidence from questionnaires, completed by over 100 teachers revealed that when faced with these contradictory imperatives or mental knots they usually opt for the easiest short-term response. Thus it was claimed that not only were the learners' needs being ignored, but also those educational precepts advocated by Paulo Freire of using the learners' cultural setting and experiences, their beliefs, interests and knowledge, as the classroom starting point. This is why, it was claimed, many of the teachers in question constantly stumble in their attempts to fit the square peg of local Brazilian cultural pedagogical norms into the round hole of global solutions, in common with those teachers described by Tsui (2005) .

In response, UFF EFL researchers have recently attempted to activate teen learners' left-brain analytic/linguistic functions by focusing their attention on newly-acquired, post-puberty abilities to reason logically and critically. This was achieved by triggering the previous experience and knowledge of learners. It has involved more than the long-standing accepted activation of content knowledge and key words through various forms of pre-reading/listening/ viewing. Here, in addition, the teachers concentrated on the learners' experience of a wide range of genres and text types in the first language, Portuguese. This tack was illustrated from three recent research/teaching projects. Each was carried out by Brazilian female EFL practitioners teaching female adolescents. Each chose to focus on digital genres identified through questionnaires as the learners' main reading interest outside the classroom. Learner choice of texts aimed at inspiring improved motivation (Prowse and Garton-Sprenger 2005). Each of these genres included descriptive elements but had a largely selling, persuasive communicative function. Further selection criteria for the genres were that learners found them easily accessible in both English and Portuguese and that they were short enough to be exploited in single classroom sessions. Book blurbs of popular novels from the Amazon website, Agony Aunt/Dear Abby letters, and pro-file segments of personal descriptions from on-line dating sites were the three genres analysed, using straightforward 'generalisation–exemplification' and 'situation–problem–response–evaluation' macro-patterns (Hoey 2001).

In all three cases, a first classroom session aimed at raising learner awareness of generic text make-up in Portuguese using simplified analytical frameworks. Learners then chose individual internet text examples in Portuguese. A second classroom session involved pairs matching their texts with the same analytical categories. A third session focused on the digital genre make-up in English. Subsequently, learners chose

English web texts and a final session involved pair-work identification of generic elements. This choice of meaningful learner-selected genres, moving from the known (Portuguese) to the unknown (English), empowerment and the intellectual excitement from the contrastive analyses, led to positive learner involvement.

Email: dshepherd@uol.com.br

9.6 ChatBox: dynamically creating a resource for e-moderators

Valentina Dodge *University of Naples, Italy* **and**
Sheila Vine *Freelance, Javelin Communication, Bad Lippspringe, Germany*

E-moderation and the problems facing e-moderators is an increasingly popular topic in the teaching community as online synchronous (i.e. lessons that occur in real-time where participants are separated by distance) and asynchronous learning become more widespread. The issues are both similar and different to those face-to-face teachers cope with. Dropouts from classes and low motivation of both teachers and students affect all types of teaching. However, at a distance, in a virtual environment, a new set of skills is also required. This swapshop aimed to describe some of the problems associated with synchronous classes and in the second part presented an online resource as one method of addressing some of these challenges. The whole swapshop was based on the principles of blended learning:

- the hybrid format of the presentation,
- predominately virtual nature of the preparation, and
- feedback is encouraged both face-to-face and virtually.

The swapshop began in a virtual manner with the presenters sitting in the audience and allowing the slides to begin the presentation which was, in line with the ethos of this project, developed entirely online with the presenters meeting in person the day before the presentation. Thanks to the audio, video clips and text slide instructions the participants were able to fully appreciate the technological tools available. The session began with introductions and the audience getting to know each other and comparing their own online experiences, all with no physical presence on stage!

At this point the presenters revealed themselves and the swapshop continued in a more traditional manner. Socialisation of online participants was discussed; it is more important than in a face-to-face course. Team development issues were outlined following Bruce Tuckman's model of face-to-face dynamics of forming storming, norming, performing and mourning and also how they fit into the online scenario.

The technical features of eChatBox were then described. It is a free exchange mechanism hosted on a Moodle (an Open Source course management system) platform using Wiki technology to encourage fast and easy access to contributions. Wikis are editable web pages which allow users to contribute, edit or comment very simply. The exchange is divided into 10 topics:

1. guide to using this exchange mechanism;
2. overview of chat-rooms and software evaluation (including Voice over Internet Protocol);
3. chatroom concepts for first time moderators;
4. chat protocols;
5. chat starters;
6. chat tasks;
7. chat round-offs;
8. a history of chats: our experiences and case studies;
9. chat moderation skills;
10. our ethos.

The third and most enjoyable swapshop phase was the 'let's try it' stage, with the audience wholeheartedly and actively engaged in doing and contributing to activities. By alternating the presenters a clear distinction between the audience acting as students and acting as teachers in a training session was made. Sheila led the 'audience as students sessions' and Valentina the 'audience as teachers' part. Participants were given prompts and in the role of students asked to respond to simple warm-up or ice-breaker tasks. The raising of a yellow STOP! card (a text-chatroom technique) signalled to participants that they should swap roles and think up some similar activities in groups. The audience scribbled suggestions on specially designed handouts, available on the seats, and posted them into yellow chatboxes. This was a simple way of simulating the virtual exchange mechanism and building of a chatroom resource bank.

The second chatroom task involved finishing idiomatic expressions. Many suggestions relevant to participants' own contexts were received. Thirdly, the use of the shared application features such as virtual whiteboards was demonstrated with a quick 'Can you see what it is yet?' guessing game activity which led on to the concept of real-time brainstorming or discussing the stages in a process (for example, making of an omelette) as an excellent way to elicit key vocabulary. The resulting chatscript (an electronic log recording, written or audio) can be used in many ways to review and expand vocabulary, or as a starting point for deeper follow-up writing activities.

The swapshop was rounded off with question time. Participants were given a key to eChatBox so that any further questions could be posed online and responded to in more depth, allowing those not present to benefit from the issues raised. Since the conference the excellent suggestions and queries have been posted to eChatBox as a special section and are there for everyone to see. To access eChatBox visit www.echatbox.com. The enrol key is '24echbx06'; you can register any username or password you like.

Email: valentinadodge@echatbox.com
sheilavine@echatbox.com

9.7 E-twinning: the Polish experience

Elżbieta Gajek *Institute of Applied Linguistics, University of Warsaw, Warsaw, Poland*

In autumn 2004, e-twinning action was launched as action 3 in a European e-learning programme within the Comenius-Socrates programme. Its web address is www.etwinning.net. E-twinning is intended for schools and their teachers of all subjects, the pupils, librarians and school administrators. All primary and secondary schools, and kindergartens located in the European Union as well as schools in Norway and Iceland can participate. It offers various possibilities for developing intercultural, technical, linguistic and communication skills.

Only schools can register for the programme (and not individual teachers). It is important that teachers are not paid for participation and schools get no money for equipment. The framework for a partnership is very flexible. It may last from one week to many years. All European languages may be used as means of communication. All subjects can be involved and also cross-curriculum projects. Partners have to use the technology that is available for them—mainly in the schools.

In 2005 I did some research on the registered partnerships. The database was closed for analysis on 1 June 2005. Polish schools, mainly at secondary level, cooperated most often with Lithuanian schools, and then with Italian and English schools. As expected, English as a lingua franca was the main language of communication, followed by German and Polish. The duration of partnerships reflected the usual school routine—a school year or a semester were the most popular. The technology was rather simple: email, PowerPoint presentations and building websites dominated.

It seems that partners need to share the work equally. Usually each partner prepared a product for the counterpart, but sometimes only one partner did something for the other. However, the most beneficial and sound procedure was when a team or teams from both schools worked on a common product.

'Glocalisation' is the next interesting issue. Learners realised at once that every culture is glocal now: that is the global and the local values are interrelated. What is more, learners noticed immediately the conflict between the global and local values, between unification and diversity. Teachers facilitated learning-by-doing, not learning-by-reading. Teachers supported learners' autonomy and developed their own autonomy.

Three methodological approaches were the most commonly used: content-based learning, cooperative language learning and task-based learning. Tasks are not only well- defined but also meaningful for learners.

Topics of the partnerships may be categorized into overlapping categories. The first category encompasses various forms of everyday culture. Children exchange information on their daily routine, hobbies and free time activities. The next category is related to teenage culture. Children compare teen music, fashion, hobbies, and search for similarities and differences in their interests. The following category relates to history, traditions, local and regional culture. For example, children compare the ideal medieval knights, knights from their national history and knights from fantasy novels. In another category environmental issues are presented in a meaningful way. Slovak and Polish children exchange information about national parks in the neighbourhood. While reflecting on nature and human activity, learners immediately identify the serious conflict between building facilities for people and protection of natural heritage.

The most entertaining partnerships are built around visual arts, theatre and music. Learners exchange national songs and dances, learn the partners' dances, make video films and exchange CDs with their videos. The smallest category encompasses non-cultural subject-related partnerships. In one, learners identify the mathematical code in nature, art and architecture. In the other, teachers exchange methods of teaching maths and learners exchange home-made electronic tools for learning maths. Reflection on money encompasses enterprise, statistics and consumerism. While solving tasks in computer science, students may communicate in English or in their Slavic languages, that is Polish and Czech. An interesting category is created by the schools which cooperate with several other schools. For example each class in an English school was assigned to a different European country.

To sum up, in e-twinning learners and teachers get hands-on experience, communicate via technology, and develop their own interest in cultures, as well as intercultural skills, autonomy, multilingual competences, and tolerance to others. When technology is changing the cultures and the ways of human communication, new teaching and learning practices needs to be introduced. E-twinning provides a safe, low-tech environment, particularly user-friendly for women. Both learners and teachers may develop their intercultural, linguistic and technical skills while collaborating through technology.

Email: e.gajek@uw.edu.pl

10 Testing

The chapter opens with reports from the symposium on teaching for institutional exams. **Rubina Khan** opened the symposium by highlighting the importance of good examination preparation for students. **DilAfroze Quader** reports on falling standards of education at Bangladeshi public universities and outlines proposed improvements in the university admission test for English. The last contributor to the symposium was **Kibiwott Peter Kurgat**, who points out that courses in academic writing skills could usefully include insights gained from an analysis of questions that are typical of the courses studied by university students.

The symposium report is followed by **Judith Mader**'s overview of test types and their associated characteristics and problems. Her spoof test illustrates several aspects of testing such as the importance of timing, of question order and of multiple correct answers. Judith Mader also suggests links between knowledge gained in the production of international examinations and classroom testing. **Michael Black** lists some general suggestions for helping IELTS candidates and then focuses on a number of specific difficulties experienced by candidates as highlighted through his study of the Cambridge International Corpus.

The last three summaries all demonstrate the growing influence of the CEFR (Common European Framework of Reference). **Spiros Papageorgiou** gives an account of a project that uses the *Manual* for relating language examinations to the CEFR in order to assign two suites of Trinity College exams to the correct levels. **Juliet Wilson and Senem Donancı Büyük** also made use of the same *Manual* to inform the syllabus of the foundation programme of an English-medium university in Turkey and in particular to produce exit level descriptors for the programme's courses. They note that students use 'can do' statements based on the descriptors to assess their own progress and that feedback from teachers and students has been mostly positive. **Maria K. Norton** is concerned with alignment to the CEFR in testing as well as other areas. She identifies some problems that a British Council Teaching Centre experienced with regard to implementing the 'can-do' approach of the framework. She goes on to describe remedial steps that were taken and reports considerable success.

Chapter 10: Testing

10.1 Symposium on teaching for institutional exams

Convenor: Rubina Khan *University of Dhaka, Bangladesh*

Rubina Khan introduced the symposium by highlighting the importance of preparing students for examinations. First, the significance of exam results on people's lives was emphasised and it was pointed out that through exams teachers put labels on people and categorise them as either excellent, good or bad. The gate-keeping function of exams was also mentioned—exam results provide access and denial to higher education, and open and close doors to certain coveted professions.

The seriousness and responsibility involved in teaching exam preparation classes was emphasised and it was stressed that exam preparation classes need to be conducted with a definite focus. The qualities of a good exam preparation teacher were outlined. It was pointed out that such a teacher is aware of the importance and value of exams, is efficient at time management, gives direct feedback on students' performance and is able to motivate students towards autonomous learning. In teaching exam classes it is imperative that teachers be aware of the format and content of the exam, the skills to be tested, time allocation and the assessment criteria.

The symposium also featured Dil Afroze Quader from Bangladesh and Peter Kurgatt from Kenya. A brief synopsis is presented below:

DilAfroze Quader *(Institute of Modern Languages, University of Dhaka, Bangladesh)* presented the alarming situation of falling standards of education at Bangladeshi public universities. She reported that a growing number of students are leaving university without appropriate skills for employment. A possibility for improvement may lie in changing the university admission test for English, at present consisting of twenty-five multiple-choice questions (MCQs). The present format is designed for teachers untrained in testing English to cope with numerous scripts in a short time. Only MCQs can assure reliability across markers, allowing transparency in performance assessment. But such items test at sentence level, not skills needed at university, such as reading and writing extensively, and presenting papers in English. Students learn poorly for lack of language skills.

Students with better skills might be inducted by changing the present entrance examination for which students prepare intensively and willingly. Once enrolled, students generally lose motivation to improve English language skills. A new entry test could put pressure on them to improve English skills before entry. The proposal is to present the test in three parts. The present multiple-choice grammar test can be retained for the first part. The second part could be a cloze test of about 150 words, which would form a bridge between sentence level testing, and reading at discourse level. It would test grammar in text, unity, and coherence, as well as reading comprehension. For paper markers, acceptable answers could be decided upon by trialling the test among the trained teachers and question setters. The third section would be a reading text of 300 words where the comprehension questions could require short answers of a few words only. For examiners, the answers would be decided upon by trialling them among trained question setters and examiners. The short answers could help retain reliability in marking across untrained examiners in formats testing more diverse skills.

Preparation for the new tests would require students to practise extensive reading, and understand cloze tests through performing on them repeatedly. Practice in replacing words while keeping meaning intact would help understanding and practice grammar. Analysis of errors and discussion of answers could lead to understanding of grammar issues and language aspects. Use of reading texts for teaching comprehension and answering questions at increasing levels of difficulty would help students understand text mechanism, discourse, and grammar in discourse. Such test requirements could ensure higher standards of student performance at university, and could have a positive backwash effect on English teaching at lower levels.

Kibiwott Peter Kurgat (*School of Arts and Sciences, United States International University, Nairobi, Kenya*) looked at undergraduate essay and examination questions in an African university. This research was mainly motivated by the fact that in analysing institutional documents for the university, it was found that written examinations are usually given more weighting than other types of written work. (The ratio of examinations to other written work is approximately 70:30.) Moreover, these examination questions contained certain features that seem to be unique to certain disciplines. In view of this, it was thought that teachers of language for academic purposes need to understand the nature of these features as well as consider teaching students to answer examination questions. In order to do this, it was necessary to look at the nature of the examination questions that students were required to answer in the various courses. In particular, features of a hundred and forty-three essay and examination questions in twenty-two disciplines were examined. An analysis was done to classify these questions using the categorisation and sub-categorisation of prompts proposed by Horowitz (1985). The results of the analysis showed that the nature of the prompts was not predictable from what may be interpreted in some cases as related subjects. For example, it was found that in two biological subjects, there was a significant difference between the types of prompts in all the categories identified. It was also found that a significant number of questions contained more than one prompt, thus requiring students to do more than one task. It was also noted that differentials in the types of prompts may be due to requirements in subject areas and that the nature of the prompts themselves could be significant in determining how students are to be taught to answer examination questions in the various subject areas. Thus, it is proposed that the input into academic writing skills could include insights gained from analysis of questions that are typical of the courses that are studied by university students.

The disparate presentations from different continents generated an interesting and lively discussion with enlightening feedback from the participants. Most questions centred around the following three issues:

Open-ended questions
In both Bangladesh and Kenya open-ended questions are marked impressionistically.

Role of external examiners
In Kenya external examiners look at a percentage of the scripts corrected by internal examiners, to see if the marking has been done according to standard. In Bangladesh, all scripts are marked by external examiners, and the two marks are averaged to attain objectivity. If the difference between the two marks on any script is more than 20 per cent of the total marks, the script is re-examined by a third examiner. The two closest marks are averaged to provide the final grade.

The emphasis on language or content
In Kenya, the focus is largely on content in scientific subjects. The same is true, not only of Bangladesh, but also of UK schools based on research data collected by Quader. She stated that teachers of science and geography maintained that the presentation of content was more important, whereas teachers of English disagreed as they believed linguistic proficiency was also necessary.

Email: rkhan@agni.com
dilafroze.qr@hotmal.com
pkurgat@usiu.ac.ke

10.2 Who really uses tests?

Judith Mader   *The European Language Certificates, Frankfurt am Main, Germany*

The aim of the session was to increase awareness of why we use tests in the classroom and how these can be used properly. For many, testing is something we all do and for which no particular training and preparation is considered necessary as long as it is only done in the classroom and with our own learners. Once we start talking about real examinations, the whole area of testing becomes rather dry and theoretical and it is often felt that it is best left to experts and academics. Where is the line to be drawn between tests and examinations and low and high stake assessment? As there is really no clear line, I feel that all tests should be prepared with equal care and that testing theory, taken in the appropriate doses, can be interesting and, more importantly, useful for all teachers. All tests are potentially stressful for their takers and often for the test-givers too. Carefully prepared tests can reduce the stress involved for all concerned.

The session was (fittingly) introduced by a test, the aim of which was to make types of tests and their underlying ideas clearer and more accessible to the participants. The 'test' was as follows:

A TEST

You have 5 minutes to answer the following questions. Read through all the questions first. You may answer them in any order you wish.

1. Put the following in the right order: (6)
   achievement test
   class test
   diagnostic test
   end-of-term paper
   final exam
   placement test

2. Translate the following into another language: (4)
   assessment
   candidate
   evaluation
   examiner

3. Define the following terms: (5)
   multiple-choice
   Cloze test
   C-Test
   criteria
   validity

4. Are the following sentences true or not true? (3)
   Every course should be concluded with a test.
   Writing skills are best tested by having candidates write long essays.
   External exams should be chosen carefully.

5. Now answer the following questions: (4)
   When was the last time you took a test?
   Did you pass or fail?
   How did you find the experience?
   How would you describe your attitude to testing?

6. And now for the final question:
   What do you think of this test? (20)

The purpose of this spoof 'test' was not only to introduce the subject of testing and some of the terms to be used in the workshop, but also to make several aspects of testing clear, for instance, the importance of timing (5 minutes is clearly far too short), how the order in which the questions are answered can affect the final marks, as well as the problem of several right answers. The intention of the final question was to lead into the following discussion and workshop. The participants realised this and a lively and, unfortunately for many, too short discussion ensued, but with the preliminary conclusion that tests should adhere to certain principles.

Although the question of why we test at all was to be discussed at the end, it came up at several points during the session. If we are only giving our learners a test to pass the time or to occupy them while we think of what to do next, then we should admit this and can more or less forget about testing theory. If, however, we are really trying to assess their competence in some way and for some sensible purpose, then we should take certain things into account, such as the validity, objectivity and reliability of the test we are setting. Only in this way can we be fair to our learners and ensure that our test is doing what it intends to do. What often actually happens in classroom tests was demonstrated by means of examples, both good and bad, and how these could be modified and improved.

Although I represent an examination board, the purpose of the session was not to advertise the examinations we produce but to show how the knowledge gained in the production of high-quality and high-stakes international examinations can be useful in the production of apparently small-scale low-stake tests. But how low-stake are classroom tests really? Possibly the lower-stake a test is considered to be, the more leeway the teacher has in its production and marking. Thus an important factor in test-taking, stress, can be reduced, making the whole thing more relaxed and accessible to all concerned and allowing all tests to test more fairly what they set out to do.

Email: j.mader@WBTests.de

10.3 Objective IELTS: meeting the challenges of IELTS

Michael Black *Freelance, Huntingdon, UK*

My report presents some suggestions for helping IELTS candidates. Candidates may be unfamiliar with some of the Reading and Listening task types: they should be reassured that if they read the rubrics carefully, they will know what to do. They should follow the instructions *exactly*: if they are asked for a maximum of two words they are throwing marks away by writing three, as this will score no marks. Some tasks can be daunting, particularly distinguishing between 'no' (or 'false') and 'not given'. A 'no/false' statement is incompatible with what is in the passage, while 'not given' means there is not enough information to determine whether the statement is compatible with the text or not. Candidates may fear that lack of familiarity with the subject matter (especially in Listening and Academic Reading) will hamper them: they should be told that the questions test understanding, not knowledge of the subject. They need to read quickly, and to skim and scan. Readers who laboriously try to understand every word in a passage may not complete the module.

Candidates should use the Speaking and Writing Modules as opportunities to demonstrate their range of linguistic knowledge. They should be active, for instance by seizing a chance to use a modal perfect or conditional. They should also remember that only their English is being assessed, so they can save time, without losing marks, by inventing information or opinions (except in Task 1 of Academic Writing). Good time management is essential: candidates should spend 20 minutes on Writing Task 1 and 40 on Task 2, which carries more marks. An imperfect attempt at both tasks will probably gain higher marks than one perfect answer with no attempt at the other task. Candidates should also allow time for planning and checking. Writing 150 words generally takes only eight or nine minutes, and even a modicum of planning and checking can pay dividends.

While writing the *Objective IELTS* courses, Annette Capel, Wendy Sharp and I had access to the Cambridge International Corpus, an extensive collection of electronic text. We were able to consult the Cambridge Learner Corpus (a 20-million word corpus of exam scripts written by candidates of IELTS and other Cambridge ESOL exams) and the Cambridge Corpus of Academic English, a collection of British and American sources of academic writing. These invaluable corpora gave us many insights into syllabus design and into ways of improving performance in the Writing Modules. Our study of the Learner Corpus indicated several areas of grammar that caused difficulty, including errors in various aspects of number, such as 'this kind of jobs'; 'many thing'; 'he live'. As expected, articles were also a problem area: alongside great confusion about the basic rules for using 'a', 'the' and zero article, we found, for example, 'a' is frequently omitted preceding an adjective + noun combination, for example, 'long time'; and 'the' is often missing in front of certain words, especially 'future', 'only' and 'same'.

Spelling errors are common in vowel combinations, as in 'beatiful', 'believe', 'collegue'; when a letter is silent, for example, 'government'; or when words are confused, for instance 'through' and 'thought' commonly being written as each other, as 'throght', or in other ways. Candidates are often uncertain when to double the final consonant of a root before a suffix, as in 'offering' and 'preferring'. The Learner Corpus also guided us in terms of how to approach academic register and its development. A lack of awareness of academic style is indicated by examples like 'I reckon', 'bloke', 'kids', 'a lot', not to mention the in-your-face style of 'It is extremely ridiculous'.

Nominalisation, a feature of academic writing, could usefully be practised. For instance 'X is a relatively recent development' is more likely than 'X developed relatively recently'. Candidates should also try to use words in appropriate collocations—particularly more formal or academic pairings like 'inspire confidence', or 'strengthen links'.

The Learner Corpus shows that in the first Academic Writing task, candidates often invent reasons or express opinions, instead of simply presenting the visual information factually in written form. They may also misinterpret the graphics: if A and B are two groups of people, 50 per cent of group A is a higher percentage than 25 per cent of group B, but not necessarily more people—particularly if group A is the population of Fiji and group B the population of China!

Our research showed that with the right advice and materials, candidates can make considerable improvements to their IELTS performance.

Email: Michael.Black@btinternet.com

10.4 Relating exams to the Common European Framework of Reference: the Trinity College London experience

Spiros Papageorgiou *Lancaster University, Lancaster, UK*

Introduction

The Common European Framework of Reference: Learning, Teaching and Assessment (CEFR) (Council of Europe 2001) is intended to provide a basis for the development of syllabuses, curricula, textbooks and tests. The impact of the Framework has been very deep in a range of areas in language teaching and testing as has been recently described in two edited volumes (Alderson 2002; Morrow 2004).

One of the aims of the CEFR is to help exam providers describe the levels of proficiency required by their tests in order to facilitate comparisons between different language qualifications. For that reason, the Council of Europe has recently published the preliminary pilot version of the *Manual* for relating language examinations to the CEFR (Council of Europe 2003). The *Manual* offers a set of activities to enable comparisons between the level of any given examination and the six CEFR levels (A1–C2), thus facilitating mobility of learners within Europe and promoting transparency and meaningfulness of test scores.

The present study reports on a project using the *Manual* in order to relate two suites of exams to the CEFR, the Graded examinations in spoken English (GESE) and the Integrated Skills Exam (ISE) by Trinity College London.

Background of the study

The *Manual* is currently piloted by a number of exam boards, providing feedback to the Council of Europe on its use in order to relate their tests to the CEFR. Within this context, the present author was invited to coordinate a project by Trinity College London in order to link GESE and ISE to the CEFR.

Twelve participants were invited, based on their involvement in the construction of the tests in question, thus creating a team of people involved in item writing, examining, marking piloting and administering exams. The group members were asked to study the CEFR and familiarize themselves with its content. Three meetings, corresponding to the first three stages of the *Manual* were held, lasting two days for Familiarisation, and three days for Specification and Standardisation. Issues from the first two stages will be discussed here, both following the methodology suggested in the *Manual*.

Familiarisation

The Familiarisation stage aimed at ensuring that participants of the project had a deep understanding of the CEFR and that judgements were reliable, otherwise the claim that a test is situated at a specific level could be questioned. Familiarisation tasks with the CEFR scales were organised, in which participants were given handouts containing descriptors without any indication of the level they belong to, which the participants had to guess. After participants had worked on each set of descriptors their judgements were shown on a screen and participants were asked to explain the rationale behind their choosing a level. The correct level was then revealed and the group members were invited to comment on the reasons for level misplacement.

Analysis of judgements yielded the following results:

Intra-rater reliability	.75–.99
Inter-rater reliability	.72–.99
Internal consistency	.98–.99
CEFR–Judge agreement	.79–1

Table 10.4.1: Analysis of judgements-summary statistics

These results, as well as use of the Rasch model, which investigated the scaling of the descriptors based on the judgements of the group, suggested that the Trinity panel made judgements reliably and there was a good understanding of the CEFR scales, thus contributing to the validity of the linking claim.

Specification

At the time of writing, the analysis of results from this stage was in progress but a number of methodological issues were still being discussed. Starting with Familiarisation activities, the organization of this stage aimed at the completion of forms from the *Manual*, using the CEFR, which would eventually result in content analysis of the tests and the building of an initial claim as to which level the exams are situated on in the CEFR. A clear rationale had to be provided regarding the selection of the *Manual* forms, other documentation used, the selection of group or individual work and the amount of justification of decisions. The group work approach was preferred, following recommendations in the literature on judgements and decision making (for example, Plous 1993) and rounds of judgements were chosen in order to ensure accurate decisions.

Conclusion

Relating exams to the CEFR is beneficial not only for exams, but for language teachers as well, who can choose the appropriate test level for their students and compare test results. It is crucial, however, that any linking claim is based on reliable judgements and transparent methodology for which evidence should always be provided. Otherwise, any linking claim could be questioned and the interpretations of test results in relation to the CEFR might be meaningless.

Email: s.papageorgiou@lancaster.ac.uk

References

Council of Europe. 2001. *Common European Framework of Reference for Languages: Learning, Teaching, Assessment.* Cambridge: Cambridge University Press.

Council of Europe. 2003. *Relating Language Examinations to the Common European Framework of Reference for Languages: Learning, Teaching, Assessment: Manual, Preliminary Pilot Version.* Strasbourg: Council of Europe.

10.5 Using the CEFR in the tertiary level context

Juliet Wilson and Senem Donancı Büyük *Sabancı University, Istanbul, Turkey*

This talk described how the CEFR was used to inform the syllabus of the foundation programme of an English medium university in Turkey. The CEFR (Common European Framework of Reference) was used primarily to produce exit level descriptors for the programme's courses. These were then used both to produce other syllabus documents such as 'can do' statements and also to check existing syllabus documents. Perhaps the most useful outcome of producing the descriptors was that it provided a check on the coherence of the programme as a whole.

Sabancı University is a newly established English-medium university in Istanbul. The aim of the foundation programme is to develop students' linguistic and academic skills to equip them for their undergraduate studies in English. Students enter the foundation programme in one of three levels (Basic, Intermediate, Upper Intermediate).

No coherent syllabus beyond an in-house produced coursebook existed prior to this work. Work started on developing the syllabus in 2003 with a thorough needs analysis. This was followed by the establishing of course objectives. At this stage, the syllabus team, in consultation with Frank Heyworth (EAQUALS), investigated how the CEFR might be used to inform the syllabus. The work described below developed as a result of this consultation.

The first and core document produced was a set of exit level descriptors designed to clarify course aims for all stakeholders. Following familiarisation with the CEFR levels using a CEFR video and the marking criteria from the *Relating Language Exams to CEFR: Manual,* the syllabus team looked at video samples of students speaking and sample student essays (6–8 per level). Using the same criteria, exit levels were agreed: Basic – A2+, Intermediate – B1, Upper Intermediate – B2. Descriptors, using the descriptors in CEFR Chapters 4 and 5 as a starting point, were written for each level. These were written for general linguistic range and for the four skills, with the four skills being further divided into the specific requirements for each skill within the context of the foundation programme. For example, under reading, separate descriptors were written for 'reading for orientation', 'reading for information and argument' and 'processing texts for oral and written production' as well as a descriptor for 'overall reading comprehension'. In all of this work, the CEFR proved a useful starting point. However, it was equally essential to be clear about out own course aims in order to produce a useful document.

The exit level descriptors document was then used to check the existing teaching programme document and also to produce 'can do' statements. 'Can do' statements were written based on the course objectives and the exit level descriptors. Sample reading texts and essays were attached to the statements to put the content of the 'can do' statements in more concrete terms. The statements were designed to help students assess their own progress and were used either in class or in tutorials two or three times a semester.

Feedback on the 'can do' statements was mostly positive from both teachers and students. Less positive were lower level students, some of whom found the statements difficult to use. It was suggested by Brian North (one of the authors of the restructured CEFR) in comments following the talk, that this may be because the 'can do' statements for the lower levels were written in terms of classroom tasks rather than 'real-life' tasks. (At the Upper Intermediate level statements were written in terms of real-life university tasks). Students perhaps had difficulty relating to them. This still remains a problem: how to describe what low level students can do within the context of a university foundation programme. Another point highlighted by feedback was the need to provide sufficient training and support to teachers of how to use the 'can do' statements with students.

In addition to being used to produce various syllabus documents, the process of producing the exit level descriptors proved to be a useful one in itself. The close scrutiny of students' competencies and the tasks required of them which writing the descriptors demanded, enabled us to check the coherence of the programme as a whole. It allowed us to check the progression between levels and the appropriateness of objectives and tasks at the three levels. It also highlighted areas of weakness in the programme and helped with the reviewing of assessment criteria.

Email: julietw66@hotmail.com
senemd@sabanciuniv.edu

10.6 A brief history of a CEFR implementation: finding a common language

Maria K. Norton *British Council, Milan, Italy*

Introduction

The British Council Teaching Centre (TC) Milan wholeheartedly embraced the three strands of the CEFR (Common European Framework of Reference): implementing the language levels, to which our courses were mapped; the Portfolio, selected pages of which were included in our Student Guide; and the 'can-do' statements which had been adapted, renamed Learning Aims and turned into syllabi. (See Manasseh 2004.) Yet there were a number of inconsistencies and issues after the first phase. The areas obstructing can-do coherence are detailed below:

- can-do descriptors were conceived of as benchmarks for performance and so lent themselves to assessment, yet we still had student grades depending on end-of-year grammar and vocabulary tests, rather than on skills-based language competencies;
- a methodology statement inconsistent with our aims to send out a coherent message to both teachers and students;
- little support of learning strategy training plus insufficient promotion of out-of-class resources to nurture learner autonomy.

Assessment and teacher involvement

In order to address the issue of inconsistencies between course aims and assessment we:

- replaced the end-of-course test with a continuous assessment system;
- set up level files housing tailor-made tasks exploiting can-do statements specified for those levels.

These steps produced a number of benefits:

- tasks resembled what teachers do in the classroom, since they were made by a team of teachers, and so were consistent with what both students and teachers do and expect;
- a backwash effect was created, motivating students to focus on reviewing and practising language.

Another aspect of this process involved the provision and communication of the can-do-based syllabi to students:

- a syllabus document listing 15–18 can-do statements covering the four skills was written for each level, selected on the basis of what can-dos teachers would most probably cover per level; a teacher version of the syllabus document was produced, with cross-referencing to alternative resource references and supplementary materials.
- strategy can-dos were included at each level so as to begin the process of supporting teaching that drew on learner training techniques.

Student and teacher feedback

One important factor built into this course design project was that of seeking feedback for ongoing evaluation. The last day of term was set aside as a training day and this is where teachers were put into level pools with the tasks of assessing a new selection of coursework pieces, sharing best practice and commenting on their term's work. This was followed by an in-service teacher training session on learner training. Structured focus groups were then held to gather even more teacher comments on all aspects of the project so far and to inform its development. Feedback on the whole was positive, in sharp contrast to the focus groups held eight months earlier.

Evaluation

At this point in the academic year indications are that far more teachers than ever before are using the CEFR's can-dos in their teaching for the British Council TC in Milan. All adult students on general English courses have performed a number of assessment tasks and have been counselled by their teachers on their progress and how to enhance their performance. The difference is that the assessment system makes counselling more meaningful as it helps to provide evidence for speaking to students. Student focus groups carried out in December reported great satisfaction with their course package and more focus groups are planned for May. More will be made of the materials available in our library and computer laboratory, which students are encouraged to use for self-study. We are currently working on a Learner Pathways project which will draw on all these materials to provide out-of-class support and encourage learner autonomy.

The first target has been reached-that of making our courses gravitate around the common denominator of can-do based assessment to chart progress. Now further steps are being taken in order to support the learner training element: Learner Pathways are being put together for September. I have written a methodology statement for inclusion in our student guide-cum-notebook, which reflects all of this work and promises courses even better able to support the CEFR can-do perspective.

Successes

The successes of this project so far are:

- courses mapped to the CEFR in a way which is meaningful to all stakeholders;
- a user-friendly continuous assessment system based on can-do statements;
- more meaningful student counselling procedures;
- teacher involvement in the Teaching Centre's academic direction;
- a clear methodology statement.

Email: maria.norton@britishcouncil.it

Reference

Manasseh, A. 2004. 'Using the CEF to develop English courses for teenagers at the British Council Milan' in K. Morrow (ed.). *Insights from the Common European Framework*. Oxford: Oxford University Press.

11 Cross-cultural matters

In her plenary paper **Ryuko Kubota** offers a new framework for looking at culture, which she calls the 'Four Ds Approach'. She argues that a discursive construction of culture is a useful, critical approach creating an understanding that many of our common beliefs about particular cultures are constructed by discourses rather than reflecting objective or scientific truths. Certain knowledge about culture and cultural difference is often used strategically for pursuing political and ideological purposes. She goes on to make some suggestions for classroom practice such as discussion focusing on a specific cultural product or practice, a mini-lesson at a teachable moment and an understanding of culture that can inform teachers' awareness or critical consciousness.

Alan Waters contributes a polemical piece in which he tackles the need to reduce the dominance in ELT of native speakers of English by looking at the problem in a novel way. He is convinced that a view of ELT based on critical theory (CT) contributes to the problem of native-speakerism by refusing to take account of data obtained directly from representative groups of NNS. He explains that his research into the innovation strategy used to implement the ELT component of the Philippines Basic Education Curriculum indicates that the preferred strategy was not a CT-oriented, normative re-educative approach, but, a more top-down, centre-periphery model.

The next section comprises summaries from the symposium on the Chinese learner convened by **Melinda Whong-Barr**. **Xiaoli Jiang**'s paper addressed how learner autonomy is interpreted in a Chinese context by Chinese learners. **Yingchun Li** presents an ethnographic study of two EFL classrooms in higher education in China, one led by a British teacher and the other by a Chinese teacher. The two classrooms were found to demonstrate different sets of 'cultural traits' but the learners perceived both classrooms as successful places of learning. **Mark Allen** notes that while international students in Britain expect a high level of service, cultural differences offer many opportunities for misunderstandings. He explains the importance of clear English and clarity as to how binding rules are. Melinda Whong-Barr was the last presenter in this symposium; she recommends making use of Chinese learners' ability to memorise, a facility that is given considerable weight in Chinese education. Her examples include memorising chunks of well-written academic language and memorising appropriate discourse moves in specific written genres.

Chapter 11: Cross-cultural matters

Keeping to the topic of Chinese culture, **Wei-Wei Shen** explores the possibility of explaining Chinese cultural keywords in English while avoiding culture-dependent concepts and terminology. Wei-Wei Shen exemplifies the procedure by interpreting six key items of Chinese cultural lexis using 'natural semantic metalanguage.'

The final contributions to this chapter range widely across different cultures and different aspects of cross-cultural communication. **Irina Perianova** investigates food as a marker of culture. She observes that eating the same food in the same way demonstrates affiliation with a particular community. Attitudes to food can emphasise difference or sameness, and demonstrate adherence to or rejection of aesthetic, social, political or historical values. **Elka Todeva** considers the best ways of building on learners' previous knowledge to teach them the core target forms of English. The goal of this is to empower them by aiding learning and facilitating cross-cultural communication. She proceeds to define some core phonological, grammatical and lexical items but sees pragmatic choices, which posit a linguistic identity embedded in culture, as a difficult area. **Nadia Benrabah-Djennane** writes about her survey of teachers' attitudes to English as a lingua franca (ELF). The majority of her NS and NNS teacher informants believed that British English, American English or other varieties of native English were the most appropriate for the classroom. It seemed that most teachers had not considered the idea of teaching 'world English' or ELF.

The volume closes with a report from the intercultural communication symposium convened by **Alessia Cogo**. **Martin Dewey**'s paper reported recent ELF corpus findings and considered the pedagogical implications. Alessia Cogo returns to the problem of cultural and linguistic identity, as mentioned by Elka Todeva. Hitherto, Alessia Cogo states, international English has been regarded as neutral, free of cultural identity. However, her research highlights a number of features of language use that suggest membership of a multilingual and multicultural community. **Ayako Suzuki** illustrates the importance of teaching the diversity of English for intercultural communication by focusing on data from Japan. The conclusion is that raising students' awareness of L2 speakers' ways of using English can be a valuable initial step in preparing students for international communication. **Sherida Altehenger-Smith** deals with intercultural problems which arise in teaching students from seventeen different countries in a university in Germany. Intercultural variance is seen in attitudes towards language learning and methods of learning which students bring with them from their home countries. Finally **Alun Phillips** looks at some practical activities for developing intercultural awareness.

11.1 Plenary: Critical approaches to culture in English language teaching

Ryuko Kubota *The University of North Carolina at Chapel Hill, Chapel Hill, North Carolina, USA*

Culture constitutes an important aspect of teaching and learning English as a second or foreign language. Scholars in the field of second/foreign language teaching have been exploring how to approach culture and how to help students develop intercultural competence (Alred, Byram, and Fleming 2003; Atkinson 1999; Byram and Risager 1999; Corbett 2003; Hinkel 1999; Holliday 1999; Holliday, Hyde and Kullman 2004; Kramsch 1993). Scholars and practitioners have increasingly been aware of the danger of essentialising or stereotyping a certain culture or viewing a group of people as the Other, constructing a rigid boundary to distinguish them from Us. This paper aims to scrutinise such essentialising trends and explore a critical approach to understanding and teaching culture (Kubota 2003, 2004).

The problematic of culture

Culture is a common term that we hear and use in our daily life. However, we often flounder when asked 'What is culture?' With some brainstorming, one can come up with a list of constitutive elements such as art, beliefs, customs, life styles, and so on. Such a list helps us explain culture in general and suggest characteristics of a certain culture. Yet, once a belief within a certain culture, such as individualism is scrutinised to see if it indeed applies to all aspects within the culture, the concept often loses its legitimacy as the unique construct that represents the culture. Culture is indeed a familiar yet illusive concept; as Geertz states, 'the more deeply it goes the less complete it is' (1973: 5).

The field of second language education and research has recently problematised the tendency to emphasise dichotomous cultural differences between the target language society's culture and the students' home culture, which often constructs essentialised images of the Self and the Other. Such a tendency has been critiqued as cultural stereotypes (Kumaravadivelu 2002) or the 'received review' of culture (Atkinson 1999: 626) and alternative perspectives have been proposed. For instance, Atkinson (1999) suggests a middle-ground approach to culture, stressing dialectics of the individual nature of culture and the group membership of humans. Holliday (1999) proposes the notion of *small cultures* that are based on cohesive social groups as opposed to *large cultures* that are based on essentialist features of ethnic or national groups. This distinction also suggests different inquiry approaches, namely, a non-essentialist heuristic interpretive process for understanding small cultures versus a prescriptive or normative process to understand categorical differences among large cultures. In the field of contrastive rhetoric (i.e. cross-cultural investigations of written discourse organisations), Al Lehner and I have proposed *critical contrastive rhetoric* (Kubota and Lehner 2004) to move inquiries away from discovering essentialist cultural differences in rhetoric toward exploring how our knowledge of cultural differences has been constructed by discourses, implicitly serving to categorise people and languages under culture-based new racism (Bonilla-Silva 2003; May 1999; van Dijk 1993), and how one can create counter-hegemonic pedagogies that recognise linguistic hybridity, multiplicity, and power relations that influence written discourse organisations.

Despite such critiques, the essentialist notion of culture seems still pervasive in our field. A recent example is a resource book on cultural and linguistic diversity for primary and secondary school mainstream classroom teachers in the United States, describing cultural characteristics of several ethnic groups of English language learners (Ariza 2006). East Asian characteristics, for example, are described as conformity to authority figures, Confucian values, politeness, favouring ambiguity, traditional family structures, respect for harmony, and so on. At the end of each chapter, discussion questions are presented to review cultural traits of each group described in the chapter. No doubt such a book is useful for teachers who work with culturally diverse learners. Texts such as this are created with good intentions. Nonetheless, any attempt to describe and explain cultural differences constructs a discourse that forms specific knowledge of who we are and who others are, potentially essentialising cultures and groups of people (cf., Kubota 1999, 2001).

This paper provides teachers and teacher educators with a framework for critically understanding culture. I call the framework the 'Four Ds Approach', which brings our attention to (1) descriptive understanding of culture, (2) diversity within culture, (3) dynamic nature of culture, and (4) discursive construction of culture. Although the first three Ds provide important insights, they contain some limitations. The final D resolves the difficulties and takes our understanding to a different dimension. Because the final D is a rather complex notion to grasp, I will discuss it in more detail. Some of the examples come from teaching Japanese as a foreign language, which is part of my professional career. Other examples are drawn from the US context, in which I currently work. Before presenting the Four Ds Approach, I will briefly discuss the background of this idea.

Background

In the United States, one significant federal educational initiative in the 1990s was establishing national standards for learning and teaching for primary and secondary education. In the field of foreign language education, a set of content standards for learners was established (National Standards in Foreign Language Project 1999). They consist of the Five Cs: namely, Communication, Cultures, Comparisons, Connections, and Communities. Within Cultures, the interrelation of three cultural components or the Three Ps—(cultural) Perspectives, Practices, and Products—are to be explored. In my experience of teaching a foreign language as well as engaging in teacher education, I have found these concrete models useful. However, I have also observed some potential problems of the Three Ps model; that is, it can easily reinforce essentialised cultural values and beliefs in explaining how they are related to cultural practices or products. The Four Ds model provides practitioners with a critical way to approach culture that augments the Three Ps.

First D: Descriptive understanding of culture

Teachers and teacher educators trying to understand cultures may seek a laundry list of characteristics of a certain culture, because such a list would fulfill their needs in an immediate and concrete manner. However, in this approach, these characteristics tend to become a prescriptive knowledge of how we/they think and behave. Instead of relying on preconceived ideas of cultural characteristics, it would be more fruitful for students and teachers to conduct observations of multiple social situations through a descriptive approach in order to understand how social hierarchy, or any other cultural aspect, emerges in diverse social contexts and interpersonal relationships in multifaceted ways. Social practices and phenomena (for example, individualism, collectivism, social hierarchy) are also likely to be observed in all cultures in slightly different ways. Thus, arriving at any broad-stroke prescriptive generalisations not only disregards the complexity of culture but also deprives students and teachers of the opportunity to learn to closely observe cultural intricacy and to understand that such skills are developed through an ongoing reflective process.

There is one caution. One of the challenges in understanding culture is to go beyond various binary notions. For example, cultural stereotypes might be understood as a result of inaccurate or false understanding of a culture (see National Standards in Foreign Language Project 1999). The corollary is that stereotypes are overcome once an accurate and true understanding is obtained. However, this true-false binary seems a bit too naïve. As Pickering argues, stereotypes do not just reflect a false image that becomes a target of abuse and discrimination; they are 'a component of the broader power/knowledge relations which produce and organise the 'truths' of the self-consolidating Other' (2001: 168). Although a descriptive understanding of language and culture is important, it does not escape the binary between true and false; that is, descriptive data could be regarded as accurate whereas prescriptive information as inaccurate. This limitation will be discussed in more detail later.

Second D: Diversity within culture

The descriptive approach to culture enables us to explore the complexity, variability, and diversity that exist in culture. Cultural practices, products, and perspectives vary according to the geographical location, gender, generation, occupation, socioeconomic status, ethnicity, religion, language, and other social, political, and economic categories. Exploring diversity is important for a non-essentialist understanding of language and culture.

In exploring diversity, students can develop in-depth understandings of politics and history. For instance, in the US context, ESL students learning about holidays and annual events can explore different meanings of Thanksgiving Day from perspectives of both White settlers and Native Americans (Bigelow and Peterson 1998). This discussion of how the holiday is celebrated or remembered can lead to learning about a history of struggle experienced by the colonised, cultural and linguistic assimilation being forced on Native American children, and the current cultural and economic plight of Native Americans. An example from Japanese food culture is geographical diversity as seen in *ozôni*, a New Year's holiday dish of rice cake in soup. There are numerous regional recipes and, moreover, the dish does not traditionally exist in Okinawa, the southern island with a history of Japanese invasion, atrocities during World War II, and US occupation. This topic can be extended to a discussion on the culture, politics, and history of Okinawa that reflect the legacy of its struggle over sovereignty, marginality, and international relations.

In exploring diversity, one caveat needs to be kept in mind. When describing a society that has traditionally embraced multiple ethnicities and cultures in a relative sense, diversity itself can become a descriptor. This, however, diverts our attention away from the hegemonic norm that exists in every aspect of the society. In the case of the United States, despite the celebratory claim for diversity as a cultural characteristic, the White middle-class heterosexual norm permeates various aspects of private and public life, creating and perpetuating social, cultural, and economic inequalities among various groups. It is important to keep in mind that giving diversity a label for cultural uniqueness can reinforce an apolitical colour-blind or difference-blind vision of society (Bonilla-Silva 2004; Larson and Ovando 2001; Nieto 1995).

Third D: Dynamic nature of culture

Whereas the second D addresses synchronic multiplicities of culture, the third D focuses on diachronic analysis of culture. One tendency of the essentialist approach is to situate culture in a frozen space in history. This is especially prevalent in constructing the images of the Other in discourses of colonialism and Orientalism (Pennycook 1998; Said 1978). Such construction serves to draw a rigid boundary between the West and the Orient or between the society constantly developing and the one preserving traditions. However, when we closely examine so-called traditions, we often find that many of them are recent inventions. (See Hobsbawm 1983.) For instance, the tradition of having a wedding ceremony at a Shinto shrine in Japan began only about 100 years ago when the crown prince and princess were married under the modern imperial system, even though the whole ambiance gives the impression that it has lasted for centuries. This suggests that social practices get invented and transformed constantly in history under the influence of politics, economics, and other social forces. Cultural values and beliefs also shift in history. For instance, respect for the elderly, especially taking care of one's own parents by living together, has often been described as a characteristic of East Asian culture, but this might be changing in many parts of the region with the Westernisation of life style including the preference for a nuclear family.

It is important to note that the dynamic and diverse nature of culture is closely related to domestic socioeconomic and political conditions as well as cross-cultural influences, especially in the era of globalisation. Technological advancement and the increased flow of people, commodities, and information across the globe have created hybrid forms of cultural practices and product. Thus cultural shift and diversification should be explored in relation to the changing domestic and international landscape.

Fourth D: Discursive construction of culture

While the above three Ds are proposed to broaden teachers' and learners' understanding of culture, there are limitations and caveats. The fundamental challenge is to overcome the modernist quest for objective truths that are inherent in these concepts.

A descriptive understanding of culture as opposed to a prescriptive approach has two limitations: the assumption that objective truths exist and the orientation toward normative thinking. First, the descriptive approach implies that descriptive analysis generates illustrative facts about a certain language and culture, whereas a prescriptive approach reinforces knowledge that does not reflect realities. In other words, it is assumed that descriptive analysis yields accurate factual information, while the prescriptive orientation leads to false or inaccurate knowledge. While a descriptive approach is an important step toward challenging the fixed and essentialised images of culture and language, the implied dichotomy between true and false indicates the assumption that observations conducted for descriptive analysis will eventually arrive at the discovery of objective truth. However, because of the complexity of linguistic and cultural phenomena produced by situational specificity and individual variation, it is difficult to identify certain observed cultural or linguistic practices as generalisable reality or objective truth. Second, descriptive understandings of culture and language tend to assume that there are certain normative cultural and linguistic codes accepted by a certain cultural group or *native speakers*. This potentially undermines possibilities of cultural and linguistic creativity—especially the kinds of creativity performed by non-mainstream populations, including second/foreign language learners. Whereas a prescriptive approach fixes the norm with little empirical evidence, the descriptive approach generates knowledge about objective and generalisable norms based on actual observations. Thus, no matter how well-intended, the descriptive approach may not escape a pursuit of the norm if it supports a positivist orientation.

A similar paradox exists in the focus on the diverse/dynamic nature of culture. A focus on diversity related to various categories, such as gender, class, ethnicity, age, and geographical location, or on cultural dynamism, aims to avoid essentialising a particular culture. However, it may not escape essentialising groups within each category or at a specific time in history. For example, in exploring ethnic diversity in the United States, one might make generalised claims about the characteristics of African Americans, Latinos, Native Americans, or Asian Americans. Also, in discussing cultural hybridity seen in Asian cultures influenced by Americanisation, for instance, American culture might be perceived as unitary and homogeneous. It is necessary to be aware that the notion of hybridity does not evade essentialism when it assumes a blend of two cultures that are pure, unique, and essentialised (May 1999).

These limitations indicate that another dimension in our cultural analysis is needed. The fourth D—discursive construction of culture—can fulfill this need. It is a perspective that our knowledge about a certain culture is constructed, perpetuated, and yet challenged by discourses in a poststructuralist sense. Weedon defines discourses as 'ways of constituting knowledge, together with the social practices, forms of subjectivity and power relations which inhere in such knowledges and the relations between them' (1987: 108). In other words, discourse with regard to cultural understanding is formed through a use of language and other modes of communication that organises our cultural knowledge about the Self, the Other, and a relationship between them in a certain way. Thus, a certain characterisation of Asian students or Asian ways of learning, for instance, can be seen as knowledge produced by a discourse that structures our ways of thinking. In this view, many of the common beliefs about an East Asian culture, such as rigid social hierarchy, respect for harmony, reticence and indirectness in communication, or collectivism, are constructed by discourses rather than reflecting objective or scientific truths. Discussing a poststructuralist approach to feminism, Weedon argues:

> ... there is no such thing as natural or given meaning in the world. Language does not reflect reality but gives it meaning. Meaning is an effect of language and, as such, always historically and culturally specific. ... meaning tends to be structured in terms of hierarchical binary oppositions, such as male/female. white/black, advanced/

primitive and so on. The fact that language is plural, that signifiers have no one fixed meaning, means that there are many competing definitions of gender difference. Following Foucault, these meanings are produced within a range of institutionally located discourses such as medicine, psychology, religion, fashion, advertising, literature, the media and the arts. Thus, from poststructuralist perspectives, the meanings ascribed to bodies are culturally produced, plural and ever changing. Moreover, these competing meanings are part of broader relations of power and have implications for both women and men. They affect femininity and masculinity as forms of lived and embodied subjectivity and women and men's positions in society.

(1999: 102)

The discursive construction of knowledge about culture can indeed be made clearer by using an analogy with how our knowledge of gender difference (for example, expectations about gender roles, attractiveness of men and women) is constructed. Through critically reading popular self-help books, such as *Men Are from Mars, Women Are from Venus, Why Men Love Bitches,* one can recognise how the descriptions of what men/women tend (not) to think, feel, say, and do in various situations constructs our knowledge of what we might actually think, feel, say, and do. Furthermore, such discourse tends to form certain norms and social expectations, guiding how we should behave. In fact, because these books aim to provide men and women with concrete guidance for better communication and successful relationships, they construct ideas of model social behaviours and expectations.

A similar trend is observed in some texts on cultural difference. For example, a book titled *The Japanese Mind: Understanding Contemporary Japanese Culture* (Davies and Ikeno 2002) targets mainly university students in Japanese studies programmes and Japanese students of English learning to explain and discuss their native culture in English to others. The chapters include commonly heard cultural traits such as ambiguity, the sense of beauty, the way of the warrior, silence in communication, an implicit way of communicating, and so on. At the end of each chapter, there are discussion activities with questions. For instance, the chapter on silence poses questions such as: 'It is thought that silence plays an important role in maintaining harmony and avoiding conflict in Japan. Do you agree?' (op. cit.: 58). These questions assume in a prescriptive way that silence is a unique cultural characteristic, constructing a specific discourse on Japanese culture or a certain way of explaining it.

While there is a dominant discourse that reinforces the hegemonic view of society, there are other competing discourses. The multiplicity of discourses implies that there are contradictions and paradoxes in cultural interpretations. For instance the Amazon.co.jp website lists two customer reviews of *The Japanese Mind* by Davies and Ikeno (2002). While one expresses a thorough disappointment with the book's tendency to strengthen the old myth of Japanese uniqueness, another enthusiastically praises it for being useful in understanding aspects of Japanese culture that are often unconscious. This example demonstrates that the answer to the question 'What characterises Japanese culture?' is neither singular nor fixed; rather, it embodies a multiplicity of meanings and interpretations that are constructed within discourses competing against each other in a struggle for power. In this view, there is no transcendent truth outside of discourses and power relations.

The notions of discourse and the discursive construction of knowledge reveal political aims behind certain knowledge about culture and cultural difference, providing an understanding that such knowledge is often used strategically for pursuing certain political and ideological purposes. A dominant discourse supporting a binary cultural difference between the West and the East, for instance, serves the ideological purpose of either maintaining an existing power hierarchy as seen in the discourse of colonialism (for example, 'The East, the backward, will never become like us as they are so different') or proclaiming resistance as seen in identity politics (for example, 'We are uniquely different from and even superior to the West'). In other words, discourses of cultural difference may serve to construct the Other as inferior, as seen in the discourses of colonialism or to create positive or unique self images of the marginalised, signifying strategic essentialism (Spivak 1993). Thus, a single value judgment cannot be made as to whether essentialism is negative or positive. The political significance of cultural essentialism needs to be analysed with situational contexts in mind.

Classroom teaching

There are various ways in which aspects of culture are addressed in language classrooms. First, most obviously, culture can become an independent topic of classroom discussion through focusing on a specific cultural product or practice. For instance, St. Valentine's Day can be critically explored through interviewing people from different generations and backgrounds about how they celebrate it and what significance it has. Through sharing their findings, students may recognise a common theme and yet multiple and dynamic ways of celebrating the occasion. Furthermore, the ways of celebrating St. Valentine's Day can be analysed as not only a benign romantic or loving event but also an economically driven project of selling love and romance and constructing certain social norms.

Second, aspects of culture can be taught as a mini-lesson at a teachable moment when a certain cultural issue comes up in a language lesson. The lesson may not be fully planned but through Freirean problem-posing in a dialogic approach between the teacher and the students (Freire 1998), a critical discussion for non-essentialist cultural understanding can be conducted. The mini-lesson can be extended to more in-depth explorations later in the classroom or as students' research projects.

Third, related to the previous point, a critical understanding of culture may not be directly connected to explicit teaching of culture but can inform teachers' awareness or critical consciousness (cf., Freire, 1998) which permeates their pedagogical engagement. In other words, critical consciousness with non-essentialist knowledge becomes a foundation of what teachers do, such as presenting written, audio, or visual materials, constructing examples, preparing discussion questions, responding to students' views and opinions, and so forth. For instance, a text might have a stereotypical depiction of a certain group of people. Rather than accepting it as it is and moving on, a critical teacher might ask students if they agree, whether there are any counter examples, how the cultural explanations justify dominant cultural images, and so on. Keeping the 4Ds approach in mind, the teacher can guide students to deconstruct cultural representations and to discuss what political and ideological consequences are involved in essentialist accounts.

In engaging in critical pedagogies for cultural explorations, a teacher's positionality as a knower becomes a contentious issue. Even when teachers are cautious about cultural essentialism, if they have not been exposed to the culture that the students bring to the classroom and lack knowledge of the dominant stereotypical discourses about the culture, how can they judge if the students' voices reflect overgeneralisation or critical views of their own culture? From what position can teachers problematise or affirm students' views—from an authoritarian position or as an equal partner in a dialogue? A Freirean dialogic approach advocates mutual dialogues between the teacher and students to come to know the real situation in which students exist in the cultural world, rather than to 'bring them a message of ''salvation'' (Freire 1998: 76). Yet without a fundamental cultural knowledge about where the students come from, constructing mutual dialogues becomes challenging. In this sense, books such as Ariza (2006) and Davies and Ikeno (2002), although problematic, can be useful resources for developing knowledge about the popular discourse that describes the culture of a specific group. After all, we cannot deconstruct a discourse without knowledge about the discourse. Critical and strategic use of these texts is required of teachers.

Toward critical reflections

Culture is an easy word to utter but indeed a challenging concept to explore critically. Discourses on cultural characteristics of various groups are constructed with good intentions to promote better understandings of the Self and the Other. However, the minute we describe, categorise, and characterise a culture, we are constructing a particular way we talk about and understand the culture. By discussing cultural categories, characteristics, differences, and similarities, we are actually creating them. Furthermore, constructing critiques of cultural essentialism is itself another discourse based on a particular epistemology. There is no easy way to overcome the predicament of culture. As teachers and teacher educators, we need to constantly reflect critically on the purposes, processes, and consequences of the construction of our cultural knowledge.

References

Alred, G., M. Byram, and M. Felming (eds.). 2003. *Intercultural Experience and Education*. Clevedon, UK: Multilingual Matters.

Ariza, E. N. 2006. *Not for ESOL Teachers: What Every Classroom Teacher Needs to Know about the Linguistically, Culturally, and Ethnically Diverse Student*. Boston, Mass.: Pearson Education, Inc.

Atkinson, D. 1999. 'TESOL and culture.' *TESOL Quarterly* 33: 625–54.

Bigelow, B. and B. Peterson. 1998. *Rethinking Columbus: The Next 500 years*. Milwaukee, Wis.: Rethinking Schools.

Bonilla-Silva, E. 2003. *Racism without Racists: Color-blind Racism and the Persistence of Racial Inequality in the United States*. Lanham, Md.: Lowman and Littlefield.

Byram, M. and K. Risager. 1999. *Language Teachers, Politics and Cultures*. Clevedon, UK: Multilingual Matters.

Corbett, J. 2003. *An Intercultural Approach to English Language Teaching*. Clevedon, UK: Multilingual Matters.

Davies, R. J. and O. Ikeno. 2002. *The Japanese Mind: Understanding Contemporary Japanese Culture*. Boston, Mass.: Tuttle Publishing.

Freire, P. 1998. *Pedagogy of the Oppressed*. New York: Continuum.

Geertz, C. 1973. *The Interpretation of Cultures*. New York: Basic Books.

Hinkel, E. (ed.). 1999. *Culture in Second Language Teaching and Learning*. Cambridge: Cambridge University Press.

Hobsbawm, E., J. 1983. 'Introduction: Invention of tradition' in E. J. Hobsbawm and T. Ranger (eds.). *The Invention of Tradition*. Cambridge: Cambridge University Press.

Holliday, A. R. 1999. 'Small cultures.' *Applied Linguistics* 20: 237–64.

Holliday, A., M. Hyde, and J. Kullman. 2004. *Intercultural Communication: Advanced Resource Bbook*. London: Routledge.

Kramsch, C. 1993. *Context and Culture in Language Teaching*. Oxford: Oxford University Press.

Kubota, R. 1999. 'Japanese culture constructed by discourses: Implications for applied linguistic research and English language teaching.' *TESOL Quarterly* 33: 9–35.

Kubota, R. 2001. 'Discursive construction of the images of US classrooms.' *TESOL Quarterly* 35: 9–38.

Kubota, R. 2003. 'Critical teaching of Japanese culture.' *Japanese Language and Literature* 37: 67–87.

Kubota, R. 2004. 'The politics of cultural difference in second language education.' *Critical Inquiry in Language Studies* 1: 21–39.

Kubota, R. and A. Lehner. 2004. 'Toward critical contrastive rhetoric.' *Journal of Second Language Writing* 13: 7–27.

Kumaravadivelu, B. 2002. 'Problematizing cultural stereotypes.' *TESOL Quarterly* 37: 709–19.

Larson, C. L. and C. J. Ovando. 2001. *The Color of Bureaucracy: The Politics of Equity in Multicultural School Communities*. Belmont, Calif.: Wadsworth/Thomson Learning.

May, S. 1999. 'Critical multiculturalism and cultural difference: Avoiding essentialism' in S. May (ed.). *Critical Multiculturalism: Rethinking Multicultural and Antiracist Education*. London: Falmer Press.

National Standards in Foreign Language Project. 1999. *Standards for Foreign Language Learning in the 21st Century*. Lawrence, Kans.: National Standards Report.

Nieto, S. 1995. 'From brown heroes and holidays to assimilationist agendas: Reconsidering the critiques of multicultural education' in C. E. Sleeter and P. S. McLaren (eds.). *Multicultural Education, Critical Pedagogy, and the Politics of Difference*. Albany, N.Y.: State University of New York Press.

Pennycook, A. 1998. *English and the Discourses of Colonialism*. New York: Routledge.

Pickering, M. 2001. *Stereotyping: The Politics of Representation*. New York: Palgrave.

Said, E. 1978. *Orientalism*. New York: Pantheon Books.

Spivak, G. 1993. *Outside in the Teaching Machine*. New York: Routledge.

Van Dijk, T. 1993. *Elite Discourse and Racism*. London: Sage Publications.

Weedon, C. 1987. *Feminist Practice* and *Poststructuralist Theory*. Oxford: Blackwell.

Weedon, C. 1999. *Feminism, Theory and the Politics of Difference*. Oxford: Blackwell.

11.2 Native-speakerism in ELT: *plus ça change* …?

Alan Waters   *Lancaster University, UK*

The main theme of my talk was the importance of redressing the problem of 'native-speakerism' in ELT—the domination of professional discourse by the native-speaker voice. However, I explained that my view was that the current main attempt to do so—via the use of a 'critical theory' (CT) approach—was making the problem worse.

I characterised CT as a politically-oriented academic ideology, whereby asymmetrical power relations in society were seen to occur because of the oppression of the less powerful by the more powerful. I saw the typical stance of CT as being to support the former (for example, 'ordinary' people) and oppose the latter (for example, government). I also explained that I viewed the CT perspective as exerting a significant amount of influence on current intellectual attitudes, both outside and within ELT.

With regard to the latter, I argued that the CT perspective was one of the mainsprings behind a number of well-established professional trends, for example, learner-centredness, the anti-textbook stance, action research and so on, since it was possible to view all of them as involving an attempt to champion the cause of a perceived 'underdog' against the hegemony of a variety of 'oppressors'. In particular, I said that I saw CT in ELT as having constructed the native speaker (NS) as automatically being in a hegemonic relationship with the non-native speaker (NNS).

In doing so, however, I argued that an unbalanced approach to countering native-speakerism in ELT was being promoted.

As a case in point, I took the question of cultural stereotyping of NNS by NS. I discussed the one-sided nature of and lack of empirical support for a CT-based interpretation of an ELT conference presentation concerned with such generalisations. Rather than stereotyping being seen in an inevitably negative light, as in the analysis in question, however, I argued that it is not so much stereotyping *per se* which is problematic, but whether it was used as a mental straitjacket or as an impressionistic heuristic. I illustrated how, by adopting the latter perspective, the same conference presentation could be viewed in a much more positive light.

Furthermore, I saw attempting to ignore cultural differences in ELT as contradicting the principle of 'appropriate methodology', which involves acknowledging the importance of respecting the way such differences affect pedagogical preferences. In short, I saw CT-based ELT as *contributing to* the problem of native-speakerism, by refusing to grant due credence to common-sense modes of perception.

I therefore also argued that countering native-speakerism in ELT called for a less ideological and more empirical stance. I exemplified this by describing recent research done with an NNS colleague into the innovation strategy used to implement the ELT component of the Philippines Basic Education Curriculum. I explained that data from the study indicated that the preferred strategy was not the CT-oriented, normative re-educative approach that prevails in the professional literature, but, rather, a more top-down, centre-periphery model. Furthermore, I pointed out that the data also indicated that the approach used was seen as an appropriate response in terms of the level of resources available in the innovation situation, as well as being viewed as compatible with prevailing socio-cultural norms.

I went on to cite a number of other studies that I felt had adopted a similar research approach, i.e. had obtained data directly from representative groups of NNS by using 'standard' research techniques, with the data being allowed to speak for themselves. I said that I saw them as having generated similar results to my own study, in the sense that their findings indicated a clear preference by the NNS for practices and perceptions which were usually construed by CT-based ELT as demeaning of them (because, for example, they showed a preference for a degree of structure and control in language learning, etc.).

In conclusion, I argued that the current CT-based approach to attempting to counter native-speakerism in ELT was creating more problems than it solved; instead, a larger conduit was needed by which the representative voice of the NNS could be more frequently and more loudly heard in its own right, via more empirical studies of the kind that I had discussed.

Email: a.waters@lancaster.ac.uk

11.3 Symposium on the Chinese learner

Convenor: Melinda Whong-Barr *Durham University, UK*

The particular challenge involved in teaching English to learners from Chinese speaking countries has gained importance in UK institutes of higher education in recent years as the number of Chinese students coming to the UK has increased dramatically. This symposium explored questions of the Chinese learner by probing both the culture of education and the practice of teaching in China before turning to current practice in the UK.

Xiaoli Jiang (*University of Warwick, UK*) opened the session with 'Concepts of learner autonomy in Chinese learners' voices', noting that despite the worldwide promotion of learner autonomy, there is no consensus as to how it is defined. This, in turn, raises questions about cultural appropriateness: while political autonomy is definitely a 'Western construct', 'psychological autonomy' lies with individuals, and is, arguably, culture free. Yet culture itself is not straightforward. A geographical association is unhelpful as a distinction between 'big culture' and 'small culture' cannot be equated with a national group. Keeping these concerns in mind, this paper addressed how learner autonomy is interpreted in a Chinese context, and in particular, by Chinese learners, and explored influences on their conceptions.

Based on fifteen Chinese learners' narratives, Xiaoli Jiang's study identifies three conceptions of learner autonomy: reactive, proactive and instrumental. These conceptions are seen to change with the increase in learning experience. For example, the majority of participants (13 out of 15) demonstrate a tendency of transition from instrumental autonomy to reactive or proactive autonomy after the Chinese National Entrance Exam.

After establishing the existence of autonomy among Chinese learners, the paper looked more specifically at Chinese learners' own ideas of good learning—some of which were said to facilitate learner autonomy and some of which seem to hinder it. The diverse self-conceptions found among the learners in this study were seen as the result of cultural commonality and individual diversity. This is perhaps unsurprising given that Chinese culture, family, school education and learners' personal factors all play a role in influencing learners' conceptions. Yet, this paper showed that these factors are significant at different learning stages as concepts of learner autonomy evolve with learners' language learning experience. Subsequently, implications of developing learner autonomy among Chinese learners at tertiary level are suggested.

The second speaker, **Yingchun Li** (*University of Exeter, UK*) presented an ethnographic study of two EFL classrooms in higher education in China in her paper 'Classroom culture and learning opportunity'. This paper investigated the construction of EFL classroom culture and its relationship with the production of learning opportunities in terms of differing teacher practices. The two EFL classrooms are both part of a Chinese provincial university, one led by a British teacher and the other by a Chinese teacher.

The two classrooms were found to demonstrate different sets of 'cultural traits'. As an inclusive and egalitarian community, the British teacher's classroom is an engaging and supportive environment where participants are involved in multilateral (among teacher and students) interactions; by contrast, the Chinese teacher's EFL enterprise is more one of a 'teacher talk, teacher asks; students listen, students answer' scenario. The interactions are mainly bilateral (between teacher and students) and mono-directional (from the teacher to students). Interestingly, there is also 'supplementary' communication inside and outside the Chinese teacher's classroom via portfolios.

Despite the divergence between these two cultural entities, both classrooms have been successful in that learners feel they have achieved 'learning' through various classroom activities. The study found the architecture of the two EFL classroom cultures to include classroom setting, participants' demographics and dispositions, explicit classroom interaction patterns and an implicit code of practice. The conclusion was that different classroom cultures afford different learning opportunities for learners, from which varied outcomes can be harvested. This finding suggests the adoption of EFL classroom methodologies that are contextualized rather than superimposed in order to optimize classroom practices.

From teaching and learning in China, the Symposium then turned to the Chinese learner in the UK. In his paper 'An idiot's guide to cultural awareness in the classroom', **Mark Allen** (*Sussex Downs College, UK*) began by noting that, while international students expect a high level of service, cultural differences offer a wealth of opportunity for misunderstandings. This talk gave participants ideas to use in the classroom to increase the cultural awareness of teachers, non-EFL support staff and students. Below are two extracts from the session:

1. Plain English
Non-EFL staff may not realise the importance of grading their language to avoid producing almost incomprehensible sentences for example, 'If you can *put up with* waiting, I'll *pop up* stairs to *sort it*. Back in *a jiffy*.' A useful activity is to collect common phrases used by these teams and suggest clearer, simpler alternatives.

2. Does 'no' mean "no"?
Some cultures tend to base their behaviour on rules and might be confused by unclear rules (for example, German/Swiss/British). Other cultures tend to value relationships more and may be confused if rules are not flexible (for example, Chinese/Arab/Latin

American). This may result in Chinese students making the same request to several teachers as they seek to find a good relationship (*guanxi*) that gives them the response they want. To promote awareness of this, students could be given a dilemma involving transgression of a rule by a friend, and asked whether they would adhere to the rule or break it to support their friend. The ensuing discussion may help awareness of this potential difference.

Throughout the session the point was made that it is important to try and avoid stereotyping and to remember that 'normality' has infinite variations. People's age, context, familiarity of the participants, sex, mood, stress levels and linguistic competence will all affect communication.

The final talk considered the Chinese learner from the context of an academic English course in UK higher education. In her paper 'Starting from strength: achieving success in EAP', **Melinda Whong-Barr** (*University of Durham, UK*) argued for an approach to teaching that builds on Chinese learners' existing ability to memorize, suggesting a models-based strategy. Two lessons were presented to illustrate the approach at the sentence and text levels. At sentence level, students can be trained to pick out models of good academic language from an authentic academic text. These models can then be analysed for lexis, register, grammar, function, productivity, and so on. The suggestion was that students memorise particularly good examples as a way of storing structures, not to reproduce in exact form, but to use as a prototype from which to produce appropriate forms in their own writing.

The concept of memorising models is also valid at the level of text with an analysis and understanding of the structure of texts. At this level, it is not sentences that are analysed and memorised, but the moves associated with particular academic texts.

The paper drew parallels in the process of learning at the sentence and text levels such that students:

- read an authentic text for understanding;
- identify useful phrases/moves in text;
- collect useful phrases/frames or structures;
- analyse sentence level grammar/texts;
- categorize useful phrases/structures;
- memorise useful phrases/structures;
- produce text using appropriate phrases/structure.

Email: Mark.Allen@sussexdowns.ac.uk
yingchunli2003@yahoo.co.uk
m.k.whong-barr@durham.ac.uk
J.Xiaoli@warwick.ac.uk

11.4 Understand Chinese culture through its keywords

Wei-Wei Shen *Feng Chia University, Taichung, Taiwan*

My presentation explored the possibility of explaining Chinese cultural keywords in English without resorting to culture-dependent concepts. I began by introducing background information on Confucius and how his teachings developed one representative Chinese culture, Confucianism. I also indicated that an important purpose of studying Confucianism is to gain access to some understanding of Chinese culture.

I particularly focused on six keywords in Confucian culture. They are *'ren'*, *'li'*, *'xiaoi'*, *'de'*, *'he'*, and *'junzi'*. One reason for selecting these keywords is because of their moral values, which are emphasised in Confucianism. In addition, they are found in classic Chinese primers like *San Zi Jin* (*The Three Character Classic*) and *Qian Zi Wen* (*The Thousand Character Classic*), which are popular as tools for literacy learning and moral education.

However, I have found that there are many complexities and difficulties encountered when translating these six key items of Chinese cultural lexis into English. In fact, the English translations used by different scholars for these words show a wide range of separate terms. Also, some English terms are used as part of the translations for the different keywords (Cortazzi and Shen 2001). Therefore, focusing on avoiding 'terminological ethnocentrism' in interpreting the meanings of specific words from one culture to another (Goddard 1999; Wierzbicka 1997), I attempted to use 'natural semantic metalanguage' (NSM), a set of semantically simple and basic lexemes existing in various languages, to interpret these Chinese cultural keywords.

When applying NSM to transcribe possible cultural explications for the selected keywords, I included the basic elements of the definitions existing in the readings of Confucianism and in dictionaries.

Explication of *'ren'* (humanity, benevolence, kindheartedness)
People can say that X is a very good person because X has this.
If X has this, X does good things for other people.
X feels for other people because X has this.
When other people feel good/bad, X feels good/bad.

Explication of *'li'* (appropriate rules, principles of the social order, proper behaviour)
People know that something is good because of this.
People know that they can say/do something to someone because of this.
X says/does something good because of this.
If people do not want/know something, X does not say/do it.
People can say good things about X because of this.

Explication of '*xiao*' (filial piety, respect of hierarchy, dutiful son)
    X does something for Y because Y wants X to do it.
    If Y asks X to do something that X can do, X feels good.
    If Y asks X to do something that X cannot do, X feels bad.
    X does not say something if Y does not want to hear/know it.
    X does this because people think that this is good.
    People can say good things about X because of this.

Explication of '*de*' (virtue, morals, integrity)
    People know/think/feel that it is good to have this.
    When X has this, X knows that something is good/bad.
    When X has this, X says true things.
    People know that X is a good person because of this.

Explication of '*he*' (harmony, peace, reciprocity)
    People feel/think that it is good to have this.
    People do things because they want to have this.
    X wants to know/do something that other people want.
    People can feel good about X and X can feel good about other people because of this.

Explication of '*junzi*' (gentleman, ideal man, superiority of character and behaviour)
    People think that it is good to be this.
    X thinks/wants/does something good for other people.
    X says things that are good/true to other people.
    People can say good things about X because X is this.

In my presentation, I identified three major benefits of using NSM to understand each of these six Chinese keywords. Firstly, core concepts and meanings may be grasped quickly. Secondly, the understanding of these cultural keywords can be freed of cultural bias through the use of universal lexis. Thirdly, within the field of semantics the problem of definitional circularity caused by using conventional translations may be avoided. All in all, cultural explications may be useful to establish learners' conceptual awareness of foreign cultural keywords. One suggestion for implementing classroom practices regarding literacy learning is asking students to develop their own explications based on their understanding of cultural keywords. However, after attempting to try out NSM to explain the concepts of these six Chinese cultural keywords, I found two questions, listed as follows, which would be interesting to discuss further.

1. How do I decide if each explication has accounted for the range of use of the particular word?
2. Where do I start and stop in composing the explication of each word?

Email: wwshen@fcu.edu.tw

11.5 Dinner at the homesick restaurant

Irina Perianova *University of National and World Economy, Sofia, Bulgaria*

Food is an important part of every culture and a favourite source of linguistic metaphors, for example, 'a hot potato', 'a piece of cake', 'a real plum'. In 1954 Maslow put forward a theory of a hierarchy of common needs, labelling food as a classic lower-level (physiological) need, which should be met before people start thinking about satisfying higher-level needs (safety, acceptance, self-actualization). But it would seem that food cuts across the whole hierarchical board.

Food staples and food taboos are culture-specific, which accounts for a different attitude to food as sustenance. The subsistence culture approach where nothing is wasted, or the advocacy of oneness and merging of all things in Buddhism, is in stark contrast to the Western alienation from food, the emergence of an assembly-line approach (fast food), and consequently the avoidance of certain animal parts, such as innards. In fact, the American national dish has often been wittily described as 'menu'; health is more important than taste, cholesterol seems to be the buzz-word of the century.

The title of this paper, the same as that of the well-known novel by Anne Tyler, illustrates the functions of food as safety (home food) and affiliation. The function of food as bonding is prominent in religious rituals and festivals. Eating the same food in the same way provides continuity and an enduring tie to the community. Bonding may be produced (a) by the act of eating together; (b) by eating the same kinds of food. As rituals always impose constraints, be it a working lunch which is a staged, goal-oriented event, or a social coffee-drinking ceremony, some traditional patterns of meals may be a cause for revolt, a non-acceptance of bonding, or a metaphor for a desire for change as in H. Munro's story *Tea*, where the main character detests the whole system of afternoon tea so much that it disrupts his marriage plans.

Quite frequently, even the smallest deviations from the established routine relating to food and meals are likely to result in branding a person or an entire group as alien or strange. What one eats is perceived to reveal what one is like and beliefs about food of the other often create stereotypes of national character: cf., 'frogs', derogatory for Frenchmen. Thus, food is a means of characterisation and signifying as well as communication. Furthermore, common meals such as lunch and dinner, have varying chronological and ritual significance in different cultures—a lunch consisting of sandwiches in the USA or UK is not the same thing as Spanish '*comida*'. Different attitudes to meals are known to have caused business failures.

Aesthetically, too, foods often ring different cultural bells. 'Pumpkin' suggests caress in the UK, but an insult in Bulgaria and Hungary. 'Cabbage' implies a person who takes no interest in anything and is a jargon word for money in Russian ('*kapusta*'). By naming different foods people signify prosperity or poverty, health or illness, voice their anger or contempt. In Bulgaria, until recently, tea-drinking was associated with disease. In England, on the the other hand, tea signifies comfort.

Food is very relevant for politics and this fact accounts for the renaming of 'French fries' as 'Washington fries' in the USA after the start of the Iraqi war as a grotesque punishment for France for its 'incorrect' stance. In many cases food is so greatly interwoven with identity (Maslow's 'acceptance and affiliation needs') that eating what is regarded as the wrong food may cause rejection and disaster: eating ethnic food is the reason for the suicide of a girl in a Jewish family in the American South in P. Conroy's *Beach Music* because it signifies failure to assimilate. The politics of food is intertwined with social changes: a surprising new food slogan is 'politically correct': cf., the following recent media discoveries: 'the least politically correct hamburger' (it contains a lot of beef), 'politically correct vegetables'.

The significance of different foods and meals is not a fixture; it is not only culture-specific but time-specific as well. This change is especially noticeable in the context of our globalised world. The above-mentioned ritual of afternoon tea, so traditional for Edwardian England, is now all but gone. Another case in point is the early 20th century metaphor of the 'melting pot' to describe multicultural diversity, which has now given way to a modern metaphor of multiculturalism as 'tossed salad', with all components preserving their distinct flavour.

As food symbolises and signifies, giving or rejecting social identity, it can place and define an individual and tell a lot not only about the person who comments on other people's foods but about the comment-maker.

Email: inogina@yahoo.com

11.6 Interesting choices and untapped potential: what and who we teach

Elka Todeva *School for International Training, Brattleboro, Vermont, USA*

The workshop explored two interrelated strands—the common core between English and any other language(s) that ESL students bring to the classroom, and the common core between different varieties of English from Kachru's (1992) 'inner, extended, and outer circle'. These two strands are important, given the realities we live in, namely students coming to English with at least one (and often more) languages in their repertoire, and also the unprecedented cross-cultural communication through English, in which the majority of interlocutors have first languages other than English. Two fundamental questions were put up for discussion: (a) how can we better tap the prior knowledge of ESL students, and (b) how can we define and best teach the core target forms of English to empower learners by expediting learning and facilitating cross-cultural communication.

For years the language teaching profession has taken a 'deficit stance' on learners, evident in terms such as LEPs (Limited English Proficiency) and LESs (Limited English Speakers). The workshop engaged participants in experiences that revealed students' prior knowledge as an asset. As this knowledge often remains a hidden resource, participants were guided through a range of ideas as to how such knowledge can be used to accelerate progress in subsequent language learning.

The second part of the workshop built on the concept of a 'cross-linguistic common core' and addressed the question of what target forms constitute the core of English with regard to pronunciation, grammar, vocabulary, and pragmatics.

Regarding pronunciation, the core was defined as all meaning-distinctive oppositions in English, such as, for instance, the difference between long and short vowels, as in 'beat' vs. 'bit'. Failure to distinguish between aspirated vs. unaspirated 'p' and 't' sounds, on the other hand, does not affect meaning. It gives one a non-native-speaker accent, but this does not have to be a core focus in teaching unless the learner has an integrative motivation for learning English.

Two aspects of 'core grammar' were emphasized in the workshop: (a) defining the core grammar categories, for example, tenses, articles, prepositions, and (b) identifying the core meaning(s) of each core category. To take just one example: tenses are key for the overwhelming majority of human languages. English has twelve tenses, but corpus linguistics has shown that most communicative acts are conducted with the five 'core tenses': the simple tenses (past, present, and future), past continuous, and present perfect. For the present simple, expressing routine actions is far more common than the other meanings associated with this tense and should therefore take precedence in the chronology of teaching.

The workshop elaborated on an early article by Michael Stubbs (1986), which defines the concept of 'core vocabulary' in fine detail and shows its power in language pedagogy and learning. Among the main criteria for core vocabulary are frequency, derivational and combinatory potential, and lack of cultural constraints. Things are much fuzzier in the area of pragmatics, where questions regarding which norms one should follow and how one can negotiate linguistic identity defy any simple answers.

The workshop concluded by examining a teacher-training framework referred to as the KASA framework, which characterizes professional growth as a development of Knowledge, Awareness, Skills, and Attitudes. Changing this acronym to A + ASK brings to the fore the fact that all growth start with awareness (A). Once we have in our awareness: (a) the changes in the demographics of speakers of English and in the status of English as an international language, (b) that there is a common core that covers all varieties of English, (c) that the core gives students the most communicative mileage right from the beginning, and (d) that learners come equipped with substantial prior language knowledge that educators can tap into, we can take steps to enhance our knowledge base (K) about all these issues. With this enhanced knowledge and awareness, we can start strategizing and sharing skills (S) with others about translating this knowledge and awareness into daily practice. Through reflection on our teaching and the progress our students are making or not making, we can assess our beliefs, educational philosophy, and our attitudes (A) about how and why teaching and learning unfold the way they do.

Recent debates at IATEFL and TESOL around English as an International Language and around multilingual competence have triggered a tectonic shift in our consciousness as a profession. It is up to each one of us to continue pushing the boundaries of this awareness and finding ways of further changing our practice in view of the new global realities.

Email: lka.todeva@sit.edu

Reference

Kachru, B. 1992. *The Other Tongue: English Across Cultures*, Second edition. Urbana, Illinois: University of Illinois Press.

11.7 Questions around ELF: investigating teachers' attitudes

Nadia Benrabah-Djennane *Université Stendhal-Grenoble III, Grenoble, France*

Over the last few years, Jenkins (2000) and Seidlhofer (2001), among others, have, either individually or jointly, argued in favour of the need to recognise ELF (English as a lingua franca) as an emerging variety of English in its own right. One must admit that the various arguments put forward in order to sustain their claim are quite convincing and cannot go unnoticed. They have also triggered varied reactions from scholars all over the world. However, if they have indeed largely contributed to the spreading of an awareness about a phenomenon that no one can now afford to ignore, their claims also raise a number of questions in the mind of many a teacher of English. One such question concerns teachers' attitudes towards that new variety of English.

A pilot experiment was, therefore, conducted with a view to exploring this, to our knowledge, so far uninvestigated area in France. A questionnaire was designed in order to elicit opinions about which variety of English should be taught. It was then submitted to thirty-one informants, all university teachers available at the time this pilot study was conducted in Grenoble, France. Two groups were created, one consisting of nineteen native English speakers, and the other of eleven French speakers of English and one bilingual (British and French). All were teaching English in France.

To the question 'Which variety of English do you think should be taught?' four choices were offered to the informants: (1) British English (BE), (2) American English (AE), (3) Neither, (4) Other.

In the native group, sixteen were speakers of BE, three of AE. Fifteen out of nineteen expressed a preference for BE and/or AE (henceforth BE/AE). More particularly, eight out of those fifteen informants felt 'BE only' should be taught, while seven felt BE/AE should be. An interesting difference was observed between the British and the American speakers. Among the sixteen BE speakers, eight chose 'BE only', while only five BE/AE. Among the AE speakers, however, none chose 'BE only', none even 'AE only', but two preferred BE/AE and one felt other varieties should be taught. Although this difference ought to be regarded with caution due to the small number of American speakers considered here, it still deserves to be investigated further in a future study.

In the French group, nine said their English had mostly been influenced by BE, two by AE. In answer to the main question, only two chose BE, four BE/AE, two preferred 'Other' and four were unable to give a definite answer exclusive of all the others.

The comments they made unveiled some interesting opinions. The variety of English that is taught seemed not to matter to the French speakers provided it is coherent and 'correct'. They seemed more open to other varieties of English. Some expressed the idea that 'in a world that is more and more globalised, learners should be able to understand any type of English'. Another recurring comment in the French group was that teachers should teach the variety of English they actually use and feel more confident with.

It seemed important to most informants from both groups that learners should be exposed to both BE and AE, but some added that then why not any other variety of English? Yet, when this was the case, usually, it meant other *native* varieties of English. In both groups, the idea that AE is predominant was present. Also, the belief that learners would necessarily have to use English with either British or American speakers was noticeable. A native informant even added that a 'considerable amount of people speak it' (i.e. BE/AE). Graddol (2000) and Crystal (1997), among others, have, however, shown that this was far from being the case.

Yet, two native informants did refer to a world variety of English, one mentioning the idea of teaching a 'model of English as an international language', and the other stating that 'teachers shouldn't reduce English to UK/US. As an international language, students require a larger exposure'. Last but not least, some comments mentioned the necessity to take the learners' needs into consideration.

The interesting results that have come out of this pilot study have shown some directions that further research could take. It might be interesting to conduct a similar but larger scale study with an equal and also larger number of informants in each group. It might also be worthwhile to include a fifth more explicit choice to the informants, i.e. ELF.

Email: Nadia.Benrabah@u-grenoble3.fr

Reference

Jenkins, J. 2000. *The Phonology of English as an International Language.* Oxford: Oxford University Press

11.8 Symposium on intercultural communication

Convenor
Alessia Cogo *King's College London, UK*

Increasingly English is taught for communication in international contexts. ELT, therefore, plays an important role in preparing students for intercultural communication (IC). This symposium aimed at introducing an intercultural perspective, starting from recent developments in English for IC, promoting ideas for developing intercultural competence and awareness in practice.

Martin Dewey *(King's College, London, UK)* reported recent ELF (English as a lingua franca) corpus findings and considered the pedagogical implications. As we continue to shift towards a situation where L1 speakers are a minority, where English is used predominantly for intercultural communication, the implications for its evolution become ever more apparent. Indeed, as Graddol (2006) observes, demographic change is among the most important factors in language shift and change.

Dewey presented lexico-grammatical features indicative of emerging patterns in spoken ELF use. All reported features are systematic, frequently occurring and communicatively effective, with no breakdown in communication in all attested examples. All of the following are therefore considered non-L1 variants rather than errors, differing from standard L1 equivalents but not erroneous or deviant (see Seidlhofer 2004):

Chapter 11: Cross-cultural matters

- use of 3rd person singular zero;
- extension of relative 'which' to include functions served by 'who';
- shift in article use, for example, preference for zero article, especially where L1 use is idiomatic;
- invariant question tags (and other similar universals, such as 'this' for 'this/these');
- shift in use of prepositions, for example, 'study about';
- additional collocations for words with high semantic generality, for example, 'take an operation';
- increased explicitness, for example, 'how long time' in place of 'how long';
- preference for infinitive over gerunds, for example, 'interested to do' rather than 'interested in doing', or 'to read is ...', infinitive as subject of a clause;
- exploited redundancy, for example, ellipsis of objects/complements of transitive verbs, 'I wanted to go with'.

The second speaker, **Alessia Cogo** *(King's College, London, UK)*, took an intercultural pragmatic perspective, exploring questions of culture and identity for intercultural speakers. Culture and identity in ELT are usually defined as the culture and identity of the language being learnt. Of course this raises certain issues related to the assumption that there is a one-to-one relation between culture and language, especially in the case of English and its role as a lingua franca in IC.

Cogo investigated how ELF speakers construct and negotiate identity in ELF conversations and how they talk about their own identity in interviews. In some studies the common assumption is that ELF is deficient in at least two ways: culturally IC is supposedly neutral, lacking a definite cultural identity, and functionally, IC is regarded as a tool for transactional functions (business-like type of communication) only, but not interactional (expression of cultural identity).

However, these assumptions are not confirmed by the data of this paper, a corpus of naturally arising casual conversations collected among ELF speakers. Cogo looked at moments of identity emerging from the data and highlighted the use of code-switching and idiomatic expressions signalling cultural identity, as well as the use of accommodation strategies to suggest membership of a multilingual and multicultural community. The second part of her data concerned the participants' interviews and their thoughts about cultural identity. Participants expressed their ability to move between cultures and identities and their resistance to having their identities essentialised. (See Kubota's 'discursive construction of culture', this volume 11.1.)

Ayako Suzuki *(King's College, London, UK)* discussed the importance of teaching the diversity of English for IC by focusing on Japan as one example. Today, ICs in English are very frequently carried out between L2 speakers whose English is different from American/British English. Therefore, if English is taught for IC, it is necessary to inform students about L2 speakers and their use of English. However, as Japanese ELT tends to focus heavily on native speakers (NSs), students are likely to have a narrow understanding of IC: they believe that their communication partners speak NS-like English. This belief would hinder students from communicating successfully with other L2 speakers.

Suzuki's case study on Japanese university students' perceptions of English investigated whether informing students about L2 speakers and their use of English, i.e. the diversity of English, can improve their narrow views of IC. Suzuki worked with several students who participated in a course which covered various issues concerned with the diversity of English at one university in Tokyo. From several interviews with the students, she found that teaching the diversity of English could widen students' narrow understanding of IC to some extent: students became more aware that they were likely to encounter L2 speakers whose English is not NS-like in IC settings. In a nutshell, teaching diversity of English can be the initial step to preparing students for IC and should be included when English is taught for IC.

Sherida Altehenger-Smith *(Karlsruhe, Germany)* dealt with various intercultural problems which can arise and their possible solutions, emphasising practical rather than theoretical approaches. The data presented in this talk were collected during the past four years of teaching at a 'private university'. This institution is part of a state university in Germany and offers foreign students the opportunity of obtaining a bachelor's degree in mechanical engineering using English as the medium of instruction. In past years, students have come from seventeen different countries. Altehenger-Smith's responsibility is to prepare them for a university entrance exam as well as for bringing their English up to par during the first year through courses in technical English, presentations, negotiating and intercultural communication. Intercultural difficulties are mirrored by various attitudes towards language learning (communicative competence vs. grammatical competence) and methods of learning (learning rules by heart, not accustomed to class participation, etc.) which students bring with them from their home countries; stereotypes each student has of students from another background; and culturally shaped expectations of teacher–student relationships and towards interpersonal relationships with other students. The classroom thus becomes an intercultural melting pot for language difficulties and accents while simultaneously being part of an island within the German culture and language. Stereotypes—both positive and negative ones—abound and must be confronted and dealt with appropriately.

Alun Phillip *(Freelance, Italy)* looked at some activities for developing intercultural awareness. Based on the premise that awareness is a necessary prelude to enhancing cognitive knowledge and practical skills, this talk illustrated how focused training activities can help participants understand the impact of intercultural differences on communication. Critical incidents, in both text and video form, represent a relatively low-risk starting point for getting learners to think about culturally-related misunderstandings. Any short dialogue (see Storti 1994) which draws on basic value differences (for example hierarchy/equality) can be used for observation and description by participants. Secondly, role play represents a motivating way of involving participants in simulated 'culture shock'. One example is where a team is sent on a vital fact-finding mission to a team representing 'Krakozhia', a fictitious culture with set verbal/non-verbal behaviours designed to disorient the time pressed fact-finding team. Awareness-raising takes place in the debriefing session where both teams reflect on their negative impression of the other side.

A third approach is simulation games, which emphasise the affective experiential element of intercultural learning. For example, the 'Barnga' card game involves giving students different (and conflicting) sets of rules to play a simple game of trumps and denies them any possibility of spoken communication to sort out misunderstanding/difficulties. This normally leads to lively and spontaneous feedback from players, and should lead to insights into how to deal with 'unexpected' behaviour.

Index of authors

Anderson, Clare, 96
Appleby, Rachel, 150
Atay, Derin, 125
Beaven, Briony, 155
Beech, Peter, 148
Belak, Mojca, 170
Benrabah-Djennane, Nadia, 233
Berman, Robert, 98
Black, Michael, 202
Bolitho, Rod, 113, 157
Bouqdib, Maggie, 11, 188
Çağlayan, Esin, 115
de Chazal, Edward, 40
Chen, Zehang, 68
Coates, Jennifer, 17
Cogo, Alessia, 235
Collie, Joanne, 54
Dawson, Alex, 93
Dodge, Valentina, 193
Donancı Büyük, Senem, 206
Dunworth, Katie, 92
ElAtia, Samira, 98
Estling Vannestål, Maria, 56
Fu, Shan, 74
Gajek, Elżbieta, 195
Garton-Sprenger, Judy, 174
di Gennaro, Kristen, 144
Ghosn, Irma-Kaarina, 78
Graham, Tim, 127
Green, Anthony, 36
Hanušová, Světlana, 152
Harmer, Jeremy, 113
Harrison, Tilly, 64

Hobbs, Valerie, 117
Hockly, Nicky, 186
Horai, Tomoko, 31
Hughes, John, 13
Hussin, Habsah, 72
Jilkova, Jana, 184
Keblowska, Magdalena, 168
Khan, Rubina, 198
Kojima, Chizuyo, 119
Kovacic, Andreja, 62
Kubota, Ryuko, 213
Lefever, Samuel, 175
Linse, Caroline, 14
Mader, Judith, 200
McCormack, Bede, 144
McCullagh, Marie, 109
Meddings, Luke, 113
Mercer, Sarah, 177
Mol, Hans, 54
Nathan, Philip, 102
Norton, Maria K., 208
Onat-Stelma, Zeynep, 142
Oxholm, Alice, 127
Papageorgiou, Spiros, 204
Pawlak, Miroslaw, 29
Peker, Bena Gül, 132
Perianova, Irina, 230
Phipps, Simon, 121
Platzer, Hans, 84
Prowse, Philip, 174
Purokuru, Riitta, 87
Rascón, Diego, 76
Rosenberg, Marjorie, 106

Index of authors

Ryynänen, Hannu, 87
Salaberri, Sagrario, 113
Savvidou, Christine, 123
Shalenko, Oleksandr, 89
Sheehan, Andrew, 146
Shen, Wei-Wei, 228
Shepherd, David, 191
Simpson, Adam J., 60
Smidowicz, Vincent, 107
Smith, Anne Margaret, 180
Stelma, Juup, 142
Swan, Michael, 10, 45
Taylor, Linda, 74
Thorn, Sheila, 34
Thorne, Aidan, 182
Todeva, Elka, 231
Todorova, Nataliya, 89
Tomlinson, Brian, 166
Torfadottir, Audur, 38
Tremarco, John, 110
Troche, Ursula, 104
Verdonk, Désirée, 84
Vine, Sheila, 193
Viswamohan, Aysha, 104
Vogel, Beate, 188
Vojtková, Naďa, 152
Wagner, Sanja, 172
Wang, Qiang, 70
Waters, Alan, 223
Watkins, Peter, 129
Whong-Barr, Melinda, 225
Wilson, Juliet, 206
Wilson, Dede, 163
Winkler, Birgit, 58
Wright, Andrew, 80
Wright, Ros, 109
Yakovchuk, Nadezhda, 100